A PROLOG
Database System

ELECTRONIC & ELECTRICAL ENGINEERING RESEARCH STUDIES

COMPUTER ENGINEERING SERIES

Series Editor: **Professor F. G. Heath,** *Heriot-Watt University, Edinburgh, UK*

2. The Anthropocentric Approach to Computing and Reactive Machines
   Stoyan O. Kableshkov

3. A PROLOG Database System
   Deyi Li

A PROLOG Database System

Deyi Li, Ph.D.

Department of Computer Science,
Heriot-Watt University, Edinburgh, UK

RESEARCH STUDIES PRESS LTD.
Letchworth, Hertfordshire, England
JOHN WILEY & SONS INC.
New York · Brisbane · Chichester · Toronto · Singapore

RESEARCH STUDIES PRESS LTD.
58B Station Road, Letchworth, Herts. SG6 3BE, England

Marketing and Distribution:

Australia, New Zealand, South-east Asia:
Jacaranda-Wiley Ltd., Jacaranda Press
JOHN WILEY & SONS INC.
GPO Box 859, Brisbane, Queensland 4001, Australia

Canada:
JOHN WILEY & SONS CANADA LIMITED
22 Worcester Road, Rexdale, Ontario, Canada

Europe, Africa:
JOHN WILEY & SONS LIMITED
Baffins Lane, Chichester, West Sussex, England

North and South America and the rest of the world:
JOHN WILEY & SONS INC.
605 Third Avenue, New York, NY 10158, USA

Library of Congress Cataloging in Publication Data:

Li, Deyi, 1944–
A PROLOG database system.

(Electronic & electrical engineering research studies. Computer engineering series; 3)
Bibliography: p.
Includes index.
1. Prolog (Computer program language) 2. Data base management. 3. Programming languages (Electronic computers) I. Title. II. Series: Electronic & electrical engineering research studies. Computer engineering series; no. 3.
QA76.73.P356L5 1984 001.64'24 83-26896

ISBN 0 86380 014 9
ISBN 0 471 90429 5 (Wiley)

British Library Cataloguing in Publication Data:

Li, Deyi
A PROLOG database system.——(Electronic & electrical engineering research studies: computer engineering series; 3)
1. Data base management 2. File organization (computer science) 3. Prolog (computer program language)
I. Title II. Series
001.64'42 QA76.9.D3

ISBN 0 86380 014 9

ISBN 0 86380 014 9 (Research Studies Press Ltd.)
ISBN 0 471 90429 5 (John Wiley & Sons Inc.)

Printed in Great Britain

Series Editor's Foreword

This is a longer Editor's introduction than usual, and is intended to give the reader a clear view of the three distinct technical aspects within the book, as well as relating them to the present state of play in world computer technology.

The most significant thread perhaps is the realisation, which built up quietly during the 1970's, that conventional programming languages had a serious deficiency in the testing and proving area. Software engineering and modular programming improved things somewhat, but in the end debugging and difficult modification would always be expensive companions of FORTRAN, COBOL and the rest. Program maintenance is a euphemism - as a colleague says "If my car needed a few mechanics working on it regularly it would not be called maintenance - it would be rectification of design faults!"

Other workers also began to see that the language structure sprang from the specific electronic computer structure which runs them - the article by J.Backus [23] is the standard text on this subject. It shows clearly that improvements will come when the von-Neumann machine (which has had a very good run for its money) shares the stage with other types of electronic processor, related to new languages and styles of computing which can give faster results with simple checkable programs.

Functional or applicative languages were developed which were totally checkable as good programs without simulation or test running. One remembers Dijkstra's famous dictum "GOTO considered harmful" from a previous period, the new warning seems to be "X := X+1 is positively disastrous!" Certainly these languages do what they promise, but they carry with them a very mathematical flavour in the symbolic logic area, and whether they can ever appeal to the typical programmer is not yet clear.

The language used in this book is PROLOG, which again developed quietly in the artificial intelligence field over the last decade. It was designed for PROgramming in LOGic, and seems to have been put together to do a particular job in a workman-like manner. Many computer engineers always thought they knew all about logic since they could handle 'AND', 'OR' and 'NOT' gates, but the extension to set theory leads to programming methods (and consequent electronic processor designs) which are quite different. LISP and SNOBOL go part of the way along this route, and were of course used by the early AI workers.

In 1981 Dr Li had completed his preparatory work with me in Heriot-Watt University, and had mastered the UNIX operating system as well as AIDS, a CAD system for parallel hardware/software design. His first task was to master PROLOG and then try to implement some of the directed graph analyses used in the AIDS system. In less than two months he had completed programs which certainly had taken more than 18 programmer-months in language C, and the program had gone from a thick wad down to 6 or 7 pages. Discounting the high productivity of a single programmer, this was an impressive result, and we immediately decided that PROLOG was the language for his main work.

The next area of computer use which was looking for a new approach was that of databases. Once in the mid-70's when I visited Manchester, Tom Kilburn who at that time had access to all the sources of computer information asked me, "What is a database?" I tried to answer, but we then had a discussion which came to the conclusion that anything stored in a computer was being called a database, and perhaps some levels of classification would be useful.

During the years that followed I realised that the very earliest data-bases had probably been developed by computer manufacturers so that their customers would not all have different data - structures in their commercial work. Consequently there was no theoretical back-up. Similarly large text data-bases grew on standard computers, and both types of system relied completely on pointers in tables to access the data. The business databases developed classes - hierarchical and networked - but these still had no fundamental theory for the designer. The simple results of this were such things as the table structure being frozen for all time, and no guarantee that a query type not included at the design stage would work. Some of the designers at that time may feel that this brief summing up is unfair, but the main point is that a system with no overall theory can only be designed by ad-hoc methods.

Relational databases came about in an attempt to provide an overall theory, and the theory of sets can provide a relational algebra and a relational calculus. E.F.Codd [15,16] energetically promoted this approach, which finally reached heights of conceptual purity in successive 1st, 2nd, 3rd and 4th "normal forms". These were limitations on the data structure which guaranteed for instance, that any relation which was in the database could be used in retrieval. There may well be a fifth normal form by now.

Suddenly relational databases became fashionable, but had a considerable technical snag. The entities in the database had to be retrieved associatively, which either meant a slow serial search by the von-Neumann processor or complex pointer systems. Text archiving can just about put-up with pointers because there is no editing, but databases are in continual flux.

The short-term commercial solution was easy - just rename your product a relational database - but slowly the true product emerged, even if not at the highest normal form, and although slow was a considerable improvement. Types of query language developed, QBE (Query-By-Example) being a pictorial or visicalc-like method, and SEQUEL being statement-based. Mathematical query languages can also be envisaged.

The third area of work has an even longer history than the others. From the earliest British computers there have been designers who wished to build functions which did not sit naturally in von-Neumann machines as special electronic processors. An early unknown pioneer was Maurice Gribble of Ferranti, who built hardware random generators for the Manchester MARK 1* (1951) and the Ferranti Argus prototype (1957).

Another function which does not fit von-Neumann is associative memory access, mentioned earlier as one of the key elements in PROLOG and relational databases. The earliest machines, such as the MARK 1*, IBM 650 and ZEBRA, could use serial associative searching on computer words because the "backing" memory was directly addressed by the CPU (i.e. not by file). With unconscious irony, one of the pioneers told me that the drum search was very useful, since they had a valve failure every ten minutes, and they got more work done that way! It is now my belief that "associative processing" may well be the speediest method, even with von-Neumann machines.

The cost of special purpose hardware probably precluded the use of special purpose processors (except those with wide appeal such as floating-point processors) although my team in UMIST designed a wide variety of them during the 60's.

The first to be designed and marketed was the ICL content addressable file store, and while one can argue about the specifics of the design, and the operating system limitations, there is no doubt that it was a bold and technically correct step.

Within Heriot-Watt University and MEMEX Information Engines, an Edinburgh based company, an associative text retrieval system [25] has been under intensive development since 1978. It therefore was natural to adopt this work into the area of PROLOG databases, since the typical reading speed of 1 M text words / 3 seconds could transform the performance. This work is contained in Chapter 9.

As the work described in this book was beginning however the Japanese announced their "fifth generation" computer design program. Not surprisingly, they chose PROLOG as a language, and relational databases as a major component. There was however no mention of associative methods, but the general tone of the announcement convinced us that we were right to work on PROLOG programming for query methods into relational databases at various levels of normal form, linked to subsequent associative addressing techniques for speed.

This work can therefore be read as an integrated whole, showing the sort of systems and methods which will slowly become common, or it can be read as a detached study of PROLOG programming, query methods for relational databases or the application of associative methods to relational databases.

PROLOG primers are easily available, so this book starts at the next level with an introductory appendix 2 with simple examples. It is then possible to study how to program the three main styles of relational retrieval in PROLOG and a common interface into the database. Chapter 9 shows how PROLOG can convert a normalised request into a system call on associative memory.

Relational databases can be studied in Chapter 2 through the three distinct query types with a proof that they are all equivalent, corroborated by the definition of a single interface for all three. This means that different languages can be used in a random mix, and that constructing any new retrieval method is a simple front-end programming task. The examples are extended from the book by C.J.Date [27] for readers who are relatively new in the field.

Finally Chapter 9 shows how fifth generation architectures can be devised by fusing together the various ideas, and unlike so much material about fifth generation systems shows, in comparatively fine detail, how it would actually be done. This last fact explains why the book can be read in two ways. You can go through it ignoring much mathematics and programming and just get a valuable feel for the new approaches in computer systems. Alternatively, at any stage you can decide that you need to know how something really works, in which case full detail and backup references are available.

F.G.Heath

Table of Contents

CHAPTER 1
Introduction

1.1 THE HUMAN SIDE OF MAN-COMPUTER SYSTEMS

1.1.1 Background

When the computer era began, only specialists worked with computer systems; and the user was often not taken into account in the process of system design. Today advancing technology has turned many people into computer users, and there is a great variety in computer use. This has raised many problems at the computer-user interface. It is a truism to remark that it can be disastrous to neglect the user. In terms of cost, speed, reliability, and most other "efficiency" measures the machine is far superior to the human, yet humans remain a crucial part of the system. To put it another way, efficiency in the use of system resources can be ineffective if a system is not designed to match the needs and abilities of its users. As the real costs of computing power have been falling rapidly whilst the manpower costs required to support this power have simultaneously been rising, the problem becomes even more severe. This fact has led to the exploration of new research areas involving the human-oriented aspects of computer systems.

In recent years some activities in user research have begun. For example, there have been tests about the relationship between system features and user behaviour; by using techniques of experimental psychology a number of experimenters in industry and academia have begun to study database query languages. A query language is a well-defined linguistic tool with a fairly limited number of functions, the expressions of which correspond to requests one might want to make to a data base. With each request, or query, there is an associated response, or an answer. In many cases, query languages are designed for use by non-programmers. Since such a user lacks computer experience, a successful language should be easy for him to learn, use, and remember. Human factors testing of a query language can determine whether it meets these criteria. More recently, not only have there been studies of a variety of different query languages, but brief surveys of these studies have already appeared in general articles and books. Directions and methods for human factors testing of general purpose query languages have been presented.

P.Reisner in her survey [1] mentioned a number of empirical studies of database query languages and some comparisons of two or more such languages for ease-of-use, which had been made to measure the ease-of-use of a query language and to provide feedback to designers for improving a language. As she concluded, people write queries in Query-By-Example [2,3] between two and three times faster than in SQL [4,5], but they have trouble with qualification in QBE; spelling mistakes and ending errors are common in SQL. Greenblatt and Waxman [6] compared the ease of learning QBE, SEQUEL [7], and relational algebra; apparently the advantage was with QBE. Also Zloof's QBE was found easy to learn and use by the study of Thomas and Gould [8]. Reisner et al [9] made a study of SEQUEL and SQUARE [10], with the result that SEQUEL was found relatively easy to learn. Lochovsky [11] studied various data models and their associated data manipulation languages. After the comparison of SEQUEL with TABLET [12], C.Welty and D.W.Stemple [13] found that people more often write difficult queries correctly using a procedural query language than they do using a nonprocedural query language.

Motivation for the work has been diverse. What the studies have in common is that they adapt techniques of behavioural science to the study of query language issues. That is they have attempted to define the vague notion of "ease-of-use" in terms that will permit quantitative measurement, and they have developed procedures for measuring it. The specific measurement techniques developed are experimental, involving people using the languages doing different kinds of complex cognitive tasks.

Unfortunately, user research is a relatively young discipline, and "user-friendliness" and "naturalness" are concepts which are often used but seldom defined in detail and there seems to be no consensus about their meanings. These comparisons mentioned above are only approximate because the separate experiments differ in several ways, e.g., training, techniques, subject populations, test questions, stringency of scoring errors. Conclusions can only be drawn with certain conditions, and one must be cautious about over-generalising any of the findings. It seems that for the time being clear guide-lines to aid design do not exist, though many of the experiments have provided some design feedback. However, there is an increasing recognition of the importance of human factors studies. If the human part of the system is not performing effectively then it is unlikely that the technical part of the system will be efficient either. The user interface of a system has to be matched with user skills and task requirements, and the only sensible approach is to give as much emphasis to the user performance as to system performance.

1.1.2 Requirements

Keeping in mind user orientation and application, a question that immediately arises is the conflict between the human part and the technical part of a system. Let us introduce the concepts of flexibility of use and operating complexity. Flexibility of use means the user's flexibility in the delegation of tasks to the system. It is determined by the number of different processes which the user can perform with the support of a special system. Operating complexity means the complexity of those operating activities the user has to perform in order to achieve the intended task. One can distinguish the objective operating complexity which is the actual complexity given by a system from the subjective operating complexity which reflects the user's personal feelings concerning the operating complexity he has to overcome.

Transferring these two concepts into the design of man-computer interfaces leads to the result that from the human point of view a great flexibility of use is desirable; whereas from the technological point of view, a low operating complexity at an acceptable cost and performance should be achieved. With these considerations an optimal man-computer interface design can be regarded as an optimisation problem between maximal flexibility of use and minimal operating complexity [14].

1.2 THE PRESENT SITUATION OF RELATIONAL QUERY LANGUAGES

1.2.1 Classification of Relational Query Languages

Query languages differ from each other in a number of ways, such as syntactic form, procedurality, or underlying data model. Because of the wide variety of query languages it may be useful to classify them in different ways.

At the external level, which is the one closest to users, a wide range of available interaction modes are designed to accommodate the variety of users who may require database interaction. These modes include:

(i) Host language embedding of new syntactic forms into well-established programming languages such as COBOL, PL/1, or FORTRAN. The embedding may be simple invocation of subprograms. Alternatively, new syntax may be added, which requires a preprocessor or modified translator. An example is the language SQL embedded in a host programming language PL/1 or COBOL.

(ii) Self-contained language which provides all the facilities for performing the available functions. This method allows the creation of an elegant language but requires the learning of new syntactic and semantic forms which are generally easy to use.

(iii) Computer-directed function specification by menu selection, fill-in-the-blank, or parametric requests. Syntax learning can be avoided, but the range of options available may be small.

(iv) Natural language interfaces which eliminate the need for syntax learning, but may include a long clarification dialogue, and an illusion of unlimited machine intelligence which inhibits careful thinking on the user's part.

No matter what the interaction mode at the external level is, the notation for expressing queries at the conceptual level is usually the most significant part of a query language. As far as the relational model is concerned, query languages essentially break down into two broad classes:

(i) Algebraic languages, where queries are expressed by applying specialised operators to relations.

(ii) Calculus languages, where queries describe a desired set of tuples by specifying a predicate the tuples must satisfy. The calculus-based languages may further be divided into two classes:

(a) Tuple relational calculus, where the primitive objects are tuples.

(b) Domain relational calculus, where the primitive objects are elements of the domain of some attribute.

The three abstract distinct kinds of query languages serve as a benchmark for evaluating existing relational query systems. Each of them is equivalent in expressive power to the others, and they were proposed by E.F.Codd [15,16] to present the minimum capability of any reasonable query language using the relational model. Real query languages usually provide the capabilities of the abstract languages and additional capabilities as well.

1.2.2 The Existing Query Languages

There have been many experimental and prototype implementations of relational data sublanguages, a selection of which is listed below.

Language Name	Language Style	Method	Associated S/W	H/W	Developer
ALPHA	Command	Tuple Cal.	-	IBM	IBM(Codd)
APL	Command	Calculus	-	IBM	General Motors
APPLE	Command	Calculus	-	-	Northwestern Uni.
ASTRID	Command	Algebra	FORTRAN	Honeywell	Aberdeen Uni.
CUPID	Forms	Tuple Cal.	QUEL	UNIX	Uni. Calif.
INQUIRE	Command	Calculus	-	IBM	Infodata
ISBL	Command	Algebra	PRTV	IBM	Peterlee
LINUS	Command	Calculus	MRDS	Honeywell	Honeywell
QUEL	Command	Tuple Cal.	INGRES	UNIX	Uni. Calif.
QBE	Forms	Domain Cal.	-	IBM	IBM(Zloof)
REGIS	Command	Calculus	-	IBM	General Motors
RENDENZ-VOUS	Nat.Lang.	Calculus	ALPHA	IBM	IBM(Codd)
SQUARE	Command	Tuple Cal.	System R	IBM	IBM
SEQUEL	Command	Calculus	System R	IBM	IBM
SQL	Command	Calculus	System R	IBM	IBM
TABLET	Command	Algebra	-	-	Uni. Massachusetts
TAMALAN	Command	Calculus	-	CDC	CDC(Belg)
THESEUS	Command	Calculus	-	-	Uni. Rochester

Fig. 1.1 Relational Query Languages

This list does not claim to be comprehensive. Corresponding to external level, language styles have been divided into Command, i.e., command-driven using a limited syntax; Forms, i.e., dialogue-driven using fixed formats to specify queries; Nat. Language, i.e., free natural language. Method shows the method of accessing structured data at the conceptual level.

Of particular interest among them are the following systems and their languages, based on which the system ILEX is built up.

(a) **System PRTY and Language ISBL:** ISBL (Information System Base Language) is a "pure" relational algebra language developed at the IBM United Kingdom Scientific Centre in Peterlee, for use in the experimental Peterlee Relational Test Vehicle (PRTV) System. The ISBL has no aggregate operators, and there are no facilities for insertion, deletion, or modification of tuples. However there exist in the surrounding PRTV system the facilities to write arbitrary PL/1 programs and integrate them into the processing of relations. ISBL and the PRTV system are discussed in Todd [17].

(b) **System INGRES and Languages QUEL and CUPID:** The system INGRES (Interactive Graphics and Retrieval System) was developed at the University of California Berkeley, and implemented on the top of the UNIX operating system. It provides the query language QUEL (QUEry Language), a tuple relational calculus language, embedded in a C program. QUEL has a particularly simple mapping into first-order logic. CUPID is a graphic language implemented on the top of QUEL. With CUPID the user can construct queries of arbitrary complexity by simple light-pen manipulation of a small number of standard symbols. The details of the design and implementation of INGRES are given in [18].

(c) **System R and Languages SQUARE, SEQUEL, and SQL:** System R is an experimental database management system developed on a standard IBM VM/370 operating system environment at IBM Research Laboratory in San Jose. The three languages: SQUARE (Specifying QUeries As Relational Expression); SEQUEL (Structured English QUery Language); and SQL (Structured Query Language) are the results of evolution in the course of the project. One may call them as the SQUARE-SEQUEL-SQL route showing the development history of the query language in System R during the past ten years. An architectural overview of the system is given in M.W.Blasgaen et al. [4,5,19].

(d) **System SBA and Language QBE:** QBE (Query-By-Example), a domain relational calculus language. QBE created by Zloof [2,3] is oriented toward the end user and is easy to learn and use, by means of the manipulation of graphic symbols on a display screen. The system SBA (System for Business Automation) is an extension of QBE discussed in [20,21].

1.3 PROBLEMS WITH INDIVIDUAL QUERY LANGUAGES

1.3.1 Diversity

After comparison of a number of query languages, we may come to the conclusion that even the best formal query language would never be universally accepted. Different types of users have very different needs and skills. Some users prefer string languages, such as QUEL or SQL, while others prefer the screen-oriented two-dimensional data sub-language of Query-By-Example. A language which is good for one may not be good for another. It seems unlikely that a query language will cater for the tastes of all user types, nor should one language be considered optimal for all users. There need to be different languages to meet different needs; and it seems virtually certain that several different query languages such as ISBL, QBE and SQL are going to co-exist for many years to come. The choice of a language will depend upon the human circumstance of its intended use. Thus, the question to be answered may not be which language is best but under what circumstance is one language superior to another.

This fact may cause confusion in the designer's mind and result in a system which is optimised for only a limited subset of the application domain. So as well as there being a growing need for different easy-to-use query languages, there is a need for query language software which solves a variety of problems in a consistent way.

1.3.2 Flexibility

As mentioned before, there have been many experimental and prototype implementations of relational data sublanguages. Because of the wide variety of language types, however, each of these implementations is directed towards a specific language by unrelated efforts and different philosophies. These implementations generally supply their own access methods and provisions for authorisation, integrity control, etc. This situation would require an installation that wished to switch from one language to another to change a large amount of its software. If it wished to support two different languages there would be a great deal of duplication of software functions. The resulting increases in cost, maintenance, etc. would obviously make this situation highly undesirable.

Moreover, each language always has its own strengths and weaknesses, and there is always room for improvement. It can be expensive to make changes to either the underlying database management system (DBMS) software or the query language itself. Developing applications can be time consuming as well.

Granted this premise the idea of a universal approach that provides as much commonness among those languages as possible seems an attractive proposition. Such an approach can ease problems of program portability and migration from system to system.

1.4 OBJECTIVES AND BENEFITS OF THE ILEX SYSTEM

In order to solve the problems with individual query languages, an intelligent relational data base system called ILEX is implemented, which provides a choice between at least two alternative languages to the user, and enables him to suit the system behaviour to his personal needs.

If research is to be worthwhile, it must be directed toward the discovery of general principles, which can then be translated into the specifics of particular system design. This demand is the general basis of our work. In the project every effort is made to balance theory and practice by including a reasonable number of programming examples illustrating the creation and manipulation of an intelligent relational data base system.

Concerning the integration of user needs into system design, a universal database interface for high level relational query languages will be presented. Although it would be absurd to suggest that the universal interface could possess all desirable characteristics of any existing query language, it is intended to show that a universal interface that is built on logic programming and relational foundations is implementable and can be communicated to with different relational query languages. It does have significant advantages over an individual language.

We list below some more detailed objectives for ILEX:

(i) The uniform approach aims to support the variety of existing query languages within the same query system. This application area has received little attention in the past.

(ii) Any language extension, no matter what function it provides, should be designed from the user's point of view rather than the system's. In other words, the design should proceed from the outside in. (i.e. each language is a result of top-down design).

(iii) Wherever possible it should exploit existing language features rather than introduce any novel language design. That is to say that the proposed uniform approach should also form a natural extension to well established modes of working by current query language users.

(iv) The universal approach itself should not be dependent on any particular query language. A variety of such relational query languages can be mapped into the universal interface; however, the universal interface is not limited to or biased towards any particular languages.

(v) A major objective of the ILEX system is to cover the three categories of the relational model - tuple calculus; domain calculus; relational algebra - in a unified and consistent manner. The support for the three classes of query languages should merge into a universal form, not three discrete sets.

(vi) The ILEX system should look like a centralised system to the user. That is, the user should not normally need to know all query languages provided by the system. Any language supported can be considered as a stand-alone one. Meanwhile, it should be allowable to use all query languages interchangeably, since a particular query might be extremely convenient for specification by a particular query language.

(vii) The system should be efficiently implementable. The software redundancy caused by the use of discrete query languages should be reduced as much as possible. For instance, the same built-in function library will serve for all query languages. As a matter of fact, the ILEX system itself could be considered as the data base of any query language supported. Efficient path accessing will be described and demonstrated for all languages as well.

(viii) The underlying software, such as data organisation, access method (optimisation), can be changed without requiring any change at the user interface. All query languages supported should be clearly-separated components and can be modified independently of the rest of the system.

(ix) It is expected that ILEX will be a good prototype for human performance evaluation studies of query languages, since it provides a universal interface with the same terminal equipment and underlying software.

(x) As data base machines receive considerable attention owing to their facilities for improving performance of installations with heavy data base activity, system ILEX is expected to be able to use associative hardware to very good advantage. The gap between a PROLOG system and a data base machine should be bridged.

It is widely predicted that knowledge information processing will be a major area of computer applications in the 1990's, where problem solving and logic inference will play the central computing rule [22]. Along this line, the foundation of the work is to combine concepts from three areas of computer science research: Artificial Intelligence (AI) and Logic Programming, Data Base Management Systems (DBMSs), and Associative Processing. From AI and Logic Programming we will use the concept of knowledge representation in deductive question-answering systems, and the concept of first-order predicate calculus; from DBMS we will build on the concept of a relational database; and finally, based on Associative Processing which may avoid the von Neumann bottleneck [23] we believe that database machines are the result of an architecture approach which distributes processing power closer to the devices on which data are stored. These ideas are married to form an intelligent relational data base system, yielding a novel and powerful collection of facilities in the system-user interface, and giving great benefits in reduced cost and increased flexibility of implementation and application.

1.5 THE SYSTEM DESIGN OUTLINE

These considerations led us to develop a database system entirely implemented in PROLOG [24], the best known and most widely available logic programming language. It was a rather ambitious project at the time, involving the implementation of three typical high level query languages. However, a useful and cost-effective implementation has been produced and is surprisingly "self-maintaining". It has been shown that a universal interface covering a number of relational query languages is implementable even in a minicomputer environment.

The system ILEX processes a query in three main stages:

```
      understanding             optimisation           execution
QUERY ------------> LOGIC ------------> PROLOG ---------> ANSWER
          (1)                    (2)                   (3)
```

Fig. 1.2 Query Modification: A Three Stage Process

Fig. 1.2 gives a very general overview of the knowledge information processing in ILEX, and corresponds roughly to:

(1) What does the query mean? --- An intuitive understanding of the problem to be solved.

(2) How shall I answer it? --- Optimisation, intended to solve the problem in the efficient way.

(3) What is the answer? --- Execution, which is expected to be able to link with a back-end architecture, such as an associative retrieval system, in the future.

A query written in a particular query language will be taken through the steps indicated in Fig. 1.3

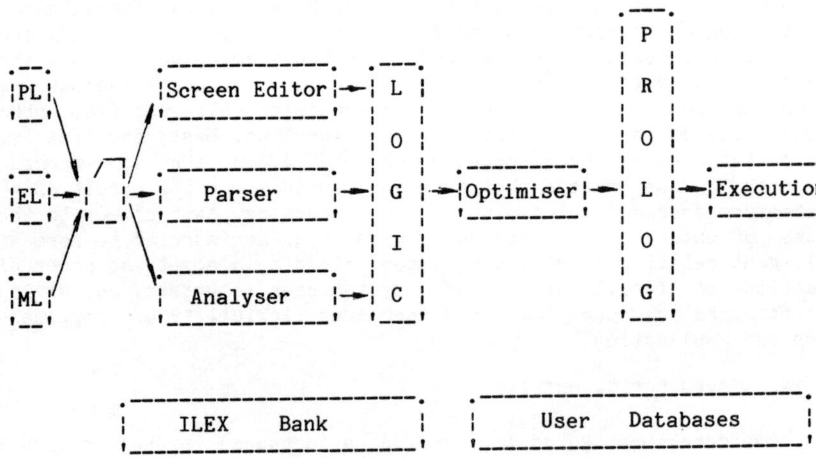

Fig. 1.3 Block Structure of ILEX

In Chapter 2 we outline terms and concepts which form the basis for the forthcoming chapters. By introducing the canonical logic expression, in Chapter 3, we set up a general knowledge representation for any query. Furthermore, Chapters 4, 5, and 6 are devoted to the translation of three quite different query languages: PL (a Picture-Like language) based on QBE, EL (an English-Like language) based on SQL, and ML (a Mathematics-Like language) based on relational algebra, into the canonical logic expression respectively. An implementation technique for negation and aggregate functions within the ILEX system is described in Chapter 7. Chapter 8 presents an effective strategy for optimisation. Some considerations of the linking between the ILEX system and the data base machine MEMEX [25] are given in Chapter 9 for hardware realisation. We conclude our approach together with the future work in Chapter 10.

CHAPTER 2
On Relational Database Systems through Logic

To pave the way for these later chapters, the present chapter gives some preliminary concepts on relational data bases and logic programming respectively. A goal of the chapter is to show how logic can provide a formal support to study relational data base problems, and in some cases, how logic can go further, helping first in their comprehension, and then in their solution. Additionally of interest is to show that relational database models fit greatly the PROLOG language by virtue of their logic nature.

2.1 THE RELATIONAL DATABASES

One of the most critical problems facing data processing installations today is the rapidly increasing cost of developing and maintaining programs. Two fundamental problems in the use of files are:

(i) The data independence problem. In nondatabase systems an application is data-dependent. It is impossible to change the storage (how the data is physically recorded) or access strategy (how it is accessed) without affecting the application.

(ii) The data redundancy problem. The fact that each application has its own private files can often lead to considerable redundancy in stored data, with resultant waste in storage space and a high risk of inconsistency.

Generalised database management systems have addressed these problems by making it possible to write data independent programs with central control of the data base.

Three well known data models are relational, hierarchical, and network models. In relational model data are assumed to be stored in the form of tables; In hierarchical model data are assumed to be stored in the form of tree structures; And in network model data are assumed to be stored in the form of general graph structures. In comparison with them, the relational approach, grounded in a well-established mathematical discipline, is a significant approach to the logic description and manipulation of data. Briefly speaking, it views the logical database as a time-varying collection of normalised relations which are flat in that no repeating groups are involved. A relational database is manipulated by powerful operators for extracting columns and join them, and involves no consideration of positional, pointer, or access path aspects. Such a high degree of logical data manipulation is not readily available in network and hierarchic data base systems. However, because of their simplicity and generality, they have been more difficult to implement efficiently. There were no full relational DBMS commercially available as of 1979, although IBM's Query-By-Example offering shows the relational orientation and the experimental relational system R is perhaps the most advanced relational implementation.

2.1.1 Terminology of Relational Model

The relational approach carries a terminology of its own and a tendency to use terms which are rather mathematically oriented. It thus has a good theoretical foundation [26]. For the future convenience we briefly summarise them as below:

[Definitions]

Relation. Given a collection of set D1,D2,...,Dn, R is a relation on those n sets if it is a set of ordered n-tuples <d1,d2,...,dn> such that d1 belongs to D1, d2 belongs to D2, ..., dn belongs to Dn. It is normal to display relations as **tables** where the attributes head the columns and the rows are tuples. Hence the **table** and **relation** are used interchangeably.

Relational Scheme. This is a set of attributes, which are names of columns for a relation. A relation scheme is assumed to remain constant over time, while the relation corresponding to it changes frequently.

Arity. The arity of a relation is the number of columns in the relation. Relations of arity one are said to be unary, relations of arity two are binary, ..., and relations of arity n are n-ary.

Attribute. An attribute of a relation is a column name in the relation; whereas the attribute values are the content of the column.

Domain. A domain is the set of values from which the set of attribute values of a relation may be taken; that is, from which a column of a table may be formed. It is important to appreciate the difference between a domain and columns; a column represents the use of a domain within a relation.

Tuple. We may consider a relation as being a mathematical set of tuples, a tuple is a row in the table. Each tuple in a relation is unique, since it is an element in a mathematical set.

Cardinality. The cardinality of a relation R, denoted by $|R|$, is the number of tuples in R.

Integrity Constraints. Database consistency is enforced by integrity constraints which are assertions that data base instances are compelled to obey. Data dependencies are special cases of integrity constraints.

Functional Dependency (FD). A functional dependency X -> Y is an assertion about a relation scheme. It asserts of any "legal" relation that two of its tuples t1 and t2 that agree on set of attributes X also agree on Y, that is, if t1[X] = t2[X] then t1[Y] = t2[Y].

Multivalued Dependency (MVD). A multivalued dependency X ->-> Y is a statement that if t1 and t2 are two tuples of a relation that satisfies X ->-> Y and X -> Y, then the relation must have the third tuple t3 that takes the Y-value from one of the tuple, say t1, and its value everywhere else from the other. In other words, X->-> Y means that the set of Y-values associated with a particular X-value must be independent of the values of the rest of the attributes.

Keys. In terms of FD and MVD of a relation, a minimum collection of attributes that can function as a unique identifier is called a candidate key. A relation may have more than one candidate key.

Normalisation. The theory of normalisation relates dependency types to desirable properties of relation schemes. By normalisation there can be no redundancy caused by dependencies of the given type in the relations for this scheme.

Normalised Relation. A normalised relation is a table with non-decomposable values, which, sometimes, is called base table, or base relation.

Databases. A database is a collection of relations, and their relation schemes collectively form the database scheme.

To sum up, a relational database DB is a collection R = { Ri }, describing certain objects of the world having certain attributes D, and the relationship among D, i.e. a set of dependencies F. Each relation Ri is characterised by a set of attributes Si = $\{Dj \mid Dj \in D\}$ called its scheme, and consists of a set of tuples. Each tuple is a map from the attributes of the relation scheme to their domains that satisfies all the dependencies of F.

Fig. 2.1 shows a relation called 'R' formed by the columns named 'AA', 'BB', 'CC', and 'DD' respectively. Each term involved in relation 'R' is given in Fig. 2.2.

R			
AA	BB	CC	DD
a1	b1	c1	d1
a1	b2	c2	d2
a1	b1	c1	d2
a1	b2	c2	d1
a2	b3	c1	d1
a2	b3	c1	d2

Fig. 2.1 A Relation (or Table)

Term	Corresponding Names	Example
relation	table/file	R
relational scheme	table heading	<AA,BB,CC,DD>
attribute	column name/field type	AA
attribute values	underlying domain	a1,a2
component	value	c2
arity	degree	4
tuple	row/entity/segment/record	<a1,b2,c2,d2>
cardinality	-	6
FD	-	BB -> CC
MVD	-	AA ->-> <BB,CC>

Fig.2.2 Terminology

A relational data base is accessed by a set of jobs submitted by user in order to retrieve, delete, insert or modify any subset of the data. In general, retrieval is an essential part of these processes. Users submit their requests for information in the form of queries, specifying the data which must be retrieved and the conditions that must be satisfied by the desired data. The task of query processing is to determine the set of data, the proper order in which the data should be accessed and the types of manipulations that must be performed on the data. This processing is referred to by different authors as query translation, access path finding, or optimisation.

2.1.2 THE EXAMPLE DATABASE

In introducing the high level query languages PL, EL, and ML we will use queries against a sample relational database extended from the book by C.J.Date [27].

The data is organised into six relations (see Fig. 2.3):

suppliers, parts, shipment, stock, department, and employee. The "suppliers" table contains, for each supplier, a supplier number (sno), name (sname), status code, and location; the "parts" table contains, for each part, a part number (pno), name (pname), colour, weight, and location where the part is stored; and the "shipment" table contains, for each shipment, a supplier number, a part number, and the quantity shipped (qty); the "stock" table shows, for each department, how many in stock to each part; the "department" describes department location and department manager for each department; the "employee" table contains the employee's name (ename), age, salary, and the department he works in. The relationships between these relations together with their keys are given in Fig. 2.4.

suppliers

sno	sname	status	city
s1	smith	20	london
s2	jones	10	paris
s3	blake	30	paris
s4	clark	20	london
s5	adams	30	athens

shipment

sno	pno	qty
s1	p1	300
s1	p2	200
s1	p3	400
s1	p4	200
s1	p5	100
s1	p6	100
s2	p1	300
s2	p2	400
s3	p2	200
s4	p2	200
s4	p4	300
s4	p5	400

parts

pno	pname	colour	weight	city
p1	nut	red	12	london
p2	bolt	green	17	paris
p3	screw	blue	17	rome
p4	screw	red	14	london
p5	cam	blue	12	paris
p6	cog	red	19	london

stock

dept	pno	qty
d1	p1	600
d2	p2	350
d2	p1	450
d3	p1	500
d3	p4	220

department

dept	city	manager
d1	london	smith
d2	perth	long
d3	london	lee

employee

ename	age	salary	dept
john	34	8600	d1
morgan	24	6300	d2
lewis	42	9000	d3
long	34	8500	d2
henry	29	12300	d1
thomas	31	7300	d3
martin	45	7500	d1

Fig.2.3 The SUPPLIERS-PARTS-DEPT Database

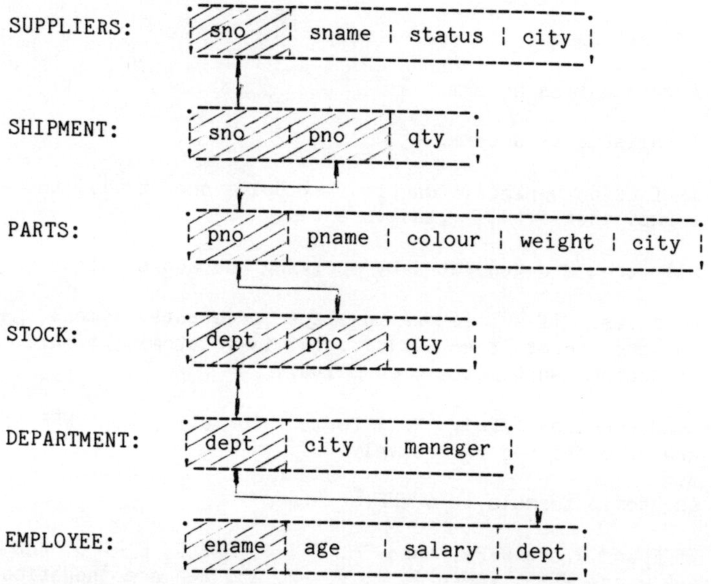

Fig. 2.4 The Relationships in the SUPPLIERS-PARTS-DEPT Database

2.2 LOGIC PROGRAMMING

Logic studies the relationship of implication between assumptions and conclusions. It was originally devised as a way of representing the form of arguments, so that it would be possible to check in a formal way whether or not they were valid. Thus we can use logic to express propositions, the relation between propositions and how one can validly infer some propositions from others (theorem proving) [28,29]. From logic point of view, a generalised DBMS is just a general-purpose question-answering system in which the set of facts necessary for question answering (or problem-solving) can be viewed as axioms of a theorem, and the question (or the problem) can be viewed as the conclusion of the theorem. Therefore, the emphasis of such a data base management system is on its deductive power. This is why logic plays such an important role in DBMSs. Recent development in automated deduction has led to the increasing use of logic as a very high level programming language and as a language for database description.

2.2.1 The First Order Predicate Calculus

A particular form of logic is called the first order predicate calculus or predicate logic. In predicate logic objects are present by **terms**. In order to express relationship between objects **formulas** are used. We give brief definitions of these concepts below:

[Definitions]

Terms. Terms are defined recursively:

(i) A constant is a term.

(ii) A variable is a term.

(iii) If f is an n-place function symbol, and t1,...,tn are terms, then f(t1,...,tn) is a term.

(iv) All terms are generated by applying the above rules.

Atomic Formulas. If P is an n-place predicate symbol, and t1,...,tn are terms, then P(t1,...,tn) is an atomic formula. No other expression can be atomic formulas.

Well Formed Formulas (WFF). Well formed formulas, or WFF for short, are also defined recursively:

(i) An atomic formula is a WFF.

(ii) If F and G are WFFs, then ~F, F & G, F # G, F -> G, and F <-> G are WFFs, where ~, &, #, ->, and <-> are 'negation', 'conjunction', 'disjunction', 'implication', and 'equivalence' connectives respectively.

(iii) if F is WFF, x is a free variable, then (∀x)F and (∃x)F are WFFs, where ∀x and ∃x are universal and existential quantifiers (quantity connectives) respectively.

(iv) WFFs are generated only by a finite number of applications of (i), (ii), and (iii).

Following these definitions we can express statements by predicate calculus formulas.

Example 1: Smith is a man.

man(smith)

Example 2: All man are mortal.

(∀x) (man(x) -> mortal(x))

Example 3: Every man is mortal, Smith is a man, therefore Smith is mortal.

(∀x)(man(x) -> mortal(x)) & man(smith) -> mortal(smith)

Example 4: Susan sits between Albert and David.

between(albert,susan,david)

Example 5: Some men are clever.

$(\exists x)$ (man(x) & clever(x))

Example 6: All men like all women.

$(\forall x)$ (man(x) -> $(\forall y)$ (women(y) -> like(x,y)))
or $(\forall x)(\forall y)$ (man(x) & woman(y) & like(x,y))

2.2.2 Clausal Form

In a WFF a connective can be expressed in terms of the other connectives. For instance:

```
F <-> G  == (F -> G) & (G -> F)
F -> G == ~F # G
~~P == P
~(F & G) == ~F # ~G
~(F # G) == ~F & ~G
(∃x)P == ~((∀x)(~P))
(∀x)P == ~((∃x)(~P))
```

A functionally complete set of connectives in Predicate Calculus, which is sufficient to express any formula in an equivalent form, could be {&,~,∀x} or {F,->,∀x}. As a result of the redundancy, there are many ways to express the same formula in an equivalent form. (The same situation in database query languages: different queries express the same request). If we wish to carry out formal manipulations on Predicate Calculus formulas, this turns out to be very inconvenient. It would be much nicer if everything we wanted to say could only be expressed in one way. So let us consider a special form, clausal form, where there are less ways of saying the same thing.

[definition]

Clausal Forms. A clause is an expression of the form

B1,B2,...,Bm <- A1,A2,...,An

where B1,B2,...,Bm, A1,A2,...,An are atomic formulas, n>=0 and m>=0. The atomic formulas A1,A2,...,An are joint conditions of the clause; and B1,B2,...,Bm are the alternative conclusions. If the clause contains the variables x1,x2,...,xk then interpret it as stating that for all x1,x2,...,xk, B1 or B2 or ... or Bm holds if A1 and A2 and ... and An hold.

There are three special cases:

(i) If n=0, that is,

B1,B2,.....,Bm <-

then: for all x1,...,xk, B1 or B2 or ... or Bm is unconditionally true.

(ii) If m=0, that is,

<- A1,A2,...,An

then: for all x1,...,xk, it is not the case that A1 and ... and An.

(iii) If m=n=0, that is the empty clause:

<-

then: this is a formula which is always false (a contradiction).

Example 1: For every X, Y, and Z, X is grandparent of Y if X is parent of Z and Z is parent of Y.

grandparent(X,Y) <- parent(X,Z), parent(Z,Y).

Example 2: For every X, X is male or X is female if X is human.

male(X),female(X) <- human(X).

Example 3: Nothing is both good and bad.

<- good(X),bad(X).

2.2.3 Horn Clauses

Clauses containing at most one conclusion are called **Horn clauses**, first investigated by the logician Alfred Horn. For many applications of logic, it is sufficient to restrict the form of clauses to Horn clauses. There are obviously two kinds of Horn clauses:

(i) **Headed Horn Clauses.**

B <- A1,A2,...,An

or

B <-

(ii) **Headless Horn Clauses.**

<- A1,A2,...,An

or an empty clause: <-

Any soluble problem (theorem-proving task) that can be expressed in Horn Clauses can be expressed in such a way that: **there is one headless clause, and all the rest of the clauses are headed** [30].

Thus, we can decide to view the headless clause as the goal which must be present for a problem to be soluble and the other clauses as the hypotheses (axioms). Because resolution with Horn clause is relatively simple, they are an obvious choice as the basis of a theorem prover which provides a practical programming system.

Example 1: The factorial of 0 is 1. The factorial of X+1 is X+1 times the factorial of X.

```
fact(0,1) <-
fact(add_1(X),Y) <- fact(X,A), times(add_1(X),A,Y)
```

where "add_1(X)" is a function indicating the X+1 function; "times(M,N,R)" is a predicate formula showing that M multiplied by N is R.

Example 2: Write Horn clauses describing the Fibbonaci function.

```
fib(0,1) <-
fib(1,1) <-
fib(add_1(add_1(X)),R) <- fib(X,R1),
                          fib(add_1(X),R2),
                          plus(R1,R2,R)
```

where "add_1(X)" is the same as that in example 1; "plus(R1,R2,R)" indicates the sum of R1 and R2 is R. This is instantly recognizable as a definition of the Fibbonaci series.

As a conclusion of this section, Fig. 2.4 gives a clear concept on logic programming.

```
.-------------------------------------------------.
| Mathematical Logic                              |
|                                                 |
|  .------------------------------------.        |
|  | First Order Predicate Calculus     |        |
|  |                                    |        |
|  |  .------------------------.        |        |
|  |  | Clausal Form           |        |        |
|  |  |                        |        |        |
|  |  |  .---------------.     |        |        |
|  |  |  | Horn Clauses  |     |        |        |
|  |  |  |               |     |        |        |
|  |  |  '---------------'     |        |        |
|  |  '------------------------'        |        |
|  '------------------------------------'        |
'-------------------------------------------------'
```

Fig. 2.5 The Onion-Layer of Logic Programming

2.3 PROLOG AS A LOGIC PROGRAMMING LANGUAGE

The language PROLOG based on Horn Clauses can be seen as a first step towards the ultimate goal of programming in logic [31].

PROLOG = Horn Clauses + Extralogical Facilities

The outstanding features of PROLOG make itself to be chosen for many applications, such as deductive reasoning over data bases, natural language, theorem proving, planning and symbol calculus. PROLOG has been chosen by the Japanese as the basis of the core language of their Fifth Generation Computer Systems [22].

2.3.1 A Brief View of PROLOG

PROLOG is by now available in many different versions. The notation of the particular PROLOG implementation used in the ILEX system can be found in [32]. The reader is suggested to consult Appendix 2 in which the PROLOG syntax and semantics are described, together with simple examples. Here only the bare essentials are given.

(a). Terms. The data objectives of the language PROLOG are called terms. A term is a constant, variable or structure.

(i) **Constants.** A constant is thought of a naming specific object or specific relationship. The constants include **integers** such as: 0, 123, 6453, and **atoms** which normally begin with a low case letter, such as: book, smith. Those made up from only symbols are also atoms, such as: ?-, :-, ->, etc. The special underline character '_' may be insert in the middle of an atom to improve legibility, for instance george_smith.

(ii) **Variables.** Variables look like atoms except they begin with a capital letter or an underline sign '_'. For example: X, Var, _value. There is a special variable named anonymous variable '_' which never shares with each other. A variable should be thought of as standing for some definite but unspecified object.

(iii) **Structures.** The structured data objects of PROLOG are the structures. A structure comprises a functor and a sequence of one or more terms called arguments. A functor is characterised by its name, which is an atom, and its arity or number of arguments. For example, the structure whose functor is named 'point' of arity 3, with arguments A, B, and C is written:

```
point(A,B,C)
```

Structures are usefully pictured as trees. For example, the term:

```
line(point(X,Y,Z),point(A,B,C))
```

would be pictured as the structure:

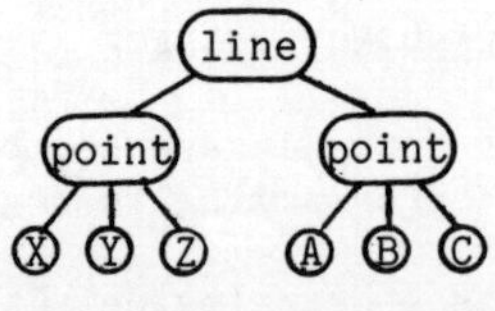

Sometimes it is convenient to write a compound term using an optional infix notation. For instance, X+Y+Z is equivalent to +(+(X,Y),Z), and instead of ;(P,Q) we may write P;Q. Finally, note that an atom is treated as a functor of arity 0.

(b). **Headed Clauses.** There are two kinds of headed clauses: **facts** and **rules.**

(i) **Facts.** A fact is an assertion which is an axiom, such as: **likes(john,mary)** stating that **John likes Mary.** When defining relationship between objects using facts, the order of objects is arbitrary, but must be consistent about it. So the fact **likes(john,mary)** is not the same thing as **likes(mary,john).**

(ii) **Rules.** A rule is a conditional assertion which consists of a head and a body. The head and the body are connected by the symbol ":-" which can be pronounced "if". For instance: to state **John likes anyone who likes wine** in PROLOG becomes:

```
likes(john,X) :- likes(X,wine).
```

The head of this rule describes what fact the rule is intended to define. The body, in this case **likes(X,wine)**, describes the conjunction of **goals** that must be satisfied, one after the other, for the head to be true. Suppose **John likes any female who likes wine**, we have:

```
likes(john,X) :- female(X), likes(X,wine).
```

(c). **Headless Clauses.** Headless Clauses in PROLOG are **Questions.** A special symbol "?-" is always put before the question. When a question is asked of PROLOG, it will search through the database, and look for facts or rules that match the question. Two facts match if their predicates are the same and if their corresponding arguments each are the same.

2.3.2 Resolution Proof Procedures of PROLOG

Any collection of the Horn clauses can be run directly as a PROLOG program in a top-down and depth-first way. A question is soluble if it is the head of some clause instance and each of the goals (if any) of that clause instance is true, where an instance of a clause (or term) is obtained by substituting, for each zero or more of its variables, a new term for all occurrences of the variable. The proof can also be interpreted as a computation.

The most important features in PROLOG are **recursion** and **backtracking.**

(a). **Recursion.** In PROLOG, recursion is the normal and natural way of viewing data structures and programs. Consider for example the Horn clause program:

```
member(X,[X|_]).                /* clause P */
```

```
member(X,[_|Y]) :- member(X,Y).  /* clause Q */
```

The clause P is to be understood as: "X is a member of the list if X is the head of the list". The clause Q is to be understood as: "X is the member of the list if X is a member of the tail of the list". Here the "[X|_]" or "[_|Y]" is the notation of a list in PROLOG, in which the head and the tail of the list are separated by the vertical bar "|".

The proof that clauses P and Q imply **member**(d,[a,b,c,d,e]) works as follows: each time the clause Q attempts to satisfy itself, the goal is given a shorter list. Eventually the clause P, which is a fact and does not cause any further subgoal to be considered, will match. The "recurrence" of the clause Q will come to an end (see Fig. 2.6).

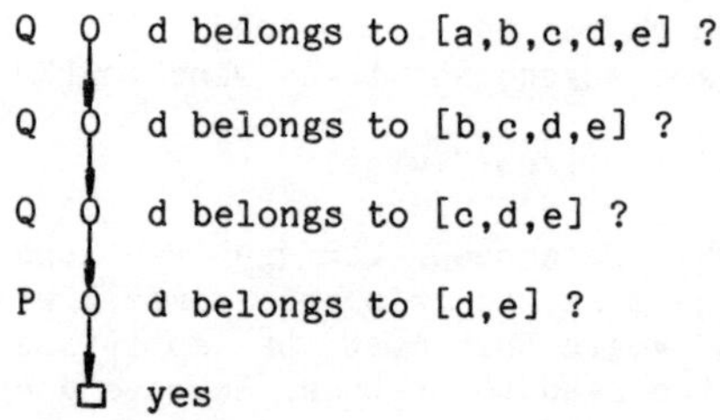

Fig. 2.6 Recursion in Proving 'member(d,[a,b,c,d,e])'

(b). Backtracking. PROLOG uses a depth-first backtracking search strategy to explore alternative branches of the search space. The order in which clauses are written determines the order in which they are tried. Thus it interprets a clause

```
A :- B,C,D.
```

as a procedure which attempts to solve A by **first** solving B **then** solving C **then** solving D. C is solved in the context created by having solved B, and so on. If a goal, say C, has failed, PROLOG then attempts to re-satisfy the next goal on the left, in this case B, by returning to uninstantiated any variables that become instantiated when this goal B was previously satisfied, and resuming searching the database, but beginning the search from where the goal's place-maker was previously put. As before, this new "backtracked" goal may either succeed or fail, which will decide whether or not to have another backtracking. For example, given clauses P and Q above the problem of finding a common element in two lists

```
?- member(X,[d,a,t,a]), member(X,[n,s,a,w,e,r]).
```

will generate a double nested loop.

2.3.3 Extralogical Facilities of PROLOG

PROLOG incorporates only a simple proof procedure. In order to be able to compensate the limitation and simulate programming styles more appropriate to conventional programming language it provides various extralogical primitives which can be used to extend the power of the language while retaining its logic foundations.

These extralogical primitives can be regarded as ways of expressing **control information** about how the proof is to be carried out. For instance, the built-in predicate **write(N)** does not have any interesting logical properties, but presupposes that the proof will have reached a certain state (with N instantiated) and initiates a communication with the programmer. The built-in predicate **name(N,L)** is saying something about the internal structure of what, in Predicate Calculus, would be an indivisible symbol. A set of built-in predicates supported by the PROLOG system has been collected in Appendix 1. The reader may find it valuable to refer to the Appendix from time to time in order to supplement his understanding of the precise meaning of the concepts. There is space to discuss only the distinctive extralogical primitive **cut** (written "!").

The **cut** is used to control backtracking. As a goal, the cut "!" succeeds immediately and can not be resatisfied. However, it also has side-effects which alter the way backtracking works afterwards. It removes the place markers for certain goals so that they can not be resatisfied. For instance, to compute the maximum of two numbers, instead of writing

```
max(X,Y,X) :- X >= Y.
max(X,Y,Y) :- X < Y.
```

a more efficient program is obtained by using "!":

```
max(X,Y,X) :- X >=Y, !.        /* clause A */
max(X,Y,Y).                    /* clause B */
```

Thus, the clause B will be used only if the clause A (before "!") fails. It avoids the redundant computation of X<Y; but it results in that individual clauses can not be understood correctly in isolation.

In PROLOG we can convert symbols to character strings, convert structures to lists and convert structures to clauses. A logical variable can be allowed to stand for a proposition appearing in an axiom. If the built-in predicate asserta is used to set up a new clause, there may be a different set of axioms at different times of proof! These operations violate the simple self-contained nature of predicate calculus propositions. There are no safeguards against using PROLOG in a manner which obscures and even conflicts with its logical foundations.

The ultimate goal of a logic programming language has not, then, been achieved with PROLOG. One day, the extralogical facilities of PROLOG will no longer be necessary. In the meanwhile they provide a valuable safety valve which allows logic programming to be practical today. For the sake of efficiency, the extralogical features of PROLOG can always be confined within high-level predicates which extend either the level of the logic or the power of the control facilities.

2.4 THE RELATIONSHIPS BETWEEN LOGIC AND RELATIONAL DATABASES

Logic has been found to be highly useful both for describing static database as well as for processing database which change. On the other hand, the evolution in database technology, particularly in relational model, has been drifting more and more toward the use of logic [33]. A considerable amount of programming logic theory can be transferred to databases. The use of logic for data description abolishes the distinction between data bases and programs. Strategies which apply to the execution of programs apply also to the retrieval of answers to data base queries. Methods for proving properties of programs apply to verification of integrity constraints. Procedures for maintaining dynamically evolving data bases apply to the evolutionary development.

As far as relational query languages and user-interfaces are concerned, there are many problems that can be conveniently transformed into logic; we shall list some of them.

(i) From the viewpoint of theorem proving, a data base system can be considered as a question-answering system where facts are represented by logic formulas; then answering a question from the facts may be regarded as proving that a formula corresponding to the answer is derivable from the formulas representing the facts; then deductive searches become important [34].

(ii) If a query is written in a very high level non-procedural query language the execution of such a query is to perform tasks that would be called intelligent. The data base system can be viewed as knowledge-based system. Starting with an initial state, one tries to find a sequence of operators that will transform the initial state into desired state - that is knowledge information processing. In this case, we can describe states and the state transition rules by logic formulas. In other words, logic programming languages, such as PROLOG, can be applied to the task of writing compilers for high level query languages [35]. The major advantage of PROLOG as a language for writing compilers is that it specifies algorithms in a human-oriented way. Such specification can be interpreted as a uniform resolution theorem-prover. It is not a great exaggeration to say that specification is the implementation. In fact, logic programming can extend any query language to a programming language.

(iii) Since a database may be viewed as a logic program, retrieval is automatically taken care of through resolution [36]. For instance, given a predicate definition for an n-ary predicate p, the retrieval of the jth argument corresponding to specific values of the others is simply obtained by posing the query:

?- p(v1,...,vj-1,X,vj+1,...,vn).

where vi are those specific values and X is a variable. Because of nondeterminism, more than one value for X may be retrieved. Because of the nondistinction between input and output, any argument or combination of arguments can be chosen for retrieval. Thus retrieval operations that are usually needed in relational databases (e.g., for the above example, projection and selection) become so simple within logic programming.

(iv) The efficiency of access strategies directly affects the performance of data base systems. Logic can indeed play an interesting role in obtaining a query less costly to evaluate [37].

The link with logic was not only found at the language level and query evaluation. For instance, an equivalence between dependencies (FDs and MVDs) and a fragment of propositional logic has been found [38,39]. It is rather straightforward that dependency statements can be expressed as first order formulas, but it goes beyond the scope of this book.

It is our belief that a wider use of logic should have a positive effect on the database field, as it provides not only a conceptual framework for formulating various database concepts, but also (in the form of logic programming) a tool for implementing them.

CHAPTER 3
A Canonical Logic Form for Query Languages

3.1 GENERAL COMMENTS REGARDING THE UNIFIED APPROACH

The ILEX system can be considered to consist of two sets of Horn clauses: the **External Data Base (EDB)**, concerning a user's database, and **Internal Data Base (IDB)**, concerning query semantic transformation, optimisation, and certain features which are standard of all query languages supported. The EDB and IDB do not correspond to two separated processes: they form a single program, part of which is user defined. The definition of a relation belongs partly to IDB and partly to EDB as our aim is to relieve the user from details that can be handled in a general manner. The control and extralogical features of PROLOG are not needed in EDB; the user, therefore, need not know PROLOG at all.

One of the most important of the objectives for ILEX is to support all three classes of relational query languages. This objective is subsequently extended to allow a new language to be mapped into the system later. The fact that these high level query languages are designed independently of each other and no consideration of the compatibility among them is made in advance may result in a great deal of redundancies and interferences.

3.1.1 Compatibility and Interference

With the observation that the existing relational query languages can be viewed as alternative ways of querying the same data base, the essential properties, which are generally hidden in the explicit descriptions of several query languages, may be much the same although the representations can be very different. Taking into account the overlappings among the various query languages, a functional bank has been built up to provide as much commonality of applications as possible across the different query languages. The bank could be considered as the knowledge database of all query languages supported, so that the software redundancy caused by the use of discrete query languages can be reduced as much as possible. However, the bank, which is consistent with the properties of data, is designed independently of any particular query language, and can be extended if necessary.

Since the independently designed query languages differ in a number of ways, such as syntactic form and procedurality, the contradiction between query languages may occur. This is called "interferences". Therefore, proper modification has to be made. Two approaches can be taken to solve this problem.

Concerning the syntactic and semantical differences between query languages, the first approach is to use read-in technique. Character strings known to a query language may be changed into their internal forms, and unacceptable readings can be discarded on the grounds of a mismatch. The second approach is used to deal with controversial operators across languages. The redeclaration can be made if necessary. Given a semantic description properties which are language-independent in a DBMS, we can define a set of meaningful operations which are consistent with the properties. This set of operations can be specified individually or locally shared with. For instance, in order to be able to understand a non-procedural query better, it is necessary to add a number of "criteria" by which the logic virtue of a query can be obtained so that the query can be proceduralised.

Fig. 3.1 shows the relationship between the different parts of the ILEX system.

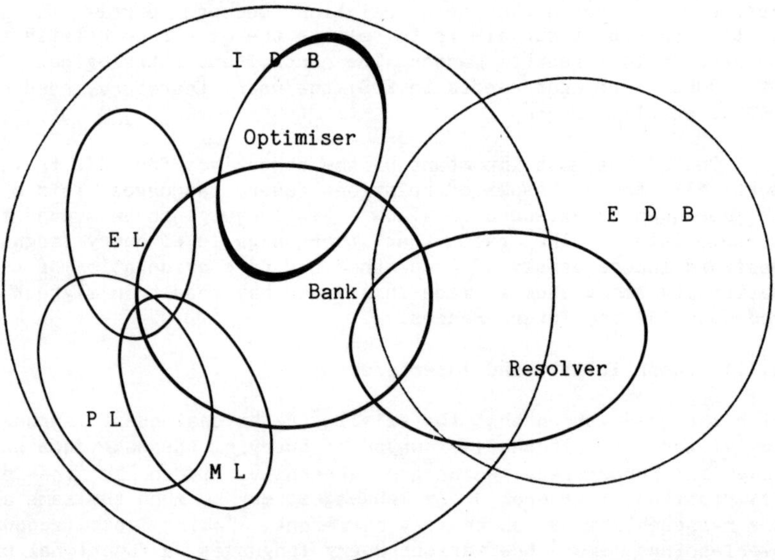

Fig. 3.1 Query Languages and Other Facilities in ILEX

3.1.2 Considerations of Query Processing

The heuristic considerations of the ILEX system are divided into three levels, each of which provides an output which is the input to the next (see Fig. 3.2).

(1) **Understanding level.** As the first step, ILEX accepts a query written in any query language by means of a universal read-in program. The necessary facilities are also provided in order to help the user formulate his query. An important idea at this stage is to translate an arbitrary query type into a canonical logic form. In terms of the language the user is using, the corresponding compiler performs the mapping from the given query to the canonical form if the query does not violate the grammar of the language.

(2) **Conceptual level.** The ILEX system takes full advantage of the canonical representation in the sense that a global program optimisation can be made rather than optimisation of individual requests specified by different query languages. An effective strategy for planning the query in canonical form is provided at the conceptual level. Based on a cost formula, an optimal order of the query is obtained in a Horn clause form which can be directly executed by PROLOG system.

(3) **Internal level.** Finally, the executor, probably incorporating associative hardware, carries out the query and gives the corresponding responses. The ILEX system normally returns the output for the user's query to the terminal used for input, but there are facilities for switching output to an alternative device. The output format is a tabular form that is system standard no matter which query language is used at that time. Besides, ILEX automatically eliminates redundant duplicates from a query result.

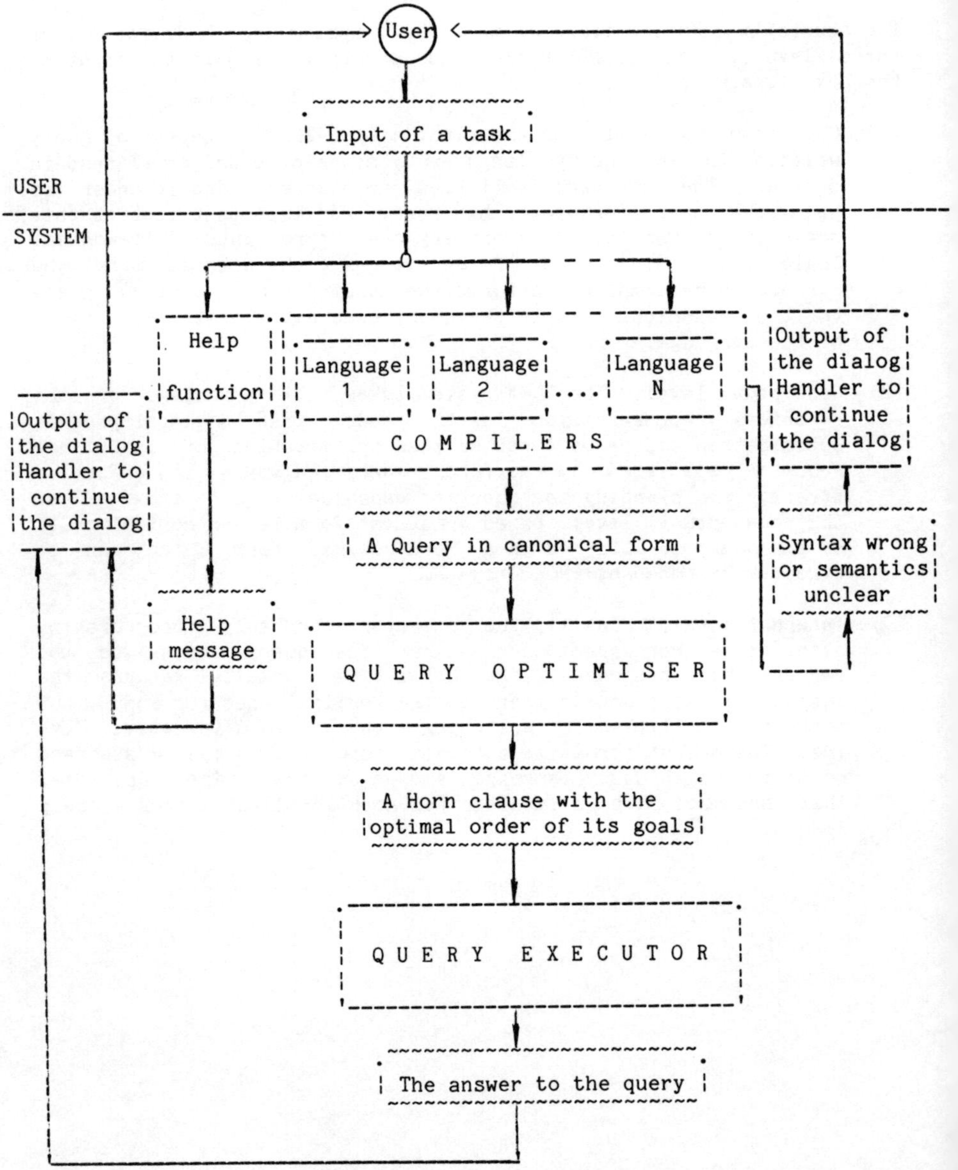

Fig. 3.2 The Organisation Levels of the ILEX System

3.2 QUERY FORMULATION

As explained in chapter 1, the complex and competing requirements of making query languages user-friendly have challenged the ingenuity of language designers and stimulated a remarkably diverse set of products. Obviously the way of formulating a query varies from language to language. For instance, with the same terminal the English-Like language EL has a definite syntax and only key words from a specified list can be used; whereas the Picture-Like language PL offers skeletons to help the user formulate his query. A new query language in the future may strive toward natural language interactive dialogue. Thus there is a need for ILEX to provide a basic facility for accepting arbitrary query types. That is the universal **read_in** facility.

The predicate **read_in** with one argument reads in a line or a sentence typed at the terminal and terminated by pressing the "return" key, and converts it to a list of PROLOG atoms. As its first step, any query is treated as a piece of information made of one or more lines from PROLOG system point of view.

PROLOG must know when one word of the input ends and the next begins. In order to do so, the definition of a word in each language must be given. Each kind of language may have its own vocabulary and grammar for how characters are strung together to form a piece of information. Any other characters just mark space between words. A line is deemed to have finished when "return" appears. An entire query is terminated by an empty input line, that is a new line with an immediate "return". This suits all query languages supported.

Let us look more closely at how the **read_in** function works. The system ILEX uses the built-in predicate **get0** to read characters from the terminal. A built-in predicate means the predicate's definition which is provided in advance by the PROLOG system (fuller detail see Appendix 1). By this point, the reader should be able to read reasonably complex programs and therefore to absorb the built-in predicates by seeing them in use. The trouble with the built-in predicate **get0** is that, once a character has been read from the terminal by it, that character has "gone for ever", and no other **get0** goal or attempt to resatisfy a **get0** goal will ever get hold of that character again. So it should be borne in mind to avoid ever backtracking over a use of **get0** in order to avoid "losing" the character it reads in. The predicate **read_in** is designed in such a way that it always reads one character ahead, and makes tests on a character inside a different rule to the one where it was read. When a character is found somewhere and can not be used at that point, it is passed back to the rules that will be able to use it. Hence, a new predicate **readword** to do with reading a single word actually has three arguments.

(i) The first is for the character that was found by whichever rule last satisfied a **get0** goal but could not find a use for the character.

(ii) The second is for the PROLOG atom that will be constructed for the word.

(iii) The last argument is for the first character that is read after the word. In order to see where a word ends, it is necessary to read up to the next character after it. This character must be passed back, because it might provide the valuable of another word.

Here, then is the program:

```
read_in([W|Ws]) :- get0(C), readword(C,W,C1), W \==[],
                   restsent(C1,Ws), !.
read_in([]) :- !.          /* An empty line  */

restsent(10,[]) :- !.      /* The rest of the sentence is empty */
restsent(C,[W1|Ws]) :- readword(C,W1,C1), W1 \==[],
                       restsent(C1,Ws).
restsent(_,[]) :- !.       /* A "return" is given after several
                              non-in-word letters typed */

readword(C,W,C2) :- in_word(C,NewC), !, get0(C1),
                    restword(C1,Cs,C2), name(W,[NewC|Cs]).
readword(10,[],_) :- !.  /* The first letter is "return" */
readword(_,W,C2) :- get0(C1), readword(C1,W,C2).
                    /* The first letter is not admissible */
restword(C,[NewC|Cs],C2) :- in_word(C,NewC), !,
                            get0(C1), restword(C1,Cs,C2).
restword(C,[],C).          /* The end of a word is distinguished
                              by an undefined letter */

in_word(X,Y) :- language(L), in_w(X,Y,L).
in_word(X,Y) :- in_w(X,Y,all).

 /* These characters can appear within a word in any languages */
in_w(95,95,_).                         /* _  */
in_w(92,92,_).                         /* \ */
in_w(45,45,_).                         /* - */
in_w(46,64,_).                         /* '.' becomes '@' */
in_w(C,C,_) :- C>96, C<123.            /* a ... z */
in_w(C,C,_) :- C>46, C<58.             /* / 0-9 */
in_w(C, C,_) :- C>38, C<44.            /* ' ( ) * +     */
in_w(C,C,_) :- C>59, C<63.             /* < = >  */

 /* These characters can appear within a word in PL   */
in_w(126,126,p).          /* "~" */
in_w(35,35,p).            /* '#' stands for an immaterial variable  */
in_w(27,27,p).            /* a call for new skeleton */
in_w(63,63,p).            /* ? */
in_w(58,64,p).            /* ":" becomes "@" */
in_w(C,C,p) :- C>64, C<91.    /* A...Z */

 /* These characters can appear within a word in ML  */
in_w(37,37,m).                         /*  "%" */
```

```
in_w(58,58,m).                                  /* ":" */
in_w(91,123,m).                                 /* "[" becomes "{" */
in_w(44,38,m).                                  /* ',' becomes '&' */
in_w(C,D,m) :- C>64, C<91, D is C+32.   /* A ... Z */

 /* These characters can appear within a word in EL          */
in_w(44,38,e).                                  /* ',' become '&' */
in_w(58,58,e).                                  /* ":" */
in_w(C,D,e) :- C>64,C<91, D is C+32.    /* A...Z become a...z */
```

It can be seen that a query expressed in any language, whatever it looks like, is always considered as a piece of information made of words or phrases separated by characters which can not be accepted by that language such as space(s) or by a "return". The alert reader will also have noticed how the interferences are avoided by the program. As a result of this definition, the program will read a query into a list, in which something may slightly changed depending on a particular language used. The given example in Fig. 3.3 is a query written in EL. As we can see, upper-case letters are automatically converted to lower-case, and the comma "," becomes "&".

```
SELECT sno FROM s WHERE City=Paris, Status>20
                    |
             .-------------.
             | read_in(Q)  |
             '-------------'
                    |
Q = [select,sno,from,s,where,city=paris&,status>20]
```

Fig. 3.3 An Example of Accepting a Query

3.3 FORMAL DEFINITION OF THE CANONICAL LOGIC FORM

As a formal basis for the design, description and comparison of high level query languages and other related researches such as query analysis and optimisation, modeling a canonical logic form is fundamental to successful interface with variety of query languages. We use the following notations to form the canonical logic expression.

Q An entire Query.

The logic operator OR, by which sub-queries are linked together. We have

Q = SUB1 # SUB2 # ... # SUBk

Hi A set of required variables in a retrieval sub query. We have

Hi = [X1,X2,...,Xj]

! An "end" notation of a sub-query.

& The logic operator AND, linking different parts within a sub query. We may have

SUBi = Hi & BODYi & !

BODYi The body of a sub-query which is a set of query tuples Ti linked together by the operator "&". We have

BODYi = T1 & T2 & ... & Tn

Ti A query tuple. We define it as following

Ti = sub_q(Ni,Ai,Fi,FFi,Vi,FUNi)

where:

Ni A relation name in the query tuple Ti.

Ai A set of arguments of the relation Ni

Vi A set of free variables in Ai

Fi A set of independent formulas in the query tuple Ti. A formula is said to be independent if it is a comparison with a constant.

FFi A set of relevant formulas in a query tuple Ti. A formula is said to be relevant if it contains variables involving other base relations.

FUNi Functional description in a query tuple Qi. It may be

!	A basic query tuple involving no aggregation.
not	A negation involved in the query tuple.
asserta	An insert operation.
retract	A delete operation.
[cnt,X,Sum]	CNT function: count number of values.
[sum,X,Sum]	SUM function: sum the values.
[max,X,Max]	MAX function: pick up the largest value.
[min,X,Min]	MIN function: pick up the smallest value.
[avg,X,Avg]	AVG function: average the values.

[all,X,Set] ALL function: collect values.

[group,X,X] partition function: group values.

[u,X,E] An update function: update values.

VJi A set of relevant variables belonging to several relations; these variables will be called join variables.

VIi A set of independent variables, standing for non-join variables.

As far as a retrieval operation is concerned, a complete query expression in the canonical logic form is:

H1 & BODY1 & ! # H2 & BODY2 & ! # ... # Hn & BODYn & !.

As for a storage operation, the general canonical logic expression is:

BODY1 & ! # BODY2 & ! # ... # BODYn & !.

Note that the symbol '!' in the canonical representation is nothing to do with the cut in PROLOG.

3.4 THE RELATIONAL PROCESSING CAPABILITY OF THE CANONICAL FORM

Relational completeness is a basic measure of the selective power of a language. A language is said to be relationally complete if any relation derivable from the given relations (i.e. the database) by means of an expression of the relational algebra can be retrieved using that language [40]. What makes ILEX so powerful is the economy with which this completeness is achieved. Any derivable relation can be retrieved using a single canonical logic representation. As a matter of fact, the term "relational completeness" is frequently taken to include this constraint (namely that any derivable relation be retrievable via a single statement), and we shall generally use the term in this more demanding sense. All query languages supported in ILEX are at least this powerful. What relational completeness means to the user is that, very loosely speaking, if the information wanted is in the database, then it can be retrieved by means of a single self-contained request. Of course, most queries will be fairly simple in practice; but from the underlying theory the user can ask arbitrarily complex questions if he wishes.

We shall show that the canonical logic form is sufficient, that is, every relational algebraic operator can be expressed in these terms. For this purpose, we assume r1, r2, r3, r4, s1, s2, s3, and s4 are relations in a mathematical database (see Fig. 3.4).

r1

aa	bb	cc
a	b	c
d	a	f
c	b	d

s1

aa	bb	cc
b	g	a
d	a	f

r2

aa	bb	cc	dd
a	b	c	d
a	b	e	f
b	c	e	f
e	d	c	d
e	d	e	f
a	b	d	e

s2

cc	dd
c	d
e	f

r3

aa	bb	cc
1	2	3
4	5	6
7	8	9

s3

dd	ee
3	1
6	2

r4

aa	bb	cc
a	b	c
b	b	f
c	a	d

s4

bb	cc	dd
b	c	d
b	c	e
a	d	b

Fig. 3.4 The Mathematical Database

There are five basic operations that serve to define relational algebra. These are: **union, set difference, extended Cartesian product, projection and selection.**

1). **Union.** The union of relations R and S, denoted R ++ S, is the set of tuples that are in R or S or both. R and S must be union-compatible, that is to say that they have the same arity. The following expression constructs r1 ++ s1.

```
[X1,X2,X3] &
sub_q(r1,[X1,X2,X3],[],[],[X1,X2,X3],!) &
! #
[X1,X2,X3] &
sub_q(s1,[X1,X2,X3],[],[],[X1,X2,X3],!) &
!.
```

```
r1 ++ s1
-------------------------
aa      bb      cc
-------------------------
a       b       c
d       a       f
c       b       d
b       g       a
```

2). **Set difference.** The difference of relations R and S, denoted R--S, is the set of tuples in R but not in S. R and S are required to be union-compatible. The following procedure constructs r1--s1:

```
[X,Y,Z] &
sub_q(r1,[X,Y,Z],[],[],[X,Y,Z],!) &
sub_q(s1,[X,Y,Z],[],[],[X,Y,Z],not) &
!.
```

```
r1 -- s1
-------------------------
aa      bb      cc
-------------------------
a       b       c
c       b       d
```

3). **Cartesian product.** Let R and S be relations of arity m and n, respectively. Then R**S, the Cartesian product of R and S, is the set of (m+n)-tuples t's such that t is the concatenation of a tuple r belonging to R and a tuple s belonging to S. The concatenation of a tuple r=[r1,r2,...rm] and a tuple s=[s1,s2,...sn], in that order, is the tuple t=[r1,r2,...rm,s1,s2,...sn]. In our canonical expression r1**s1 becomes:

```
[X,Y,Z,A,B,C] &
sub_q(r1,[X,Y,Z],[],[],[X,Y,Z],!) &
sub_q(s1,[A,B,C],[],[],[A,B,C],!) &
!.
```

r1 ** s1

11	22	33	44	55	66
a	b	c	b	g	a
a	b	c	d	a	f
d	a	f	b	g	a
d	a	f	d	a	f
c	b	d	b	g	a
c	b	d	d	a	f

4). **Projection.** The project operator transforms one relation into a new one consisting of selected attributes of the first, including duplicate elimination. Project relation r1 on attributes cc and aa, denoted r1 [cc,aa], is formed by taking each tuple in r1 and forming a new tuple from the third and first components of r1 in that order. In the canonical form we have:

```
[C,A] &
sub_q(r1,[A,#,C],[],[],[A,C],!) &
!.
```

r1 [cc,aa]

cc	aa
c	a
f	d
d	c

5). **Selection.** Let F be a formula involving

(i) operands that are constants or attributes,

(ii) the arithmetic comparison: =, \=, <, >, =<, >=,

(iii) the arithmetic operators: +, -, *, /,

then R:F is the set of tuples t in R such that when all attributes occurring in F are substituted by the corresponding components of t, the formula F becomes true. For example, to select tuples from relation r3 where bb>2, denoted r3 : bb>2, write:

```
[X,Y,Z] &
sub_q(r3,[X,Y,Z],[Y>2],[],[X,Y,Z],!) &
!.
```

r3 : bb>2

aa	bb	cc
4	5	6
7	8	9

In addition, there are a number of useful algebraic operations that can be expressed in terms of the previously mentioned operations, but which have been given names in the literature and sometimes used as primitive algebraic operations. These are **intersection, quotient, join, and natural join.**

6). **Intersection.** The intersection of two (union-compatible) relations R and S, denoted R :: S, is the set of all tuples t belonging to both R and S. We have:

R :: S == R -- (R -- S)

The intersection of r1 and s1, r1::s1, can be obtained as following:

```
[X1,X2,X3] &
sub_q(r1,[X1,X2,X3],[],[],[X1,X2,X3],!) &
sub_q(s1,[X1,X2,X3],[],[],[X1,X2,X3],!) &
!.
```

r1 :: s1

aa	bb	cc
d	a	f

7). **Quotient.** Let R and S be relations of arity m and n, respectively, where m>n. Then R **%%** S is the set of (m-n)-tuples t such that for all s-tuples u in S, the tuple tu in R. We have

R%%S == R[1,2,...r-s]--((R[1,2,...r-s])**S--R)[1,2,...r-s]

This is a rather complicated case but still can be expressed in the canonical form by means of function description such as 'group' and 'all'. For instance, to compute r2 **%%** s2 we have:

```
[A,B] &
sub_q(r2,[A,B,C,D],[],[],[A,B,C,D],([group,[A,B],[A,B]]) &
sub_q(s2,[C,D],[],[],[C,D],([all,[C,D],L1]) &
sub_q(r2,[A,B,C,D],[],[],[A,B,C,D],([all,[A,B,C,D],L2]) &
sub_q(subset,[L1,L2],[],[],[L1,L2],!) &
!.
```

r2 %% s2

aa	bb
a	b
e	d

8). **Join.** The O-join of R and S on columns r1,r2,...ri,s1,s2,...sj written R**S : F, where F is a formula involved with these columns and defined as the same as that in selection operation, is a set of tuples t in the Cartesian product of R**S such that when all attributes occurring in F are substituted by corresponding components of t the formula F becomes true. To compute r3 ** s3 : dd>bb [aa,bb,cc,dd,ee] write:

```
[X1,X2,X3,X4,X5] &
sub_q(r3,[X1,X2,X3],[],[],[X1,X2,X3],!) &
sub_q(s3,[X4,X5],[],[X4>X2],[X4,X5],!) &
!.
```

r3 ** s3 : dd > bb [aa,bb,cc,dd,ee]

a	b	c	d	e
1	2	3	3	1
1	2	3	6	2
4	5	6	6	2

9). **Natural join.** If O is "=" in O-join operation, it is called an equijoin denoted by R <=> S. To compute R <=> S we have:

```
R<=>S == (R**S:R.A1=S.A1&R.A2=S.A2&...&R.Ak=S.Ak) [i1,i2,...im]
```

For instance, r4 <=> s4:

```
[A,B,C,D] &
sub_q(r4,[A,B,C],[],[],[A,B,C],!) &
sub_q(s4,[B,C,D],[],[],[B,C,D],!) &
!.
```

r4 <=> s4

aa	bb	cc	dd
a	b	c	d
a	b	c	e
c	a	d	b

The canonical logic representation is not only sufficient for relational completeness; many other functions, including updating and deleting of tuples, the ability to group together certain tuples and aggregate functions such as CNT, SUM, MAX, MIN, AVG, etc, can also be converted to the uniform (discussed in chapter 7). As we have seen in the canonical form, the existential quantifier ($\exists x$) in relational calculus is used implicitly; while the universal quantifier ($\forall x$) is replaced by the functional description 'all' which implies a second-order predicate. More structural compatibility between the proposed logic form and existing high level languages is therefore achieved. Besides, the canonical logic form provides "function extensibility" -- i.e. the ability to extend its power, for instance, to include an arbitrary set of new built-in functions. The characteristic of logic programming in PROLOG is also able to represent and utilise recursive definitions. From this point of view, a class of "recursion queries" which retrieve the data of relations with a specific ordering among tuples and can not be expressed in relationally complete query languages can be handled as well. Thus the logic representation appears to be sufficient for the implementation of many realistic and useful query languages.

It is highly significant that we could begin with a query, regardless of what language is used, reduce it to the canonical logic representation, optimise the logic form, and then implement the optimised query using any data management software. If this conversion is accomplished automatically, many different relational languages can be implemented using the same underlying software. Furthermore, the underlying access method can be altered by making minimum changes in the conversion method - without requiring any changes at the user interface.

3.5 AN INTRODUCTORY EXAMPLE

In the next three chapters, we shall develop three quite different query languages and consider their translations into the canonical logic form. Before getting into details of each particular high level query language we present an introductory example to illustrate the different states at the three levels during the query processing.

> **Get supplier names and their locations for supliers who supply part P2 with the quantity greater than 200.**

The transformation is shown in Fig. 3.5.

A QUERY WRITTEN IN ML, PL AND EL

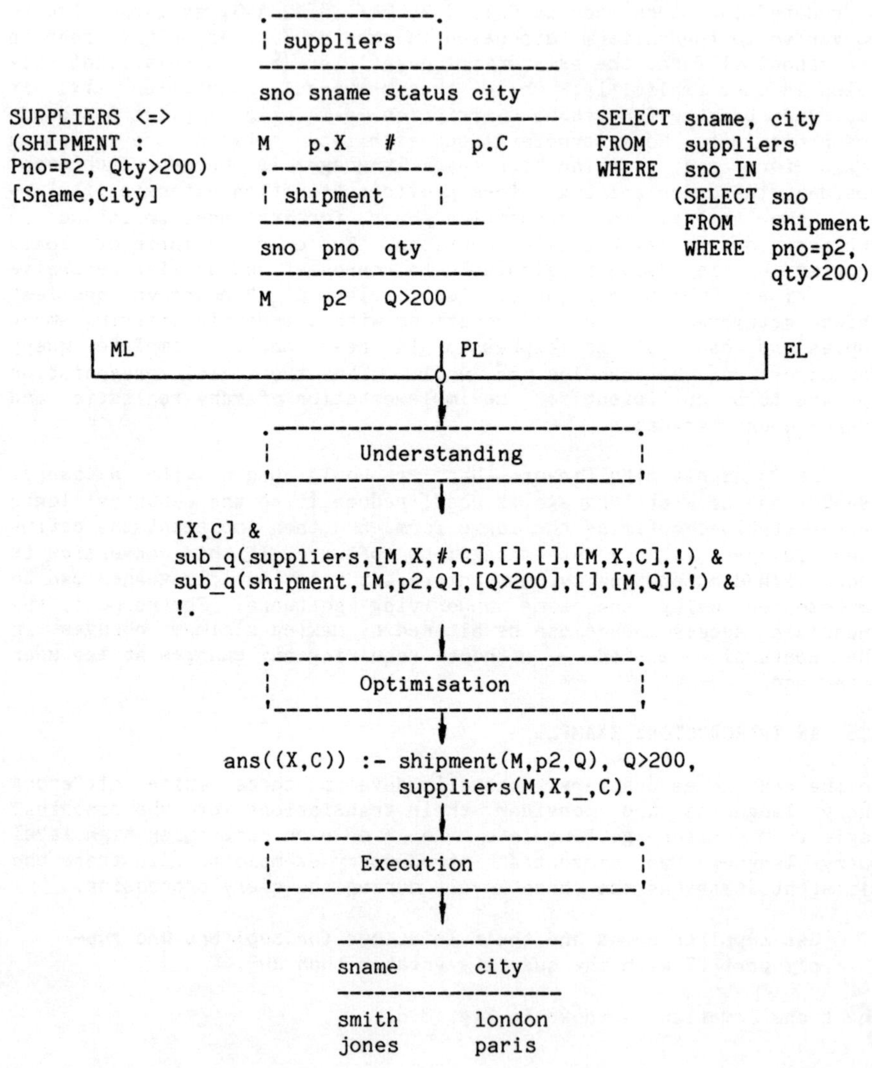

Fig. 3.5 An Introductory Example

CHAPTER 4

A Picture-like Language

One of the objectives of the proposed approach is to exploit existing query language features rather than introduce new ones wherever possible. Along this line the Picture-Like language PL, one of query languages supported by the ILEX system, is based on the domain calculus language QBE, and actually could be considered as the extension of QBE.

4.1 QBE AS A CANDIDATE OF THE ILEX SYSTEM

Query-By-Example (QBE) is a query language for use by non-programmers querying a relational data base. Originally it was developed at the IBM Yorkton Heights Research Laboratory. The name of "Query By Example" is used to refer both to the system itself and to the user language the system supports. It is designed for use with a visual display terminal: not only are results presented in the form of displayed table, but all requests from the user are also specified by filling in tables on the screen. These tables are constructed partly by the system and partly by the user. Since operations are specified in tabular form, we say that QBE has a two-dimensional syntax. Most traditional computer languages, by contrast, have a linear syntax.

The philosophy behind QBE is to require the user to know very little to get started and to minimise the number of objects and concepts that he subsequently has to learn in order to understand and use the whole language. In comparison with other query languages, QBE represents a very natural way of interfacing man and machine, and demonstrates the simplicity that is needed for widespread end-user communication. It has undergone a certain amount of human factors testing with very favourable results [6,8]. Various psychological studies of the language have shown that naive users acquire the skill to make complicated queries in less than three hours. It is hard to imagine a powerful formal language which could be learned much more rapidly than QBE.

The unique features of QBE can be concluded as follows:

(i) The user has the perception of manual table manipulation and a pre-established frame of references, i.e. the table.

(ii) The user can easily pre-identify the relation to be used, resulting in an early reduction in the scope of the data base.

(iii) Users rarely confuse disjunctive and conjunctive queries, and they have little trouble linking attributes within a single table or linking multiple tables together.

(iv) The user has multi-degrees of freedom in that the sequence of filling in the tables and the rows within the tables is immaterial. The sequence of filling different tables in a query is also immaterial. This implies that given a data base the system does not constrain the user's thinking process in any way while he is formulating the query. Thus, the system is capable of capturing the different ways in which different users approach the problem.

(v) QBE allows the user to divide the query into decoupled segments, making it declarative and highly non-procedural. Therefore, it can handle rather complicated queries without giving up its simplicity.

Because of the attractive features stated above, QBE is immediately chosen as a candidate of the ILEX system. The weak-point of QBE is the specification with qualification which people frequently confuse. In addition, the condition boxes used in QBE seem slightly to spoil the natural style of QBE. The effort will be made to improve them by proper modification.

4.2 THE LANGUAGE PL

The best way of introducing the language PL is through a series of examples. We assume that the suppliers-parts-dept database (see 2.1.2) has been defined and entered. Query examples on retrieval and storage operations will show how well the PL can be easily used.

4.2.1 Retrieval Operations

Let us start with a simple query to retrieve information from a single table. The task "(Q4.1) Get part numbers for all parts supplied" is accomplished by filling the table in the way:

shipment		
sno	pno	qty
#	p.No	#

As soon as the table name 'shipment' is given, the attributes of the table with the skeleton will automatically come out. So the user only need to fill it. And the "p." stands for "print"; it indicates a retrieval operation. "No" is a variable indicating the target of the query, i.e., the values that appear in the result. The "#" stands for something which is not concerned (for simplicity of our implementation only). The second "#" can be omitted since the user has already finished specifying all information concerned at that row.

A fundamental concept in PL is variables. A variable begins with a capital letter so it can be distinguished from constant elements. There are two kind of constants: integers and atoms. Atoms normally begin with a lower-case letter. Therefore the following query

suppliers			
sno	sname	status	city
#	p.Name	S>20	paris

instructs the system to display supplier names for suppliers in Paris with status>20 (Q4.2). Observe how the condition "status>20" is specified; any of the comparison operators =, \=, <,>, <=, >= can be used in this way (except that '=' is normally omitted, as in the city column above). Also, any of these operators can be preceded by "p." if we desire to print the value concerned. For example, we could have specified "p.S>20" under status above, if we had wanted to print the status values too.

Conditions specified within a single tuple are considered as AND-linking together. However, the distinguishable variable in separate tuples will imply an OR-linking. For example: "(Q4.3) Get supplier numbers and names for suppliers who are located in Paris or have status > 20" will be:

suppliers			
sno	sname	status	city
p.M	p.A	#	paris
p.N	p.B	S>20	

As far as the "OR" function is concerned, the retrieval targets by OR-linking are hoped to be union compatible which means that each target has the same number of components, that is, same arity, as the example above. However, if not, no confusion will be caused but to the user himself.

The variable concept is easy to understand but covers a wide variety of database operations, including cross-referencing between tuples, formulating comparison on values, moving data from one object to another, deriving new tuples, etc. Examples of these operations follow.

Cross-referencing between tuples. Suppose a user wants to find supplier numbers for suppliers who supply both p1 and p2 (Q4.4).

```
.-------------.
| shipment    |
-----------------------
sno     pno     qty
-----------------------
p.N     p1
  N     p2
```

Here the variable N which must be used twice is called join variable; we need two tuples to express the query because we need to link two conditions with "AND" on the same attribute.

Another example showing linking between tuples is: (Q4.5) Get supplier names and status for suppliers who live in London and supply at least one red part. For this task, three skeletons are displayed on the screen. The final formulation of this query is as follows:

```
.-------------.
| suppliers   |
-----------------------------
sno     sname   status  city
-----------------------------
M       p.Name  p.S     london


.-------------.
| shipment    |
-----------------------
sno     pno     qty
-----------------------
M       N


.-------------.
| parts       |
---------------------------------------
pno     pname   colour  weight  city
---------------------------------------
N       #       red
```

A query may even be complicated by utilising variables, such as: (Q4.6) Get those part numbers which weight is greater than 18, or located in Paris, or supplied by Jones.

parts				
pno	pname	colour	weight	city
p.X	#	#	W>18	
p.Y	#	#	#	paris

shipment		
sno	pno	qty
M	p.Z	

suppliers			
sno	sname	status	city
M	jones		

Retrieval using negation. (Q4.7) Get supplier names and status for suppliers who do not supply part P2.

suppliers			
sno	sname	statue	city
N	p.A	p.S	

shipment		
sno	pno	qty
~N	p2	

Notice the NOT operator (~) against the query tuple in table "shipment". The query may be paraphrased "Print supplier names and status for supplier N such that there is no case that the supplier N supplies part P2".

In order to make PL look natural, we strive to express desired conditions within the framework of the query skeleton(s) rather than using an extra condition box as QBE did. The task (Q4.8) List the supplier names and locations for supplier whose status is greater than Smith's can be accomplished in the way:

```
.-------------.
| suppliers   |
--------------------------------
sno     sname   status  city
--------------------------------
#       smith   S
#       p.Name  X>S     p.City
```

As far as the retrieval operation is concerned, occasionally it is difficult to express some desired target within the original skeletons or the user wishes to get a new table heading in his result. PL allows the user to collect his results in a new table named "*" as the following example illustrates: **(Q4.9) Construct an output table containing supplier names, part names, and quantities supplied for suppliers in London.**

```
.-------------.
| suppliers   |
--------------------------------
sno     sname   status  city
--------------------------------
M       Name    #       london


.-------------.
| shipment    |
-----------------------
sno     pno     qty
-----------------------
M       N       Qty


.-------------.
| parts       |
----------------------------------------
pno     pname   colour  weight  city
----------------------------------------
N       Part


.-------------.
|   *         |
------------------------
supplier  part  quantity
------------------------
Name      Part  Qty
```

The last table is an output table the user creates by mapping data from the base tables. The headings of this table specified by the user need not correspond to the headings of the original tables.

4.2.2 BUILT-IN FUNCTIONS

In order to enhance basic retrieval power, PL provides a number of special built-in functions:

- **cnt.** number of values.
- **sum.** sum of the values.
- **avg.** average of the values.
- **max.** largest value.
- **min.** smallest value.
- **g.** grouping values, that means to rearrange values into partitions or groups, such that within any one group all tuples have the same value for the grouped attribute.

By using these functions, except cnt and g, the attribute concerned must contain numeric values.

Supposing the user wants to know **how many suppliers in London** (Q4.10), we can express the query in PL:

```
.-------------.
| suppliers   |
---------------------------------------
sno            sname   status  city
---------------------------------------
p.cnt.N        #       #       london
```

Consider the query: (Q4.11) **Find the names of employees who aged under 30 earn more than the average salary for all employees.**

```
.-------------.
| employee    |
-------------------------------
ename   age    salary   dept
-------------------------------
#       #      avg.X
p.Name  A<30   S>avg.X
```

Even a more sophisticated query could be expressed in a rather simple way. For instance, the following

```
.-------------.
| employee    |
-----------------------------------
ename   age    salary    dept
-----------------------------------
#       M>40   avg.X
p.Name  A<30   S>avg.X   D
```

```
.--------------.
| department   |
----------------------------------
dept    city    manager
----------------------------------
D       london
```

indicates to find **employee's names for employees who are under** 30 **years of age, work in London, and earn more than the average salary for all employees aged over** 40 (Q4.12).

The next example shows the use of group **g.** (Q4.13) **For each part supplied, get the part number and the total quantity supplied of that part.**

```
.--------------.
| shipment     |
--------------------------
sno     pno     qty
--------------------------
#       g.N
#       p.N     p.sum.Q
```

A statistical function is quite often followed by the query tuple with trigger g.. A more complex example is "(Q4.14) **How many people who earn less than $8000 at each department?"**

```
.--------------.
| employee     |
------------------------------------
ename     age    salary   dept
------------------------------------
#         #      #        g.D
p.cnt.N   #      S<8000   p.D
```

4.2.3 Storage Operations

So far in our discussion of PL only retrieval is concerned. Let us turn to storage operations. One of three actions: "i.", "d.", and "u.", indicating insert, delete, and update respectively, can take place upon a term.

i. Insert a new tuple in the corresponding table only if the tuple specified is succeed. The trigger must be put upon the key attribute of a table.

d. Delete tuples in the corresponding table only if the tuple specified is succeed.

u. Update those tuples in the corresponding table only if the specified condition is satisfied. The tuple to be updated is identified by its key attribute value. Key attribute value cannot be updated.

A number of examples are shown below to illustrate the features of PL on storage operations.

(Q4.15) Add part p7 (name WASHER, colour GREY, weight 2, city ATHENS) to table "parts"

parts				
pno	pname	colour	weight	city
i.p7	washer	grey	2	athens

As far as the update operation is concerned a new operator ":" which means "such that" is introduced. For instance, the "u.red:green" indicates to change red colour into green. The meaning of u.X:Y is to update X by Y. Let us see the query: **(Q4.16) Double all status of all suppliers in Paris.**

suppliers			
sno	sname	status	city
#	#	u.S:2*S	paris

(Q4.17) Delete parts supplied by Smith from table "parts" whose colour is red and weight is less than 15.

parts				
pno	pname	colour	weight	city
d.K	#	red	W<15	

shipment		
sno	pno	qty
M	K	

suppliers			
sno	sname	status	city
M	smith		

(Q4.18) Raise Morgan's salary to be the same as his manager's.

```
.--------------.
| department   |
------------------------
dept   city   manager
------------------------
D      #      Mgr
```

```
.--------------.
| employee     |
--------------------------------
ename   age    salary   dept
--------------------------------
Mgr     #      X
morgan  #      u.S:X    D
```

The versatility of PL illustrated in the examples above shows that PL is a really intelligent query language. One significant advantage over most other query languages is the amount of **freedom**, the user enjoys very much, which allows to construct the query in whatever manner seems most natural. Specifically, the query may be built up in any order the user likes. For instance, Q4.17 could be specified in the totally reversed way:

```
.--------------.
| suppliers    |
--------------------------------
sno     sname   status  city
--------------------------------
N       smith
```

```
.--------------.
| shipment     |
------------------------
sno     pno     qty
------------------------
N       M
```

```
.--------------.
| parts        |
----------------------------------------
pno     pname   colour  weight  city
----------------------------------------
d.M     #       red     W<15
```

Another user may describe Q4.18 as follows:

```
.--------------.
| employee     |
---------------------------------
ename   age     salary  dept
---------------------------------
morgan  #       u.S:X   D
```

```
.--------------.
| department   |
-------------------------
dept    city    manager
-------------------------
D       #       Mgr
```

```
.--------------.
| employee     |
---------------------------------
ename   age     salary  dept
---------------------------------
Mgr      #      X
```

In conclusion PL is a highly nonprocedural language that is capable of supporting several different ways of thinking about a problem; it does not force every user to perceive the problem in exactly the same way.

4.3 The Syntax of PL

4.3.1 Query Table Entry

A query table is a skeleton in which a query or a sub-query will be filled. By using a special baton on the terminal, the user can call a new query table. In the position of a table name displayed on the screen, the following is legal:

```
.--------------.
|    ?         |
```

The "?" means an interrupt to obtain all table names in the current database while querying.

```
.--------------.
|      *       |
```

The "*" brings a result skeleton collecting the answer to a query. Following that, a set of attribute names is intended to be given, no matter what it is.

```
.--------------.
| shipment     |
```

A base table name in the current database, say, shipment, is given indicating that a sub-query being typed relates to "shipment" relation.

```
.--------------.
|  X           |
```

A variable, which results in an interrupt while querying. Perhaps, the user wants to get some information in finishing a particular query. For example, seek a suitable table name containing certain attributes given by the user.

```
.--------------.
| p.stock      |
```

A base table name, say stock, with trigger "p.". This is a short hand of an entire query asking for all information in the table specified.

```
.-------------.
| d.suppliers |
```

A short hand of deleting the whole table named "suppliers" unconditionally.

```
.--------------.
| i.employee   |
```

A new table name, say employee, is going to be created.

4.3.2 Query Tuples

A query tuple, which is always associated with a specific table, is a single row of the query skeleton illustrated by the user. Characters accepted by PL are given in 3.2. Terms made of characters in a query tuple are separated by any character which is unacceptable in PL, such as a space. A term in a query tuple may be any of the following forms:

Basic forms:

(f1) an atom, such as london, smith, red, and so on.

(f2) an integer, such as 35, 0.

(f3) a variable, such as Name, Mgr, X.

(f4) an independent formula, such as S>3000, Colour\=red.

(f5) A relevant formula, which is a comparison between variables, such as X>Y.

(f6) A relevant formula, which is a comparison between variables with offset, such as X>Y+5.

(f7) The special symbol "#" showing something which is not concerned.

Basic forms with triggers.

(f8) Any of the forms f1-f3 with negation, such as ~smith, ~100, ~K.

(f9) Any of the forms f1-f6 with the trigger "p.", such as p.No, p.S>3000, p.X>Y.

(f10) Any of the forms f1-f3 with the trigger "i.", but must be in the key attribute of the current table asked. Such as i.K, i.p7.

(f11) Any of the forms f1-f3 with the trigger "d.", such as d.X, d.smith.

Complex terms involving built-in functions.

(f12) A variable with a function. such as cnt.X, avg.Y, g.N.

(f13) The trigger "p." with f12, such as p.cnt.X, p.avg.S, p.max.S.

(f14) u.X:E, that is, update trigger with any of the forms f1-f3. The "E" may be an arithmetic expression, an integer, or an atom. Such as u.X:yellow, u.S:2*S.

4.4 THE SCREEN EDITOR OF PL

The major task of PL is to understand a query specified by the user in the natural interactive way that the PL offers, and translate it into a canonical logic form. The screen editor of PL plays a central role for this goal. The transformation will be performed in four stages. The first stage, **user-system interaction**, involves grouping the characters of the user query into a list of basic symbols called "tokens". The second stage, **conversion**, is responsible to convert the tokens into a PROLOG term. The third stage, **digestion**, produces a basic structure by analysing the PROLOG term. Finally, the effort to recognise OR-linking implied in the user query is made by the fourth stage, **recognition**, if necessary.

4.4.1 User-System Interaction

We first look at the top level of PL. The flow chart of the user-system interaction is given in Fig. 4.1.

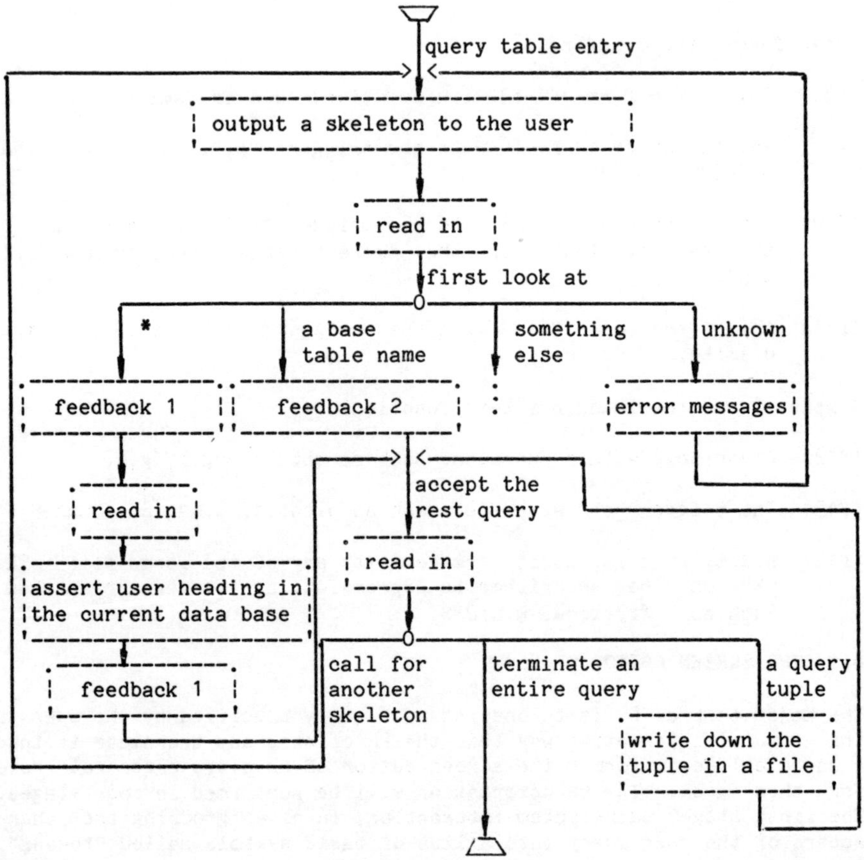

Fig. 4.1 User-System Interaction in PL

Using a conventional programming language this is a straightforward way. Our emphasis will be on how well PROLOG, as a logic programming language, performs this task. A simplified PROLOG program for this purpose is as follows:

```
table_entry :- skeleton, read_in(TableName), first_look(TableName).
first_look(*) :- feedback_1, read_in(Heading),
                 asserta(user_h(Heading)),
                 feedback_1, accept_rest_query(!).
first_look(N) :- table(N,Scheme), feedback_2(Scheme),
                 accept_rest_q(N).
first_look(S) :- do_something_else(S).
first_look(_) :- error_message, table_entry.
accept_rest_q(N) :- read_in(Query_tuple), go_on(N,Query_tuple).
go_on(_,Q) :- name(Q,[27]),
              table_entry.  /* call for another skeleton */
```

```
go_on(_,[]) :- tell(q), write('!.'),
               nl, told.   /* terminate an entire query */
go_on(N,Q) :- tell(q), write(q(N,Q)), put(44),
              tell(user), accept_rest_q(N).
```

It is easy to see from this program that PROLOG is an efficient implementation of recursion although it dispenses with GOTO, DO, FOR, and WHILE loops. The iteration is accomplished by executing recursive Horn clause procedures. It can also be achieved by using backtracking. The alternative to construct loops in our implementation is to use the combination of built-in predicates: "repeat", "cut", and "fail". In general, whereas iteration searches a tree whose depth is determined by the number of loops which nested, backtracking searches an arbitrarily deep tree of alternatives. Therefore, we have come to the conclusion that PROLOG, as a logic programming language, does provide facilities for programming in a conventional way.

At this stage the tokens of an original entire query, in general, may be made up as follows:

(i) q(!,X). X is a set of desired objects in a retrieval operation.

(ii) q(Table_name,Query_tuple).

Notice that there is neither fixed order nor maximum of the number of tokens. Furthermore, tokens are always linked each other by "&" and terminated by a special symbol "!". For instance, the tokens of Q4.3 and Q4.5 given in the previous section are:

```
Q4.3  q(suppliers,[p@M,p@A,#,paris]) &
      q(suppliers,[p@N,p@B,S>20,#]) &
      !.

Q4.5  q(suppliers,[M,p@Name,p@S,london]) &
      q(shipment,[M,N,#]) &
      q(parts,[N,#,red,#,#]) &
      !.
```

In the current database the clause, user_h(heading_list), specifying the heading of the result table will be created if and only if the query is a retrieval operation.

4.4.2 Conversion

This stage is relatively uninteresting and will not be discussed further. Only one thing we need mention here is why we do not make the conversion immediately after read_in.

By means of the read_in facility, queries typed by the user are always considered as atoms. It is necessary to change them into PROLOG terms without misunderstanding, particularly, about the correspondence of variables in an entire query. In doing so, only when an entire query which may be made of several sub-queries has been entered, can the translation of the query into terms be carried out. On the other hand, since the PL is intended to be a non-procedural one; it is the user's freedom to specify a query in the order he likes. Only in this way can the goal be reached.

4.4.3 Digestion

Now, let us look at how the screen editor can perform the task of understanding a PL query, in other words, how PROLOG can be applied to the task of writing a compiler. The usual way one attempts to make precise the definition of a language is through a collection of rules called grammar. The rules of a grammar define which strings of words or symbols are valid. In addition, the grammar generally gives some kind of analysis of the source language into a structure which makes its meaning more explicit. A fundamental class of grammar is the context-free grammar (CFG). The analysis of a string according to a CFG is a parse tree, showing the constituents of the string and their hierarchical relationships. Since the context-free rules can be expressed as Horn clauses, the problem of recognising, or parsing, a string of a language is then transformed into the problem of proving that a certain theorem follows from the definite clause axioms which describe the language.

Based on the syntax of PL, a set of such clauses illustrates the grammar of PL. We shall show very briefly what these rules should be:

```
split(X,X,!,!,!,!,!) :- atomic(X).
split(X,X,!,!,!,X,!) :- var(X).
split(~(X),X,!,!,!,X,not) :- var(X).
split(~(X),X,!,!,!,!,not) :- atomic(X).
split(@(p,X),X,X,!,!,!,!) :- atomic(X).
split(@(p,X),X,X,!,!,X,!) :- var(X).
split(@(i,X),X,!,!,!,!,asserta) :- atomic(X).
split(@(i,X),X,!,!,!,X,asserta) :- var(X).
split(@(d,X),X,!,!,!,!,retract) :- atomic(X).
split(@(d,X),X,!,!,!,X,retract) :- var(X).
split(@(g,X),X,!,!,!,X,[group,X,X]) :- var(X).
split(@(@(p,K),X),X,'Xu',!,!,X,[K,X,'Xu']) :- atom(K), var(X).
split(@(K,X),X,!,!,!,X,[K,X,'Xu']) :- atom(K), var(X).
split(T,X,!,T,!,X,!) :- arg(2,T,N), atomic(N),
                        arg(1,T,X), var(X).
split(T,X,!,!,T,X,!) :- arg(1,T,X), var(X),
                        arg(2,T,Y), var(Y).
split(T,X,X,G,!,X,!) :- arg(2,T,Y), atomic(Y), functor(T,F,2),
                        arg(1,T,@(p,X)), G=..[F,X,Y].
split(T,X,!,!,G,X,!) :- arg(1,T,X), var(X),
                        arg(2,T,Y), functor(T,F,2),
                        (functor(Y,@,2), G=..[F,X,'Xu'];
                        G=..[F,X,Y]).
split(T,X,X,!,G,X,!) :- arg(1,T,@(p,X)), arg(2,T,B),
                        functor(T,F,2),
                        (functor(B,@,2), G=..[F,X,'Xu'];
                        G=..[F,X,B]).
split(@(@(u,X),E),X,!,!,!,X,[u,X,E]).
```

```
split(T,X,!,!,G,X,[K,X,'Xu']) :- T=..[F,@(K,X),M], G=..[F,'Xu',M].
```

By using "split(T,M,P,F1,F2,V,S)", a given term T can be split into M, P, F1, F2, V, and S. That is: 1. extract the main word M, which may be a variable or a constant; 2. pick up the asked variable P if retrieval required; 3. pick up the independent formula F1 if any; 4. pick up the relevant formula if any; 5. pick up the main variables V; 6. a treatment for a special function, such as: cnt, sum, max, min, avg, group, update, retracta, asserta, not, etc. Otherwise using the symbol "!" instead. For instance:

```
?- split(p@X>Y+9,M,P,F1,F2,V,S).
```

then M becomes X, P becomes X, F1 becomes '!', F2 becomes X>Y+9, V becomes X, and S becomes '!'.

The digestion of a complete source program may be expressed by the following clauses:

```
digestion(!,!,!) :- !.
digestion((q(!,V),Q),#(V,H),B) :- digestion(Q,H,B).
digestion((q(N,L),Q),Heads,(sub_q(N,Ms,Fs1,Fs2,Vs,Sth),B)) :- !,
           analyse(L,Ms,Cs,Fs1,Fs2,Vs,[Sth]),
           cases(Cs,Q,Heads,B).

cases([],Q,H,B) :- digestion(Q,H,B).
cases(Cs,#(Cs,H),B) :- digestion(Q,H,B).

analyse([],[],[],[],[],[],[]).
analyse([T1|T2],[M1|M2],Ps,F5,F6,Vs,Fu) :-
                        split(T1,M1,P1,F1,F2,V1,S1), !,
                        analyse(T2,M2,P2,F3,F4,V2,S2),
                        (P1==!, Ps=P2; Ps=[P1|P2]),
                        (F1==!, F5=F3; F5=[F1|F3]),
                        (F2==!, F6=F4; F6=[F2|F4]),
                        (V1==!, Vs=V2; Vs=[V1|V2]),
                        (S1==!, Fu=S2; Fu=[S1|S2]).
```

By means of the predicate **split**, the predicate **analyse** is defined to examine each query tuple. Therefore, the predicate **digestion** with three arguments Q, Head, and Body will analyse sub-queries from the given Q and classify them into two parts: Heads and Body in a standard form. After the processing of digestion, the original query has been changed a lot. Again taking the examples of Q4.3 and Q4.5, the execution of the predicate **digestion** will produce:

```
Q4.3      [M,A] &
          sub_q(suppliers,[M,A,#,paris],[],[],[M,A],!) &
          ! #
          [N,B] &
          sub_q(suppliers,[N,B,S,#],[S>20],[],[N,B,S],!) &
          !.

Q4.5      [Name,S] &
```

```
sub_q(suppliers,[M,Name,S,london],[],[],[M,Name,S],!) &
sub_q(shipment,[M,N,#],[],[],[M,N],!) &
sub_q(parts,[N,#,red,#,#],[],[],[N],!) &
!.
```

4.4.4 Recognition

The only form of the knowledge information processing described so far is the translation of a PL query into a conjunctive logic form. There are reasons for adding some further understanding check at the compile time. let us look at such a reasonable query:

suppliers

sno	sname	status	city
#	jones	S	C
#	p.X	S1>S	
#	p.Y	#	C

Obviously, the user wants to find supplier names for suppliers whose status is greater than Jones's, or who live in the same city as Jones's (Q4.19). This is a query implicating both OR-linking and AND-linking among the three query tuples. In order to resolve the problem, as we always hope to give users flexibility, we put the burden on the screen editor and let it make an intelligent recognition.

Since PL seems to have a great potential power for expressing various queries, we give the following assumptions:

(i) In recognising AND- or OR-links, there is nothing to do with any constant involved in a query. The two "smith"s in the following query, for example, play no role in making the decision of AND or OR. Only variables need be considered.

employee

ename	age	salary	dept
smith	#	#	p.X

department

dept	city	manager
p.Y	#	smith

(ii) If there are distinguishable variables with the trigger "p." in different query tuples, then these query tuples must be OR-linking. As for the result skeleton named "*", all query tuples are considered to be OR-linking.

(iii) If query tuples, regardless of whether table names involved are the same or not, contain join-variables, then they must be AND-linking.

(iv) A relevant formula will lead two involved query tuples to be AND-linking.

These general rules result in a path finding problem. The breadth-first and depth-first search can be used for this purpose. The task is accomplished by repeatedly applying procedures to unrecognised sub-queries until the initial query has eventually been recognised, so that a canonical logic form is generated.

In conclusion, we give a comprehensive example here. Find the department and its location, where there is at least one part in stock the quantity of which happens to be the total number of the same part supplied by all suppliers (Q4.20). The query could be written in the way:

```
.--------------.
| department   |
------------------------
dept    city    manager
------------------------
p.D     p.C


.--------------.
| stock        |
------------------------
dept    pno     qty
------------------------
D       M       Qty


.--------------.
| shipment     |
------------------------
sno     pno     qty
------------------------
#       g.M
#       M       sum.Q=Qty
```

The screen editor produces the corresponding canonical logic form as follows:

```
[D,C] &
sub_q(department,[D,C,#],[],[],[D,C],!) &
sub_q(stock,[D,M,Qty],[],[],[D,M,Qty],!) &
```

```
sub_q(shipment,[#,M,#],[],[],[M],[group,M,M]) &
sub_q(shipment,[#,M,Q],[],[X=Qty],[M,Q],[sum,Q,X] &
!.
```

CHAPTER 5
An English-like Language

In this chapter we begin with the introduction of the English-Like language EL, which is heavily based on SQL, by using examples on the suppliers-parts-dept database. Then we proceed to a discussion of the language syntax, which is followed by our implementation of the language in order to install it in the ILEX system. The emphasis will be on how well the transformation of an EL query into the canonical logic form can be made by using a parser - a set of deductive axioms - therefore, how well the language can be supported by the ILEX system.

5.1 SQL AS A CANDIDATE OF THE ILEX SYSTEM

As mentioned in Section 1.2, system R is an experimental database system constructed at the IBM Research Laboratory in San Jose to show that the usability advantages of the relational data model can be realised in a system with complete functions and high performance. The SQUARE-SEQEUL-SQL route shows the development history of the query language in system R during the past ten years. The implementation of the SQL language was a team effort and subsequent refinements to the language have been continuously made up to the time of writing.

Experience and human factors testing have shown that the SQL was generally felt to be successful in achieving its goals of simplicity, power, and data independence [6,13,41]. The language is simple enough in its basic structure so that users without prior experience were able to learn a usable subset on their first sitting. At the same time, when taken as a whole, the language provided the query power of the first-order predicate calculus combined with operators for grouping, arithmetic, and built-in functions, such as SUM and AVERAGE. Perhaps the aspect of SQL which was most consistently praised by users was the uniformity of its syntax across the environments of application programs, ad-hoc query, and definition of views. Users who were formerly required to learn inconsistent languages found it easier to deal with the single syntax. It may be fair to say that languages like SQL provide a common core of features that will be required in all such high languages. From the user standpoint, SQL is probably the most important relational retrieval sublanguage at the present.

As some people confidently expected, every major relational system will provide for SQL in the years to come.

For these reasons it is incumbent upon us to take a close look at the most important features of the language, and install it into our universal interface. Since there are always suggested extensions to SQL it is hard to find a fixed version of it. In terms of our implementation we call the marriage of SQL and PROLOG as an English-Like language EL.

Keeping in mind what the PL language discussed in the previous chapter looks like, the reader will find extremely different aspects between EL and PL, such as syntactic form, procedurality. However we would like to note some similarities between the two; these similarities are useful as an aid to understanding of the whole ILEX system.

(i) They have the same language level - the top level of the ILEX system. No matter which interactive query language is used, the canonical logical form of an original query will always be deduced by a corresponding reasoning.

(ii) They both use the same data model - Codd's relational model, and they are both relationally complete.

(iii) They both use the same terminal equipment. The output for the user's query to the terminal is system standard. Redundant duplicates are always eliminated in the result.

5.2 THE LANGUAGE EL

We now proceed to illustrate the major features of EL by means of a set of examples, based on the suppliers-parts-dept database of Fig. 2.3.

5.2.1 Retrieval Operations

The fundamental operation in EL is a SELECT-FROM-WHERE block. The SELECT clause specifies the attributes of the target result; The FROM clause specifies the names of relations which involve in forming the result, both in conditioning selection and in actually supplying result value; The WHERE clause specifies the condition(s) on which the result is to be obtained. A query, the user might wish to see a display of supplier names and status for suppliers in Paris (Q5.1), can be typed as follows:

```
SELECT  sname, status
FROM    suppliers
WHERE   city = Paris
```

The query could have been written within one line:

```
Select SNO, STATUS from SUPPLIERS where CITY = PARIS
```

EL does not require a query in a fixed format; it does not care about more spaces between words. Both upper and lower case letters are all acceptable. The only thing the user must remember is to avoid spelling mistakes. If a mistake is made in entering a query, the system will respond with an error message.

(Q5.2) Get full details of all employees.

```
SELECT  *
FROM    employee
```

The asterisk * is a shorthand for an ordered list of all attribute names in the FROM table. The query shown is thus equivalent to

```
SELECT  ename, age, salary, dept
FROM    employee
```

Qualified retrieval. **(Q5.3) Get supplier numbers for suppliers in Paris with status > 20.**

```
SELECT  sno
FROM    suppliers
WHERE   city = Paris,
        status > 20
```

The conditions following WHERE may include the comparison operators =, \=, >, <, <=, >=; The comma "," appearing in the specification represents the Boolean operator "AND".

Joining in EL is described by placing attributes from more than one relation in the SELECT clause, placing the multiple relation names in the FROM clause, and including a join criterion in the WHERE clause. For example, **(Q5.4) For each part supplied, get part number and names of all cities supplying the part.**

```
SELECT  pno, city
FROM    shipment, suppliers
WHERE   shipment.sno = suppliers.sno
```

The user may name several relations in the FROM clause, and use the relation names as qualifiers in the SELECT clause to resolve ambiguities if necessary (or for clarity). The SELECT clause in the previous query could have been written

```
SELECT  shipment.pno, suppliers.city
```

if desired. The criterion following WHERE can be any expression, involving arithmetic comparisons (=, >, <, \=, <=, and >=) on attributes. Therefore, say, **(Q5.5) to get less-join of relation "r3" and relation "r4" on the attributes "bb" and "dd", based on the mathematical database of Fig. 3.4, we have:**

```
SELECT  r3.aa, r3.bb, r3,cc, s3.dd, s3.ee
FROM    r3, s3
```

```
        WHERE   r3.bb < s3.dd
```

Of particular interest is retrieval using equijoin. **"(Q5.6) Get supplier names for suppliers who supply part P2"** could be written as:

```
SELECT  sname
FROM    suppliers, shipment
WHERE   suppliers.sno = shipment.sno,
        shipment.pno = p2
```

EL actually provides several ways of handling equijoin. Since the query differs from the two previous queries in that the result is entirely extracted from a single relation "suppliers", though it is true that two relations, "suppliers" and "shipment", must be inspected to determine that result, it should therefore be possible to express the query in the form:

```
SELECT  sname
FROM    suppliers
WHERE   sno =
             (SELECT  sno
              FROM    shipment
              WHERE   pno = p2)
```

The expression in parentheses is a **subquery**. In general, the condition

```
f = (SELECT Sth FROM ...)
```

evaluates to true if and only if the value f is equal to at least one value in the result of evaluating the "SELECT Sth FROM ...". Similarly, the condition

```
f < (SELECT Sth FROM ...)
```

evaluates to true if and only if f is less than at least one value in the result of evaluating the "SELECT Sth FROM ...". The operators <=, >=, \=, and > are analogously defined. Of the various comparison conditions, easily the most useful is

```
f = (SELECT Sth FROM ...)
```

This form may equivalently (and more clearly) be written as

```
f IN (SELECT Sth FROM ...)
```

Retrieval with multiple levels of nesting. **(Q5.7) Get supplier names for suppliers who supply at least one red part.**

```
SELECT  sname
FROM    suppliers
WHERE   sno IN
             (SELECT  sno
              FROM    shipment
```

```
                    WHERE   pno IN
                                   (SELECT  pno
                                    FROM    parts
                                    WHERE   colour = red ))
```

Subqueries can be nested to any depth. It is also allowable to retrieve with a subquery where the same relation name is involved in both blocks. For instance, (Q5.8) Get supplier numbers for suppliers who supply at least one part supplied by supplier S2.

```
SELECT  sno
FROM    shipment
WHERE   pno IN
               (SELECT  pno
                FROM    shipment
                WHERE   sno = s2 )
```

Retrieval with negation. (Q5.9) Get supplier names for suppliers who do not supply part P2.

```
SELECT  sname
FROM    suppliers
WHERE   sno NOT_IN
                   (SELECT  sno
                    FROM    shipment
                    WHERE   pno = p2)
```

The condition in the WHERE clause:

```
f NOT_IN (SELECT Sth FROM ...)
```

evaluates to true if and only if for all values V's in the result of evaluating "SELECT Sth FROM ..." none of them is f.

SQL uses the usual set operators - UNION, INTERSECT, and MINUS - to combine the results of independent SELECT-blocks. These operators are algebraic in nature, and are procedural components. In order to reduce the procedurality, EL dispenses with INTERSECT and MINUS by using IN and NOT_IN combined with a set of attributes instead. The specification of obtaining the intersection of relation "r1" and "r2" based on the mathematical database of Fig. 3.4 (Q5.10) is given as follows:

```
SELECT  aa, bb, cc
FROM    r1
WHERE   (aa, bb, cc) IN
                        (SELECT  dd, ee, ff
                         FROM    s1 )
```

To get the difference of the relation "r1" and relation "s1" (Q5.11), we have

```
SELECT  aa, bb, cc
FROM    r1
```

```
WHERE   (aa, bb, cc) NOT_IN
                      (SELECT  dd, ee, ff
                       FROM    s1 )
```

We believe that the modification of the specification about intersection and difference gives a better understanding to ad hoc users, while keeping the uniformity of the language. However, EL retains the UNION operator.

Retrieval using union. (Q5.12) Get part numbers for parts that either weight more than 18 pounds or are currently supplied by Jones (or both).

```
  SELECT  pno
  FROM    parts
  WHERE   weight > 18
UNION
  SELECT  pno
  FROM    shipment
  WHERE   sno IN
                (SELECT sno
                 FROM   suppliers
                 WHERE  sname = Jones)
```

5.2.2 Built-in Function

The retrieval power of the basic language can be easily extended by provision of built-in functions. As with PL, the functions currently supported by EL are CNT, SUM, AVG, MAX, MIN, and GROUPED_BY.

Function in the SELECT clause. (Q5.13) Get the number of shipments for part P2.

```
SELECT  CNT(sno)
FROM    shipment
WHERE   pno = p2
```

Function in a subquery. (Q5.14) Get employee names for employee who earn more than the average of all employees in the "d1" department.

```
SELECT  ename
FROM    employee
WHERE   salary >
                  (SELECT  AVG(salary)
                   FROM    employee
                   WHEHE   dept = d1)
```

Use of GROUPED_BY. (Q5.15) For each part supplied, get the part number and the total quantity supplied of that part.

```
SELECT      pno, SUM(qty)
FROM        shipment
GROUPED_BY  pno
```

The GROUPED_BY operator conceptually rearranges the FROM relation into partitions or groups, such that within any one group all tuples have the same value for the GROUPED_BY attribute. In the example, relation "shipment" is grouped such that the first group contains the tuples for part P1, the second contains the tuple for part P2, and so on. The SELECT clause is then applied to each group of the partitioned relation. Each expression in the SELECT clause must be single-valued for each group; that is, it can be either the GROUPED_BY attribute itself, or a function such as SUM that operates on all values of a given attribute within a group and reduces those values to a single value.

(Q5.16) For each department, get the total number of employees with their average age and average salary.

```
SELECT      dept, CNT(ename), AVG(age), AVG(salary)
FROM        employee
GROUPED_BY  dept
```

Use HAVING and GROUPED_BY. **(Q5.17) Get part number for all parts supplied by more than two suppliers.**

```
SELECT      pno
FROM        shipment
GROUPED_BY  pno
HAVING      CNT(sno) > 2
```

The HAVING clause is only used to restrict a partitioned relation so HAVING is always used with GROUPED_BY. The expression in a HAVING clause must be single-valued for each group.

A comprehensive example. **(Q5.18) How many people earn less than $8000 in each department?**

```
SELECT      dept, CNT(ename)
FROM        employee
GROUPED_BY dept
WHERE       Salary < 8000
```

It is important to make the distinction between HAVING and WHERE clauses. In comparison with Q5.17, both the WHERE clause and the HAVING clause are followed by GROUPED_BY, but they differ in that expression in a HAVING clause involves a built-in function showing the property of each group whereas a WHERE clause only specifies a simple condition in a grouped relation.

5.2.3 Storage Operations

Just as PL, the EL provides three storage operations: update, insert, and delete.

Update operation. **(Q5.19) Change the colour of part P2 to yellow.**

```
UPDATE  parts
SET     colour = yellow
```

```
WHERE   pno = p2
```

Within a SET clause, any reference to an attribute on the right-hand side of an equal sign refers to the value of that attribute before the updating has been done. Hence, the query, **double the status of all suppliers in Paris** (Q5.20), can be written as the following:

```
UPDATE  suppliers
SET     status = 2 * status
WHERE   city = Paris
```

Update with complex conditions. (Q5.21) **set the quantity to zero for all suppliers in London.**

```
UPDATE  shipment
SET     qty = 0
WHERE   sno IN
              (SELECT  sno
               FROM    suppliers
               WHERE   city = London)
```

Single-tuple insertion. (Q5.22) **Add part P7 (name "WASHER", colour "GREY", weight 2, city "ATHENS") to table "PARTS".**

```
INSERT_INTO  parts:
                (p7, washer, grey, 2, athens)
```

Single tuple deletion. (Q5.23) **Delete all part records in which weight is greater than 17**

```
DELETE  parts
WHERE   weight > 17
```

Multiple-relations deletion. (Q5.24) **Delete those parts from relation "parts" which colour is red, weight is greater than 10, and is supplied by people in London.**

```
DELETE  parts
WHERE   colour = red,
        weight > 10,
        pno IN
              (SELECT  pno
               FROM    shipment
               WHERE   sno IN
                             (SELECT  sno
                              FROM    suppliers
                              WHERE   city = London))
```

From the discussion above, it can be seen that EL is a self-contained structured English-keyword language that avoids the use of mathematical notations and concepts. The form SELECT...FROM... is an expression which, as far as the user is concerned, produces a set of objects. The use of such expressions greatly simplifies the process of constructing a query. Many problems can be expressed in EL more easily and concisely. However, the nonprocedurality of EL is open to question. The designers of SQL describe it as nonprocedural (descriptive) since a SELECT-block specifies only what data is wanted, not a procedure for obtaining that data. Others classify SQL as procedural since there are some procedural elements, such as UNION and GROUPED_BY, in that language. The problem is that procedurality is a continuum. EL may be nonprocedural when compared with ML which will be discussed in the next chapter, but procedural when compared to PL. Thus, we may call EL a half-procedural language.

5.3 THE SYNTAX OF EL

In contrast to conventional languages, the syntax of EL is not at all obvious, It is necessary to be familiar with the structure of an EL expression. The definition of the syntax uses the Backus Normal Form meta-language:

```
<a task written in EL> ::=
     <retrieval operation> | <update operation> |
     <insert operation> | <delete operation>
<retrieval operation> ::= <select-blocks>
<update operation> ::=
     UPDATE <relation>
     SET <attribute> = <arithmetic expression> |
     UPDATE <relation>
     SET <attribute> = <arithmetic expression>
     WHERE <conditions>
<insert operation> ::= INSERT_INTO <relation> : <constants>
<delete operation> ::= DELETE <relation> |
     DELETE <relation> WHERE <conditions>
<select-blocks> ::= <select-block> |
     <select-block> UNION <select-blocks>
<select-block> ::=
     SELECT <target list> FROM <relations> |
     SELECT <target list>
     FROM <relations> WHERE <conditions> |
     SELECT <target list>
     FROM <relation> GROUPED_BY <attribute> |
     SELECT <target list> FROM <relation>
     GROUPED_BY <attribute> HAVING <function> |
     SELECT <target list> FROM <relation>
     GROUPED_BY <attribute> WHERE <condition>
<target list> ::= <target> | <target> , <target list>
<target> ::= <attribute> |
     <relation> . <attribute> | <function>
<conditions> ::= <condition> | <condition> , <conditions>
<condition> ::= <simple condition> | <chaining condition> |
     <join condition> | <set requirement>
<simple condition> ::=
     <attribute> <comparison operator> <constant> |
     <relation> . <attribute> <comparison operator> <constant>
<chaining condition> ::=
     <attribute> <chaining operator> <select-block>
<join condition> ::= <relation> . <attribute>
```

```
     <comparison operator> <relation> . <attribute>
 <set requirement> ::=
     ( <attributes> ) <chaining operator> <select-block>
 <arithmetic expression> ::= <constant> |
     <something> <arithmetic operator> <something>
 <chaining operator> ::= IN | = | NOT_IN | > | < | >= | <= | \=
 <comparison operator> ::= < | > | = | \= | <= | >=
 <arithmetic operator> ::= + | - | * | /
 <function> ::= <built-in function> ( <attribute> )
 <built-in function> ::= CNT | MAX | MIN | SUM | AVG
 <something> ::= <integer> | <attribute>
 <relations> ::= <relation> | <relation> , <relations>
 <relation> ::= <relation name>
 <attributes> ::= <attribute> | <attribute> , <attributes>
 <constants> ::= <constant> | <constant> , <constants>
 <constant> ::= <atom> | <integer>
```

We conclude this section with a brief mention of the difference between SELECT-blocks and SELECT-block, which is shown in Fig. 5.1. It is easy to see that the syntax specification is recursive, permitting a SELECT-block to be nested within outer SELECT-block. In the vast majority of EL retrievals we construct one or more "SELECT FROM ..." blocks, and such a block specifies a set of tuples, that is a relation. To handle relationships, we typically specify a tuple from one such block in another nested block, or that a block contains the tuples of another block.

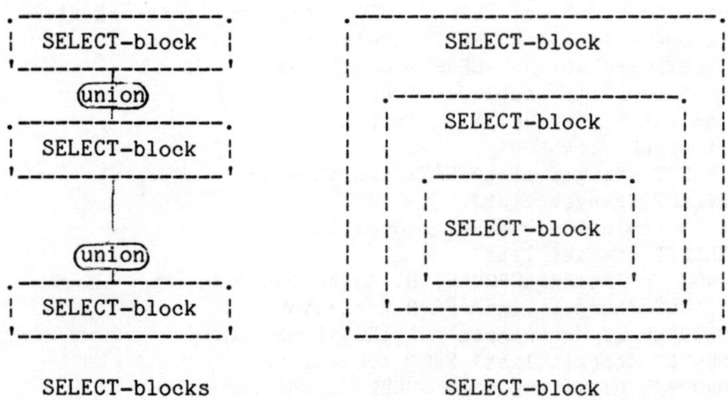

Fig. 5.1 SELECT-blocks and SELECT-block

5.4 THE PARSER OF EL

This section is devoted to an implementation technique for the English-Like language EL. As a matter of fact, the technique is general and may be used for other structured query languages. The emphasis is on those aspects which have been put to practical use in the programming language PROLOG showing how a structured query is understood by logic-program solving. There is an additional purpose of demonstrating the particular advantages of PROLOG for compiler writing.

5.4.1 Considering Keywords as Operators

One of important strategies in writing the parser of EL is that each structured English keyword in EL is considered as an operator in PROLOG by declaring it in advance. These operators not only provide syntactic convenience when reading or writing, but also allow the use of simple expressions for what would otherwise have to be implemented through more complicated code containing explicit control structures such as iteration. Each operator has three properties: a position, precedence, and associativity. The position can be postfix, prefix, or infix. That is, an operator with one argument can go after or before it; an operator with two arguments can go between them. The precedence is an integer and makes expressions unambiguous where the syntax of the terms is not made explicit through the use of parentheses; The associativity makes expressions unambiguous in which there are two operators with the same precedence. If we wish to declare that an operator with a given position, precedence, and associativity is to be recognised when terms are read and written, we use the built-in predicate op. If name is desired operator (the atom that we want to be an operator), prec the precedence (an integer within the appropriate range), and spec the position/associativity specifier, then the operator is declared by providing the following goal:

```
?- op(prec,spec,name).
```

Here we give the declaration of operators involved in EL.

```
declare :- op(40,xfx,in), op(40,xfx,not_in),
           op(180,xfy,&), op(185,yfx,having),
           op(190,yxf,where), op(192,yfx,grouped_by),
           op(195,yfx,from), op(195,yfx,set), op(195,yfx,':'),
           op(200,fx,select), op(200,fx,update),
           op(200,fx,insert_into),
           op(200,fx,delete), op(215,xfy,union).
```

It is important to note how these operators have been defined since in declarations a little bit of syntactic sugar makes a big difference. All particular query structures will be based on the definition. The precedence comparison of operators with one another is given in Fig. 5.2.

```
                                                      .-----------
                                                   40 | IN, NOT_IN
                                                 .----'
                                             180 | &
                                           .-----'
                                       185 | HAVING
                                     .-----'
                                 190 | WHERE
                               .-----'
                           192 | GROUPED_BY
                         .-----'
                     195 | FROM, SET, ':'
                   .-----'
               200 | SELECT, UPDATE, DELETE, INSERT_INTO
             .-----'
         215 | UNION
```

Fig. 5.2 The Comparison of Operators in EL

It is this declaration that permits the nesting of operators and such nesting may be carried to any depth, so that queries in EL could be constructed with arbitrary complexity. By means of the declaration, an EL query is internally represented as a function or function form. We shall use "E" to denote its internal representation of an EL query "Q". The rules for the translation are illustrated as follows:

```
Q1:  update N set Attr = Exp
E1:  update(set(N,=(Attr,Exp)))

Q2:  update N set Attr = Exp where Conds
E2:  update(set(N,where(=(Attr,Exp),Conds)))

Q3:  insert_into N : NewTu
E3:  insert_into(:(N,NewTu))

Q4:  delete N
E4:  delete(N)

Q5:  delete N where Conds
E5:  delete(where(N,Conds))

Q6:  select Attrs from N
E6:  select(from(Attrs,N))

Q7:  select Attrs from N where Conds
E7:  select(from(Attrs,where(N,Conds)))

Q8:  select Attrs from M,N
E8:  select(from(Attrs,&(M,N)))

Q9:  select Attrs from M,N where Conds
E9:  select(from(Attrs,where(&(M,N),Conds)))
```

```
Q10: select Fun(Attr) from N where Conds
E10: select(from(Fun(Attr),where(N,Conds)))

Q11: select Fun(Attr) from N
E11: select(from(Fun(Attr),N))

Q12: select Attr,Fun from N grouped_by Attr where Conds
E12: select(from(&(Attr,Fun),grouped_by(N,where(Attr,Conds))))

Q13: select Attrs from N grouped_by Attr having Fun
E13: select(from(Attrs,grouped_by(N,having(Attr,Fun))))

Q14: select Attrs from N grouped_by Attr
E14: select(from(Attrs,grouped_by(N,Attr)))

Q15: select A from M where C1 union select B from N where C2
E15: union(select(from(A,where(M,C1))),select(from(B,where(N,C2))))
```

Let us look at an example. Consider such a query, (Q5.25) **Get part numbers whose weight is greater than 18 pounds or supplied by s2 or supplied by people in London.** The query could expressed in EL as follows

```
    SELECT pno FROM parts WHERE weight > 18
UNION
    SELECT pno FROM shipment WHERE sno = s2
UNION
    SELECT pno FROM shipment WHERE sno IN
        (SELECT sno FROM suppliers WHERE city = London)
```

The internal representation of the query, that is, the structure of the query, could be more easily visualised as the tree structure shown in Fig. 5.3.

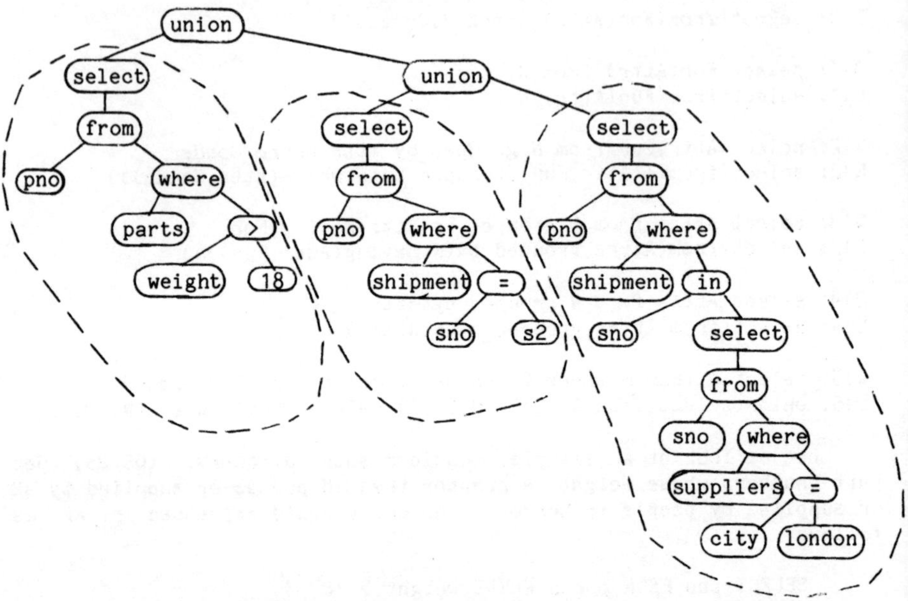

Fig. 5.3 The Tree Structure of the Function of Q5.25

Since the EL parser has a different entry for each possible EL query, unacceptable queries can be discarded on the grounds of a mismatch. This technique allows us to resolve query ambiguities with comparatively little effort.

5.4.2 Creation of Variables

The important technique of translating the EL function into the canonical logic representation is the creation of variables. Let us now consider how we can create a variable to stand for the values of an attribute specified in an EL query, and then the variable can be used to determine possible instantiation states for the attribute. Afterwards, all information about this will be derived from where the variable appears in the canonical logic expression. Basically, the value of a variable can be affected by knowledge about any of the positions in which that variable has appeared. The EL parser provides a way of generating such variables.

First of all, the predicate user_head_xs creates a set of variables to represent the target list specified in the SELECT clause of the outermost level SELECT-block, if a retrieval operation is required. In the meantime, it keeps the heading required by the user for formating the final answer to the query. The set of the variables will form the head Hi of the subquery SUBi in the canonical logic expression.

In assimilating an EL function, we have the problem of dealing with the situation when a new attribute is discovered. If the attribute has been encountered before, then the created variable corresponding to the attribute is a join variable that will appear in the canonical logic form; otherwise, we must ensure that the new variable we assign to it does not accidentally coincide with one representing any other attribute. In both cases, it is important to keep the correspondence between the attributes and the variables. However, it is not always easy to maintain the correspondence. For instance, an extra variable should be introduced if a built-in function has been encountered.

While dealing with an attribute, it is helpful not only to remember whether the corresponding variable is desired by the user but also to understand whether the variable is a join-variable or just an independent one. However, there is no need to classify variables into different types in the physical implementation since an EL query, with a fixed function or a function form, implies the procedurality so that the artificial variables corresponding to the attributes can be created step by step, while parsing.

Another important implementation technique is to decide when these variables are considered as real variables by the PROLOG system. Because of the fact, that variables in PROLOG behave in a very active way, but they are taken to be local to each clause (i.e. unrelated to variables in other clauses, even when their identifiers might coincide), therefore, it is sensible to postpone the conversion as late as possible, both for the sake of efficiency and correspondence.

5.4.3 The Treatment of Conditions

In general, a SELECT-block will be translated into a sub query SUBi located in the canonical logic form. The most difficult job in parsing an EL query is to understand the WHERE conditions on which the answer to a query is to be obtained.

Let us consider the following example:

```
SELECT  attri11, attri21
FROM    relation1, relation2
WHERE   relation1.attri11 > relation2.attri21
        relation1.attri13 = 5,
        relation2.attri22 IN
               (SELECT  attri31
                FROM    relation3
                WHERE   attri32 = smith)
```

It is easy to see that there are three kinds of conditions:

(1). **Join conditions.** The comparison between two attributes belonging to different relations, such as

relation1.attri11 > relation2.attri21

(2). **Chaining conditions.** One of chaining operators ("IN", or "=", or "NOT_IN") is used in the comparison in order to select information from one relation based on the contents of another relation, such as

```
relation2.attri22 IN
   (SELECT attri31 FROM relation3 WHERE attri32 = smith)
```

(3). **Simple conditions.** Comparison with a constant (integer or atom), such as

```
relation1.attri13 = 5
```

Specifically, the parser provides a different entry for each possible combination to an arbitrary SELECT-block specification. There are nine cases of specification about SELECT-block in our implementation. The recursive processing is accomplished by a matched predicate **get_sub_qs(Spec,Vars,FunDes)** in which the three arguments Spec, Vars, and FunDes must be all given:

Spec: Specification of the SELECT-block.

Vars: Variables, which are going to match with the target list of the SELECT clause of the block.

FunDes: Function description from the out level of the block.

We only discuss one case here. Suppose the specification of the SELECT-block is the form:

```
select A from I,J,K where .....
```

What happens at execution time of the predicate **get_sub_qs** in dealing with the SELECT-block is illustrated in Fig. 5.4.

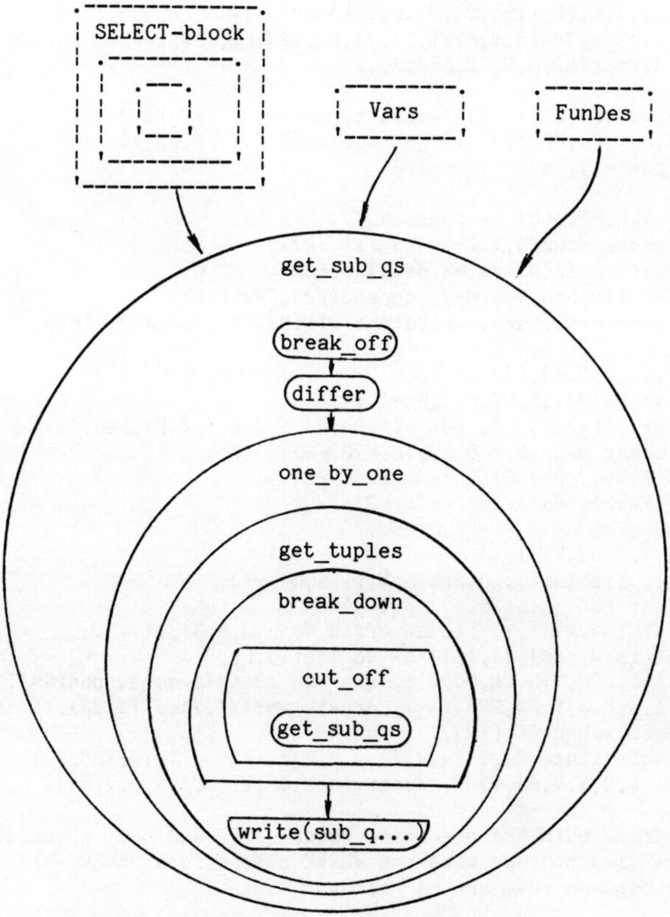

Fig. 5.4 Compilation of a SELECT-block

A top level PROLOG implementation corresponding to the recursive processing is given below:

```
get_sub_qs(from(X,where(&(Y1,Y2),Z)),Var,!) :- !,
            to_list(&(Y1,Y2),Names),
            to_list(X,Cols), to_list(Z,Conds),
            break_off(Cols,Var,Conds,S,V,F,FF),
            differ(Names,S,V,F,FF,R), one_by_one(R).

break_off(S,V,[],S,V,[],[]).
break_off(S1,V1,[A|B],S,V,F,[A1|FF]) :-
            join_cond(S1,V1,A,S2,V2,A1),
            break_off(S2,V2,B,S,V,F,FF).
break_off(S1,V1,[A|B],S,V,[A|F],FF) :-
            break_off(S1,V1,B,S,V,F,FF).
```

```
differ([],_,_,_,_,[]).
differ([N1|N2],S,V,F,FF,[(N1,S1,V1,F1,FF1)|R]) :-
            pick_up(N1,S,V,F,FF,S1,V1,F1,FF1,F2,FF2),
            differ(N2,S,V,F2,FF2,R).

one_by_one([(N,S,V,F1,F2)|[]]) :- get_tuples(N,S,V,F1,F2,!).
one_by_one([(N,S,V,F1,F2)|B]) :- get_tuples(N,S,V,F1,F2,!),
            put(44), one_by_one(B).

get_tuples(N,S,V,C,F2,Sth) :- table(N,H),
            break_down(S,V,C,Ss,Vs,Fs1,F21),
            reform_f2(Ss,Vs,F2,Sss,Vss,F22),
            sort(H,Sss,Vss,Ms), append(F21,F22,Fs2),
            degree(Ms,Var), write(sub_q(N,Ms,Fs1,Fs2,Var,Sth)).

break_down(S,V,[],S,V,[],[]) :- !.
break_down(S1,V1,[A|B],S2,V2,Fs1,Fs2) :-
            A=..[I,J,K], !, cut_off(S1,V1,I,J,K,S,V,F1,F2),
            break_down(S,V,B,S2,V2,F12,F22),
            (F1==!, Fs1=F12; Fs1=[F1|F12]),
            (F2==!, Fs2=F22; Fs2=[F2|F22]).

cut_off(S,V,in,J,K,S1,V1,!,!) :-
            to_list(J,L), subst(S,V,L,Xs,S1,V1),
            get_sub_qs(K,Xs,!), put(44).
cut_off(S,V,=,J,K,S1,V1,!,!) :- cut_off(S,V,in,J,K,S1,V1,!).
cut_off(S,V,not_in,J,K,S1,V1,!,!) :- to_list(J,L),
            subst(S,V,L,Xs,S1,V1), get_sub_qs(K,Xs,not), put(44).
cut_off(S1,V1,I,J,K,S,V,F1,F2) :- !, create_var(S1,V1,J,Y1,Y2),
            get_sub_qs(K,[Y2],!), put(44),
            substitute(S1,V1,=,J,Y1,S,V,F1), F2=..[I,Y1,Y2].
cut_off(S1,V1,I,J,K,S,V,F1,!) :- substitute(S1,V1,I,J,K,S,V,F1).
```

In the program, both the predicate "break_off" and the predicate "break_down" are used to cope with the WHERE clause in a SELECT-block. The differences between them are as follows:

a). The predicate "break_off" is used to break off such a SELECT-block in which the FROM clause contains several relations. As a result, by creating join variables, the join conditions specified in the WHERE clause will be replaced by relevant formulas. There are seven arguments associated with the predicate:

```
break_off(Attrs_1,Vars_1,Conds,Attrs_2,Vars_2,IndeFs,ReleFs)
```

Given attributes **Attrs_1**, variables **Vars_1** which match with the attributes, and the conditions **Conds** specified in the WHERE clause, the predicate "break_off" parses the conditions **Conds**. The new list of attributes **Attrs_2** and their corresponding variables **Vars_2** will be obtained. All conditions will be classified into independent formulas **IndeFs** and relevant formulas **ReleFs**. However, at this stage, the predicate ignores any chaining conditions and treats them as simple ones.

b). The predicate "break_down" is only used to break down such a SELECT-block in which the WHERE clause may contain chaining conditions. As a result, by creating join variables, the chaining conditions will be broken down into pseudo-independent formulas and relevant formulas. There are also seven arguments related to the predicate:

break_down(Attrs_1,Vars_1,Conds,Attrs_2,Vars_2,IndeFs,ReleFs)

Given attributes **Attrs_1** which have been encountered so far, variables **Vars_1** which have been created, and the non-join conditions **Conds**, the predicate "break_down" will parse the conditions **Conds**. The new list of attributes **Attrs_2** and their corresponding variables Vars_2 will be obtained. All conditions will be classified into independent formulas **IndeFs** and relevant formulas **ReleFs**.

The function of the predicate **differ** is that from the collection of all attributes S, variables V, non-join conditions F, and relevant formulas FF which is the result of the execution of **break_off**, each relation picks up its own attributes S1, variables V1, non-join formulas F1, and relevant formulas FF1 respectively, then puts them into the box R in the particular order:

[(N1,S1,V1,F1,FF1),(N2,S2,F2,FF2),......]

The box R will be dealt with by the predicate **one_by_one**. As the sub goals of the predicate **one_by_one**, the predicate **get_tuples** performs the writing of the query tuple in the canonical logic form. The predicate has six arguments:

get_tuples(Name,Attrs_1,Vars_1,Conds,ReleFs,FunDes)

where:

Name The relation name.

Attrs_1 Attributes which have been encountered in the relation.

Vars_1 Variables, which correspond to attributes Attrs_1.

Conds Non-join conditions (i.e. chaining conditions or simple conditions).

ReleFs Relevant formulas, probably obtained from "break_off".

FunDes Function description which may be any form given in Section 3.3.

The relationship among sub goals of the predicate "get_tuples" is shown in Fig. 5.5. By means of proper changing and sorting, the canonical form is obtained.

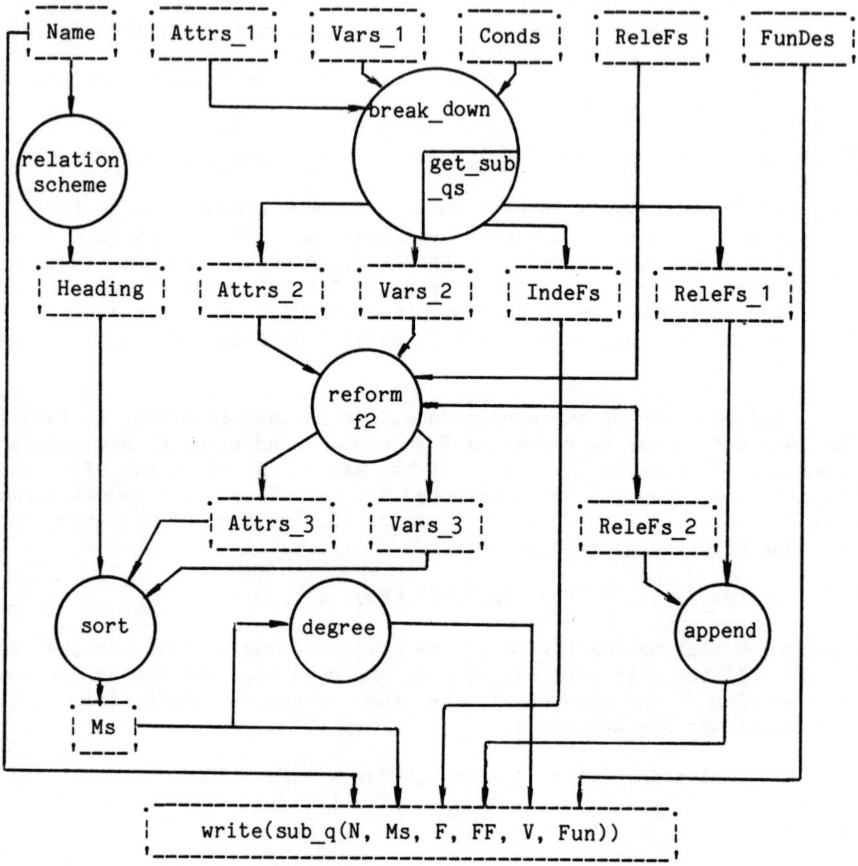

Fig. 5.5 The Function of the Predicate 'get_tuples'

If there exists another nested chaining embedded in the chaining condition then the predicate **get_sub_qs** will be called again and again until the **break_off** and **break_down** processing hits the bottom of the recursion.

We conclude this chapter with a rather sophisticated example showing the original EL query and its canonical logic expression given by the EL parser. Suppose one wants **to find the department and its location where there is at least one part in stock the quantity of which happens to be the total number of the same part supplied by all suppliers.** The EL expresses the query in the way:

```
SELECT  dept, city
FROM    department
WHERE   dept IN
```

```
(SELECT  dept
 FROM    stock
 WHERE   (pno, qty) IN
                        (SELECT pno, SUM(qty)
                         FROM   shipment
                         GROUPED_BY pno))
```

The canonical logic form deduced from the EL parser is:

```
[X1,X2] &
sub_q(shipment,[#,X3,#],[],[],[X3],[group,X3,X3]) &
sub_q(shipment,[#,X3,X5],[],[],[X3,X5],[sum,X5,X4]) &
sub_q(stock,[X1,X3,X4],[],[],[X1,X3,X4],!) &
sub_q(department,[X1,X2,#],[],[],[X1,X2],!) &
!.
```

It can be seen that the nested query is decomposed into a simple collection of query tuples in its canonical form, and the result is the same as that given in Section 4.4, where the query was expressed in PL language and the canonical expression was obtained from the PL editor.

CHAPTER 6
A Mathematics-like Language

Chapters 4 and 5 have been concerned with the calculus-based languages PL and EL, and have shown how a PL query or an EL query can be translated into the canonical logic expression by the PL editor and the EL parser respectively. In this chapter we turn our attention to another class of relational query languages: algebraic languages. Our goal is to develop a Mathematics-Like language called ML, where, in marked contrast to both PL and EL, queries are generally effected by the specification of a sequence of algebraic operators.

Apart from the description of ML, this chapter is mainly devoted to showing the unification of arbitrary algebraic expressions and the compatibility between algebra and calculus in the course of automatic reduction of arbitrary ML queries to their canonical forms.

6.1 RELATIONAL ALGEBRA OPERATIONS

Relational algebra is a collection of operations on relations. Each operation takes one or more relations as it operand(s) and produces another relation as its result. We discussed a set of such operations in Section 3.4 as the basis for proving the relational completeness of the proposed canonical logic expression. Based on the E.F.Codd's original algebraic operations, Numerous variations have been proposed. The existing query language ISBL (Information System Base Language) developed at the IBM UK Scientific Centres in Peterlee [17] could be considered as a "pure" relational algebraic language.

It is often said that relational calculus-based languages are higher-level than algebraic languages because the algebra is a procedural or navigational language specifying the order of operations, while the calculus expression does in fact tell only what is wanted, not how to get it. Nevertheless, the algebra is still important. The basic reason is that it provides a yardstick against which other languages can be measured. The algebra also lays a foundation for research into several other aspects of database management, such as database design, view definition, and restructuring. For these reasons we have put the algebraic language ML in the ILEX system.

However, we discuss only the policy decisions made in ML with retrieval examples, since a pure relational algebraic language is less "user-friendly".

6.2 THE LANGUAGE ML

6.2.1 The Syntax of ML

Together with the correspondence to ISBL, the ML notations to algebraic operators are shown in Fig. 6.1, where R and S are relations or sub-algebraic expressions, which are the combination of operations such as selection, projection, intersection, difference, union, equijoin, and Cartesian product; "Conds" is a set of formulas specifying related conditions, i.e., formulas are linked together by commas indicating logic function "AND"; "Attrs" specifies a list of attributes.

Algebra	ISBL	M L
union	R + S	R ++ S
difference	R - S	R -- S
intersection	R . S	R :: S
selection	R : Conds	R : Conds
projection	R % Attrs	R [Attrs]
natural join	R * S	R <=> S
product		R ** S
general join		R ** S : Conds

Fig. 6.1 Correspondence Between Algebra, ISBL and ML

The definition of each algebraic operator can be found in Section 3.4. Fig. 6.2 illustrates the precedence comparison of operators in ML. It is useful to keep in mind these precedences while writing algebra queries. We will discuss these operators in detail with examples. As usual, all examples are based on the suppliers-parts-dept database.

```
                              .-----------------------------------
                          190 | difference "--", intersection "::"
                              | equijoin "<=>", product "**"
                     .--------'
                 195 | selection ":"
            .--------'
        200 | projection "[]"
   .--------'
   215 | union "++"
```

Fig. 6.2 The Precedences of Relational Algebra Operators in ML

6.2.2 Simple Retrieval

Operations in relational algebra are very high level, and much may be accomplished in a single operation. We shall first discuss projection and selection.

Projection. The projection operator yields a "vertical" subset of a given relation. No attribute may be specified more than once in a projection operation. An example of projection is **(Q6.1) to get all part names and their colours.**

```
PARTS [Pname,Colour]
```

As in EL, the user is free to choose the upper or lower case letters for clarity, while an algebra query is being given. The order of the listing in the projection can be changed by request. Let us consider that one **wants to get full details of all suppliers (Q6.2).** Again, this is a projection operation, and the query could be written in the way:

```
SUPPLIERS [Sno,Sname,Status,City]
```

Since specifying a list containing all attributes of the given relation in their left-to-right order is equivalent to omitting the list of attributes in ML, the expression for Q6.1 could be simplified by specifying the relation name only:

```
SUPPLIERS
```

Selection. The selection operator yields a "horizontal" subset of a given relation - that is, the subset for which the specified comparison conditions are satisfied. **(Q6.3) Select all information about suppliers in London with status > 20.**

```
SUPPLIERS : City=London, Status>20
```

Selection-Projection. This is a very common form in ML, involving a selection and projection on a single relation. **(Q6.4) Get supplier names for suppliers in Paris with status > 20.**

```
SUPPLIERS : City=Paris, Status>20  [Sname]
```

6.2.3 Select-Project-Equijoin Expressions

A more complicated type of query involves taking the **equijoin.** For simplicity, we make the common assumption that the attribute names in different relations are significant and identificational. ML will equal-join relations based on whether or not those attribute names are the same. Our example query is **"(Q6.5) Get supplier numbers who supplier at least one red part".**

```
(PARTS : Colour=red) <=> SHIPMENT [Sno]
```

The class of expressions we have in mind in the query is formed from the operators select, project, and equijoin. First, select tuples in relation PARTS such that the colour is red; Second, equijoin the result relation with relation SHIPMENT; Finally, project the attribute Sno from the result relation. Intuitively, many queries can be viewed as taking an entity (described by the selection operator ":"), connecting it to an entity of another type (described by equijoin operator "<=>"), and then printing some attributes of the latter entity (the projection "[]" determines the attributes printed). We call such expressions select-project-equijoin expressions. The user also could express the previous query in more detail by adding two extra projection operation to the relations, PART and SHIPMENT, respectively, that is:

```
(PART : Colour=red [Pno]) <=> (SHIPMENT [Sno,Pno]) [Sno]
```

The parse tree of the expression is shown in Fig. 6.3.

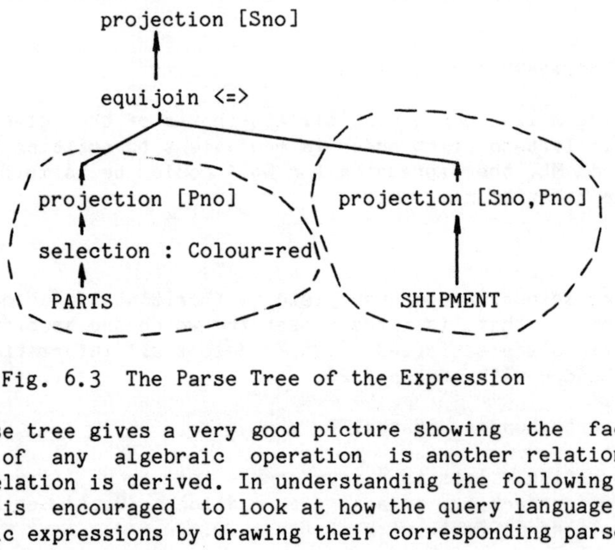

Fig. 6.3 The Parse Tree of the Expression

The parse tree gives a very good picture showing the fact that the result of any algebraic operation is another relation and how the final relation is derived. In understanding the following queries, the reader is encouraged to look at how the query language ML specifies algebraic expressions by drawing their corresponding parse trees.

(Q6.6) Get supplier names for suppliers who supply part P2.

```
(SHIPMENT : Pno=P2 [Sno]) <=> (SUPPLIERS [Sno,Sname]) [Sname]
```
or
```
(SHIPMENT : Pno=P2) <=> SUPPLIERS [Sname]
```

(Q6.7) For each part supplied, get part number and names of all cities supplied the part.

```
(SHIPMENT [Sno,Pno]) <=> (SUPPLIERS [Sno,City]) [Pno,City]
```
or
```
SHIPMENT <=> SUPPLIERS [Pno,City]
```

The difference between Q6.6 and Q6.7 is that the result attributes in

Q6.7 are obtained not only from the second relation but also from the first one.

(Q6.8) Get supplier names for suppliers who are located in London and supply part P1.

```
(SUPPLIERS : City=London) <=> (SHIPMENT : Pno=P1) [Sname]
```

6.2.4 Complex Queries

A more **general join** or **Cartesian product** of several relations is also available. For instance, we could express the query: **"(Q6.9) Get supplier names for suppliers who supply at least one red part."** in the way:

```
(PARTS ** SHIPMENT : Colour=red, PARTS.pno=SHIPMENT.pno [Sno])
<=> SUPPLIERS [Sname]
```

Although the attributes are distinct in the ML assumptions, it is necessary to specify relation names in a relevant formula involved in a general join, say, R.aa>S.dd, otherwise there would be an ambiguity of whether the "dd" stands for an attribute or a value under the attribute "dd". Q6.9 can also be written in the way:

```
(PARTS <=> SHIPMENT : Colour=Red [Sno]) <=> SUPPLIERS [Sname]
```

Let us now consider the **difference** and **intersection** operators. We only apply the two operators to relations of the same attributes. We assume the result relation "R -- S" or "R :: S" has the same attribute names. **(Q6.10) Get supplier numbers for suppliers not currently supplied any parts.**

```
(SUPPLIERS [Sno]) -- (SHIPMENT [Sno])
```

(Q6.11) Get supplier names for suppliers who do not supply part P2.

```
((SUPPLIERS [Sno])--(SHIPMENT : Pno=P2 [Sno])) <=> SUPPLIERS [Sname]
```

(Q6.12) Get supplier numbers for suppliers who are located in London and supply at least one red part.

```
(SUPPLIER : City=London [Sno]) ::
(SHIPMENT <=> (PARTS : Colour=red) [Sno])
```

Union. We only apply the union operator to relations of the same arity which are said to be union compatible. We assume the attributes of R and S have the same names as those of "R++S". To illustrate union operator, we give two examples. **(Q6.13) Get supplier names for suppliers who either are located in London or supply part P1.**

```
(SUPPLIERS : City=London [Sname] ) ++
(SUPPLIERS <=> (SHIPMENT : Pno=P1) [Sname] )
```

(Q6.14) Get part number for parts that either weigh more than 18

pounds or are currently supplied by Jones (or both).

```
(PARTS : Weight>18 [Pno]) ++
((SHIPMENT <=> (SUPPLIERS : Sname=Jones) [Pno] )
```

The relational algebra is basically a retrieval language. The union "++" and the difference "--" could be used to handle insert, delete, and update operations. However, these storage operations, which, we think, would be done in a more attractive notational form, will not be further discussed here.

6.3 THE ANALYSER OF ML

6.3.1 The Strategy of Algebra Manipulation

There are a large number of ways to construct algebraic operations for a query in ML, although the essential requirement might be exactly the same. In order to achieve versatility, the ML analyser has means for unifying the "outside world" into standardised models.

Before any algebraic manipulation, we must understand clearly when two expressions are equivalent. According to our assumptions in ML, a relation is a set of mappings from attributes to values. More importantly, in any application of which we are aware, each column of a relation is labeled by the proper attribute name. Where possible, we adopt names for attributes of a relation that is the result of an algebraic expression, from the names of attributes for the expression's arguments. We also require that names be provided for the result of an intersection, difference, and union. Two expressions E1 and E2 in relational algebra are equivalent, written E1 == E2, if they present the same mapping, that is, when we substitute the same relations for identical names in the two expressions, we get the same result.

With this definition, we can list some useful algebra transformations to bridge the gap between an arbitrary algebra given by the user and an expression needed to be translated into the canonical logic form.

The use of a rule-based formalism for unification of arbitrary algebra queries has proven quite beneficial. A rule based system is defined as one that consists of a collection of antecedent-consequent rules. The rules might be conditional statements that describe how to unify algebraic expressions when certain patterns are recognised. Powerful pattern-matching routines are obtained by the recursive processing:

```
unify(A,C) :- rule(A,B), (B==A, C=A; unify(B,C)).
```

The process works as follows. Rules are checked to find one that could make a contribution to the unification. When such a rule is found its conditions, if any, are examined: if they are true, the rule succeeds. If all other rules fail, the last rule "rule(X,X)" will always succeed. Therefore, further unification continues recursively until no more change could be made. By the way, the use of the rule system should have a positive effect on efficiency.

6.3.2 The Rule System

Let us now concentrate on what these rules should be.

1) Cascade of projections.

    R [Attrs1] [Attrs2] ... [Attrs_n] == R [Attrs_n]

The cascade of several projections can be combined into one. Note that the attribute "Attrs i+1" must be the subset of attribute "Attrs i" for the cascade to be legal.

2) Cascade of selections.

    R : Cond1 : Cond2 ... : Cond_n ==
    R : Cond1 & Cond2 .... & Cond_n

The cascade of selections can be combined into one selection that checks for all conditions at once.

3) Commuting selections and projections.

    (R [Attrs]) : Conds == R : Conds [Attrs]

The conditions, Conds, specified in the projection operation, could involve any attribute in R

4) Unify any combinations of projections and selections. Such as:

    R [Attrs1] : Conds1 : Conds2 [Attrs2] [Attrs3] : Conds3 ==
    R : Conds1 & Conds2 &Conds3 [Attrs3]

5) Commuting selection with a union.

    (R ++ S) : Conds == (R : Conds) ++ (S : Conds)

6) Commuting selection with a set difference.

    (R -- S) : Conds == (R : Conds) -- (S : Conds)

7) Commuting selection with an intersection.

    (R :: S) : Conds == (R : Conds) :: (S : Conds)

8) Commuting projection with a union.

    (R ++ S) [Attrs] == (R [Attrs]) ++ (S [Attrs])

9) Commuting equijoin with a union.

    (R ++ S) <=> P == (R ++ P) <=> (S ++ P)

10) Convert difference to predicate "not_in".

```
(R [Attrs]) -- S  ==  R : Attrs not_in S [Attrs]

(R : Conds) -- S  ==  R : Conds & R not_in S

R -- S  ==  R : R not_in S
```

The predicate "not_in" has two arguments which may be a relation name or a set of attributes. By means of the rule, the intersection operation "--" will no longer appear in its result; a select condition has been added instead.

11) Convert intersection to predicate "in".

```
(R [Attrs]) :: S  ==  R : Attrs in S [Attrs]

(R : Conds) :: S  ==  R : Conds & R in S

R :: S  ==  R : R in S
```

The predicate "in" has two arguments which may be a relation name or a set of attributes. By means of the rule, the intersection operation "::" will no longer appear in its result; a selection condition has been added instead.

12) Convert equijoin to predicate "equal".

```
(R [Attrs1]) <=> (S [Attrs2])  ==
R ** S : equal(Attrs1, Attrs2)

(R [Attrs]) <=> S  ==  R ** S : equal(R,S)

R <=> (S [Attrs])  ==  R ** S : equal(R,Attrs)  if R is an atom.

(R : Conds1) <=> (S : Conds2)  ==
R ** S : equal(R,S) & Conds1 & Conds2   if R and S are atoms.

R <=> (S : Conds)  ==  R ** S : equal(R,S) & Conds

(R : Conds) <=> S  ==  R ** S : equal(R,S) & Conds
```

The predicate "equal" has two arguments which may be a relation name or a set of attributes. The rule transforms an equijoin into a Cartesian product with a selection whose condition is specified in the predicate "equal".

Note there could be some other rules, such as rules for pushing a selection ahead of a Cartesian product or a join (which are ignored at this stage for reasons to be explained later). In logic programming, these inference rules are a set of Horn clauses which have been carefully ordered. The corresponding PROLOG program is given below:

```
simplify(A,C) :- unify(A,B), short_hand(B,C).
```

```
short_hand(A,{(A,*)) :- atom(A).
short_hand(A,{(A,*)) :- functor(A,F,2), (F==':'; F=='**').
short_hand(A,A).

unify(A,C) :- rule(A,B), (B==A, C=A; unify(B,C)).

rule({({(A,_),S),{(A,S)).
rule(:(:(A,Z2),Z1),:(A,&(Z2,Z1))).
rule({(A,:(S,Z)),{(:(A,Z),S)).
rule(:({(A,S),Z),{(:(A,Z),S)).

rule({(++(A,B),S),++({(A,S),{(B,S))).
rule(:(++(A,B),Z),++(:(A,Z),:(B,Z))).
rule(:(--(A,B),Z),--(:(A,Z),:(B,Z))).
rule(:(::(A,B),Z),::(:(A,Z),:(B,Z))).
rule(<=>(++(R,S),P),++(<=>(R,P),<=>(S,P))).

rule(--({(A,S),B),{(:(A,not_in(S,B)),S)).
rule(--(:(A,Z),B),:(A,&(Z,not_in(A,B)))) :- atom(A).
rule(--(A,B),:(A,not_in(A,B))) :- atom(A).

rule(::({(A,S),B),{(:(A,in(S,B)),S)).
rule(::(:(A,Z),B),:(A,&(Z,in(A,B)))) :- atom(A).
rule(::(A,B),:(A,in(A,B))) :- atom(A).

rule(**(:(A,Z),B),:(**(A,B),Z)).
rule(**(A,:(B,Z)),:(**(A,B),Z)).
rule(**(A,**(B,C)),**(A,&(B,C))) :- atom(B), atom(C).
rule(**(**(A,B),C),**(A,&(B,C))) :- atom(B), atom(C).

rule(<=>({(A,S1),{(B,S2)),:(**(A,B),equal(S1,S2))).
rule(<=>({(A,S),B),:(**(A,B),equal(S,B))) :- atom(B).
rule(<=>(A,{(B,S)),:(**(A,B),equal(A,S))) :- atom(A).
rule(<=>(:(A,Z1),:(B,Z2)),:(**(A,B),&(equal(A,B),&(Z1,Z2)))).
                         :- atom(A), atom(B).
rule(<=>(:(A,Z),B),:(**(A,B),&(equal(A,B),Z))) :- atom(A), atom(B).
rule(<=>(A,:(B,Z)),:(**(A,B),&(equal(A,B),Z))) :- atom(A), atom(B).
rule(<=>(A,B),:(**(A,B),equal(A,B))) :- atom(A), atom(B).
rule(<=>(A,:(**(B,C),Z)),:(**(A,&(B,C)),&(equal(A,B),&(equal(A,C),Z))))
                                          :- atom(A), atom(B), atom(C).
rule(<=>(:(A,Z1),:(**(B,C),Z2)),:(**(A,&(B,C)),&(equal(A,B),
             &(equal(A,C),&(Z1,Z2))))) :- atom(A), atom(B), atom(C).

rule({(A,S),{(B,S)) :- rule(A,B).
rule(:(A,Z),:(B,Z)) :- rule(A,B).
rule(::(A,B),::(C,D)) :- rule(A,C), rule(B,D).
rule(--(A,B),--(C,D)) :- rule(A,C), rule(B,D).
rule(<=>(A,B),<=>(C,D)) :- rule(A,C), rule(B,D).
rule(**(A,B),**(C,D)) :- rule(A,C), rule(B,D).

rule(X,X).
```

All these rules will be tested against all algebraic expressions in the top-down way until a match is found. It is easy to add new rules in order to be able to expand the power of the rule system.

As far as the implementation is concerned, it should be pointed out that, without consideration of efficiency, the group of rules before the last one given above could have been simplified in the way:

```
rule(E1,E2) :- E1 =..[F,A,B], rule(A,C), rule(B,D), E2=..[F,C,D].
```

Another point of interest is the alternative method of recursion by omitting the rule "rule(X,X)" with the following program:

```
unify(A,C) :- rule(A,B), unify(B,C).
unify(A,A).
```

This strategy suffers from an unexpected backtracking which, for instance, causes the algebra query "(R -- S) <=> P" to fail to be standardised.

6.3.3 Unification of Arbitrary Algebra Queries

The rule-oriented system is exactly an expert inferential system which would be able to cope with a wide range of algebra queries. Because of its importance, it is worth studying on more practical cases. The following results were obtained by the execution of the program indicating how an arbitrary algebra is standardised. R, S and P represent relations. "Attrs" represents attributes to be projected, while "Conds" describes the conditions in a select operation. The selection operator "[]" is replaced by "{" while a ML query is being accepted. The universal "read_in" facility has got the responsibility for doing so (see Section 3.2).

AN ALGEBRA QUERY

R <=> S [Attrs]

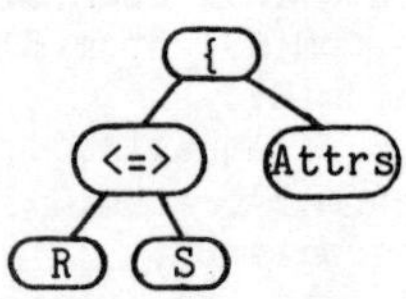

THE STANDARDISED QUERY

R ** S : equal(R,S) { Attrs

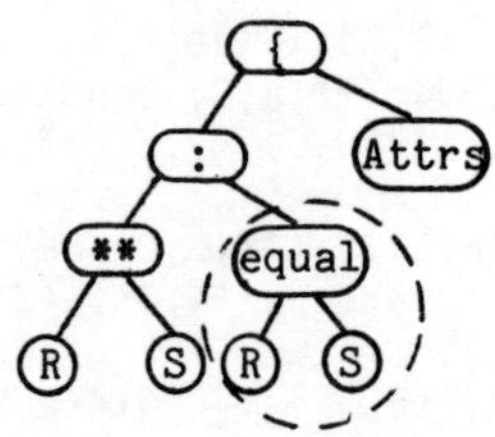

(R [Attrs])--(S [Attrs])

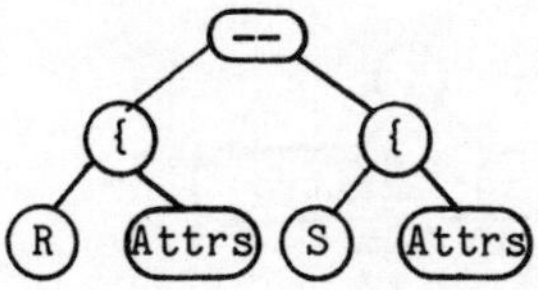

R : Attrs not_in S { Attrs

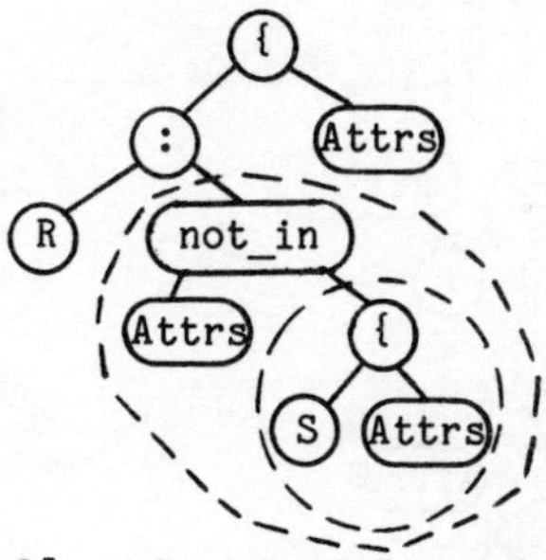

(R : Conds1 [Attrs1]) : Conds2 [Attrs2]

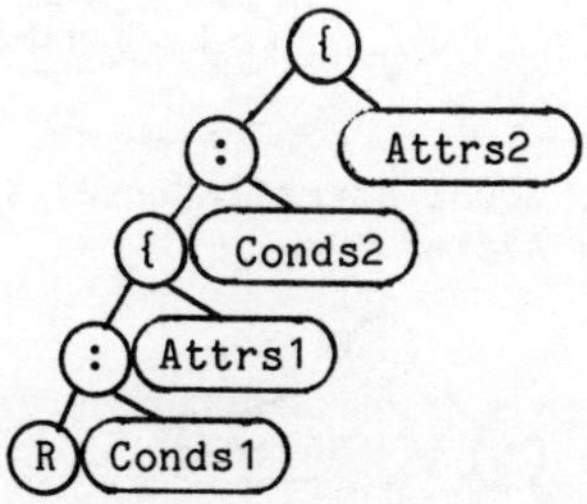

R : Conds1 & Conds2 { Attrs2

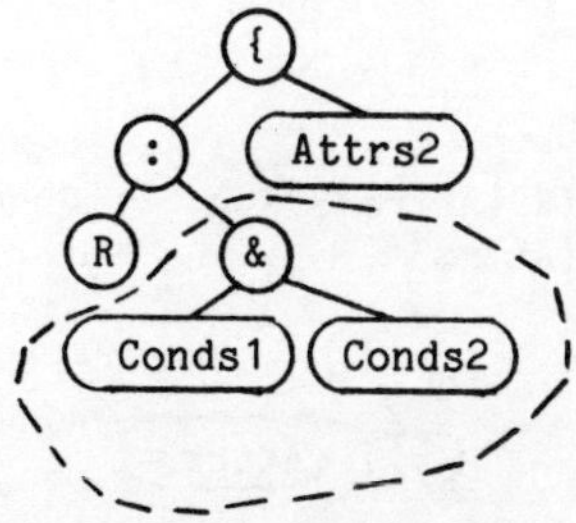

R <=> S : Conds [Attrs]

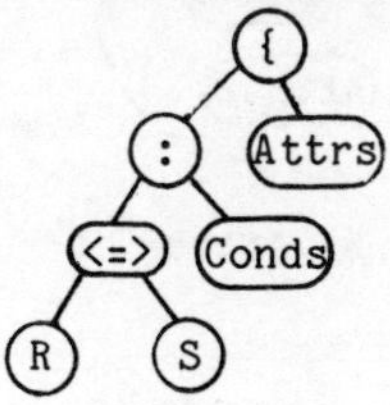

R ** S : equal(R,S) & Conds { Attrs

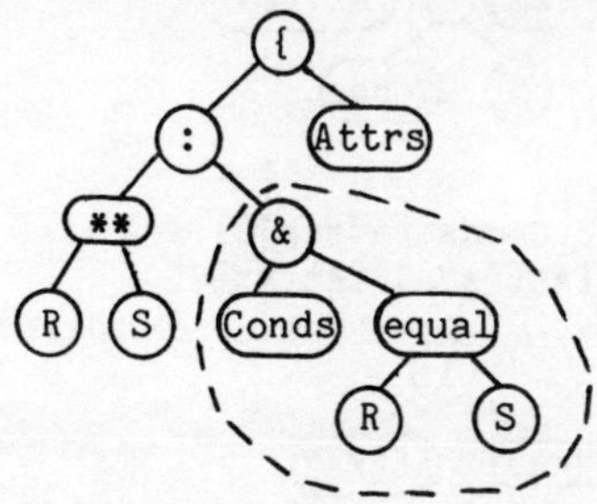

(R:Conds [Attrs1])<=>S [Attrs2]

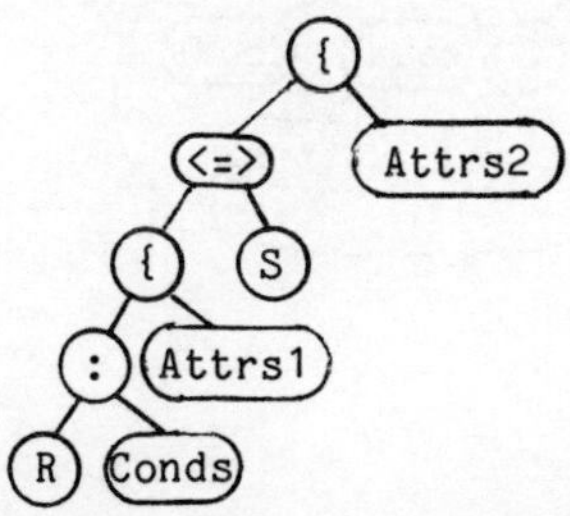

R**S:Conds&equal(Attrs1,S) { Attrs2

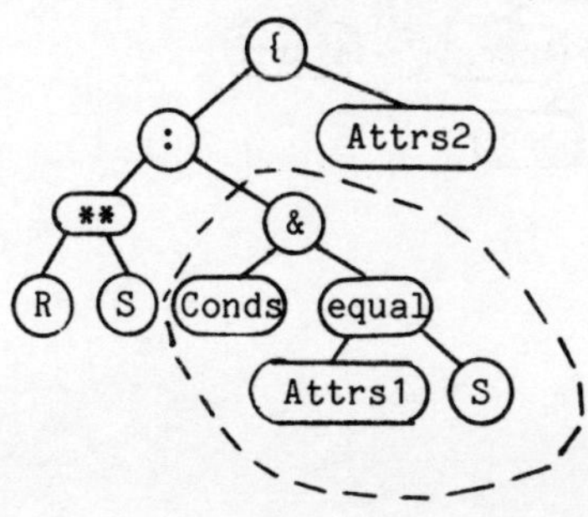

((R [Attrs])--(S:Conds [Attrs]))
<=> P [Attrs1]

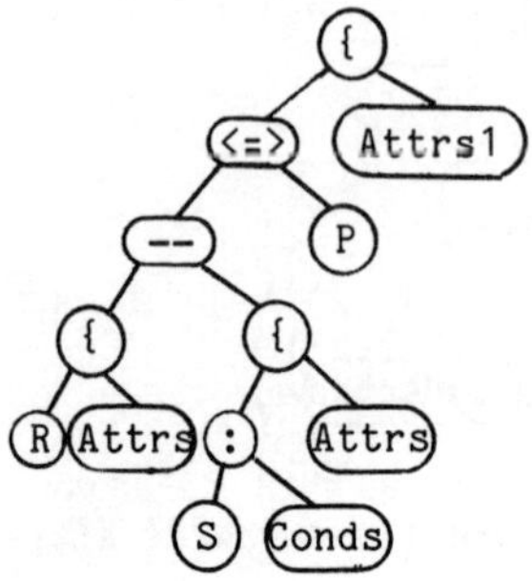

R**P : equal(Attrs,P) & not_in
(Attrs,(S:Conds{Attrs)) { Attrs1

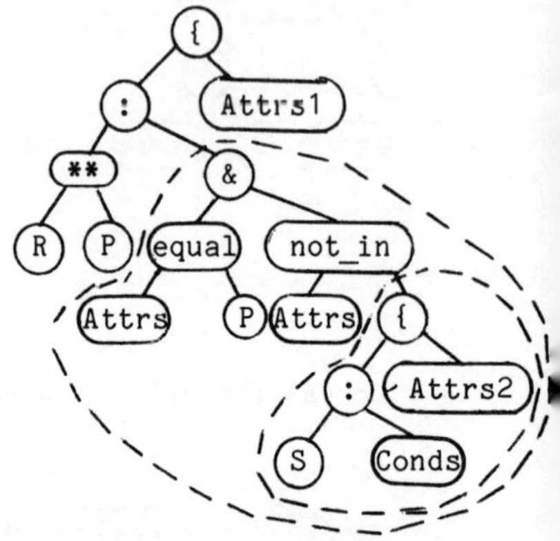

(R [Attrs1])<=>(S : Conds [Attrs2])
[Attrs3]

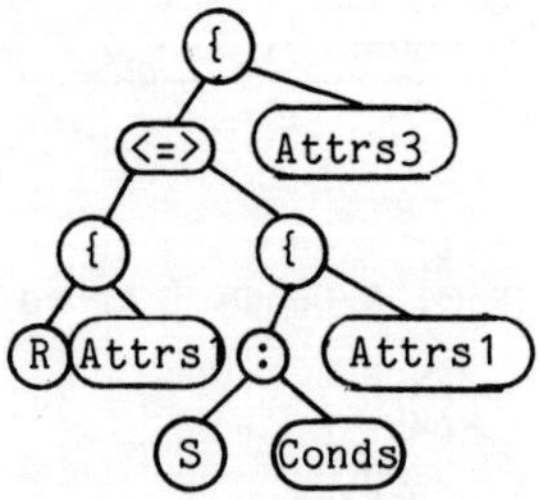

R** S : equal(Attrs1,Attrs2) &
Conds { Attrs3

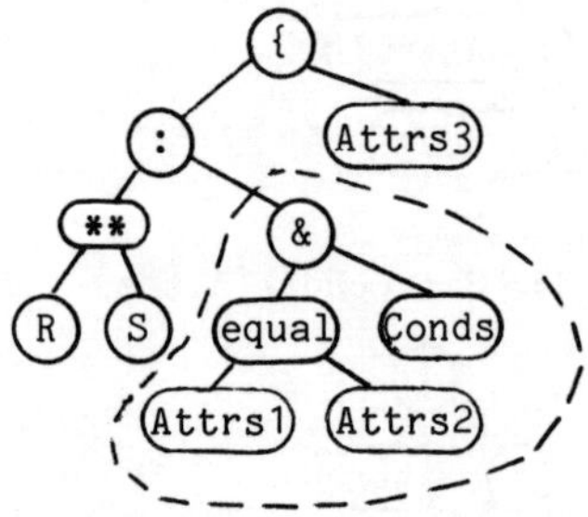

(R : Conds [Attrs1]) <=>
(S [Attrs2]) [Attrs3]

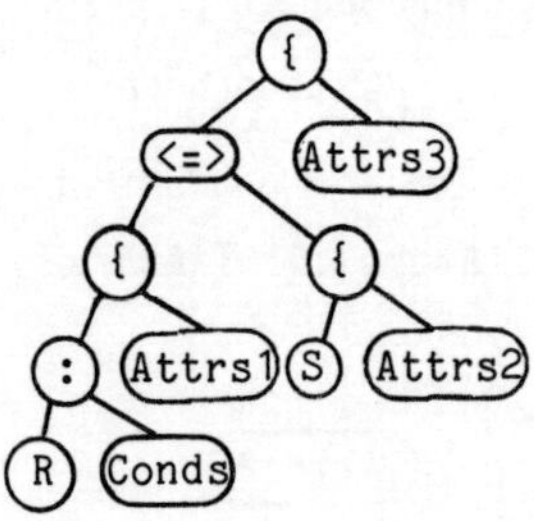

R**S : equal(Attrs1,Attrs2) &
Conds { Attrs3

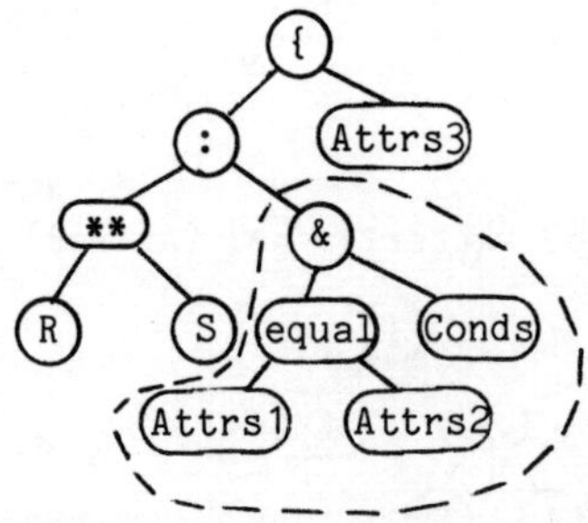

(R [Attrs1]) <=> (S [Attrs2])
[Attrs3]

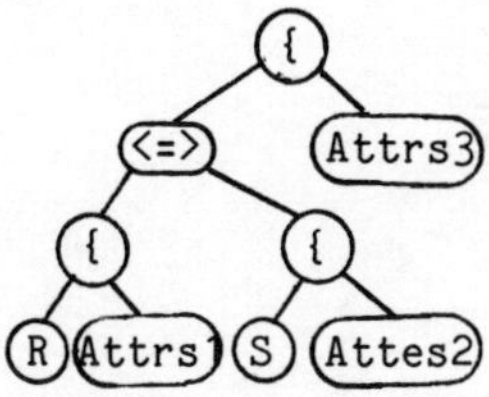

R ** S : equal(Attrs1,attrs2)
{ Attrs3

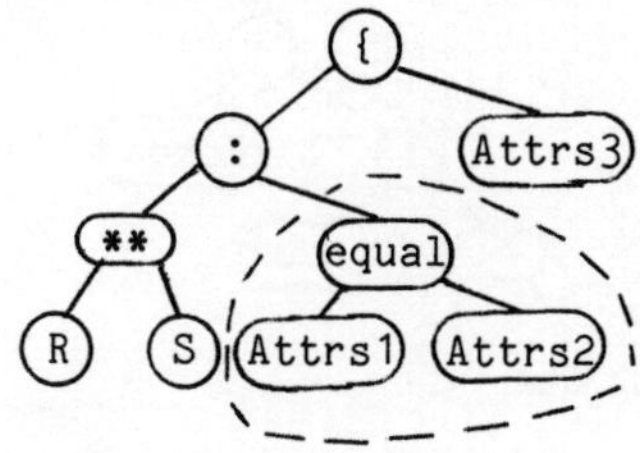

((R [Attrs])--(S : Conds [Attrs]))
<=> (P [Attrs1]) [Attrs2]

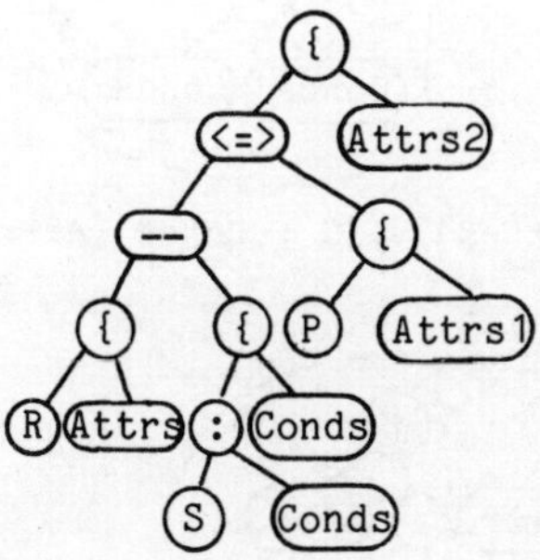

R ** P : equal(Attrs,Attrs1) &
not_in(Attrs,(S : Conds { Attrs))
{ Attrs2

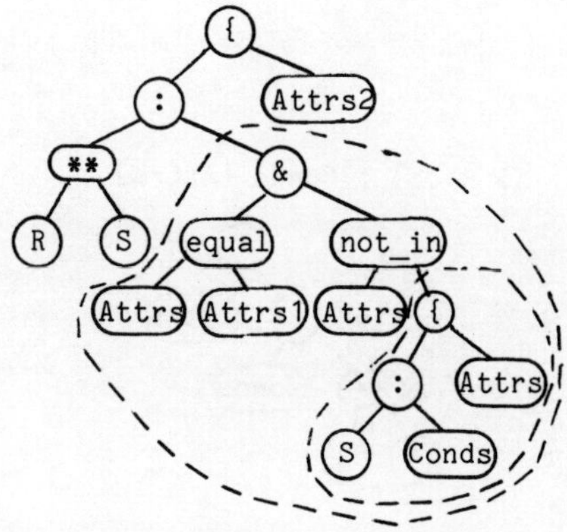

(R**S : Conds [Attrs1]) <=>
P [Attrs2]

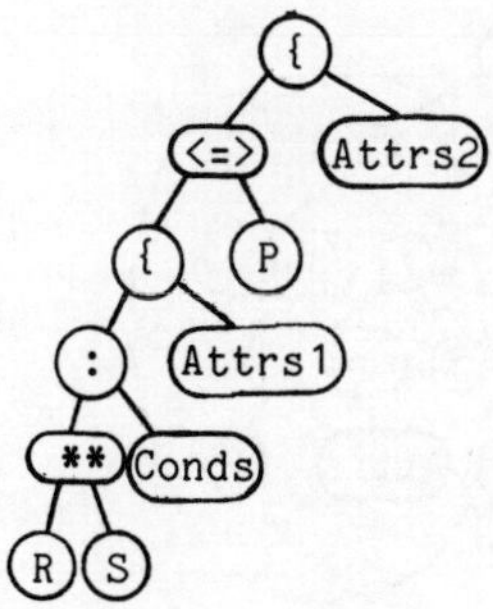

R ** S & P : equal(Attrs1,P) &
Conds { Attrs2

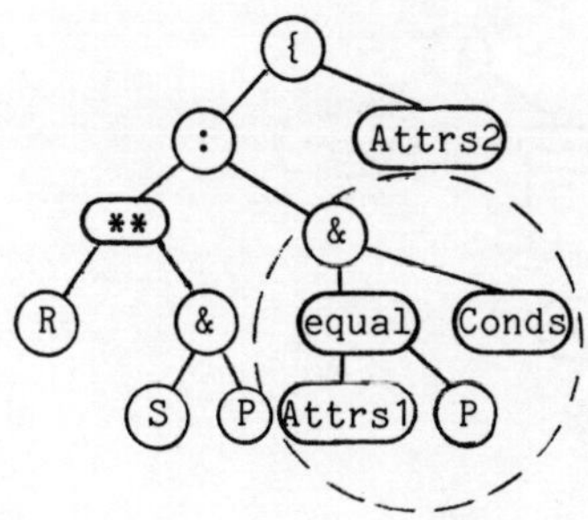

(R -- S) : Conds1 : Conds2

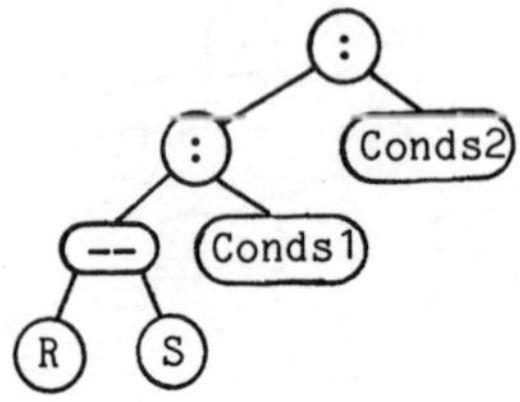

R : Conds1 & Conds2 & R not_in
(S : Conds1 & Conds2) { *

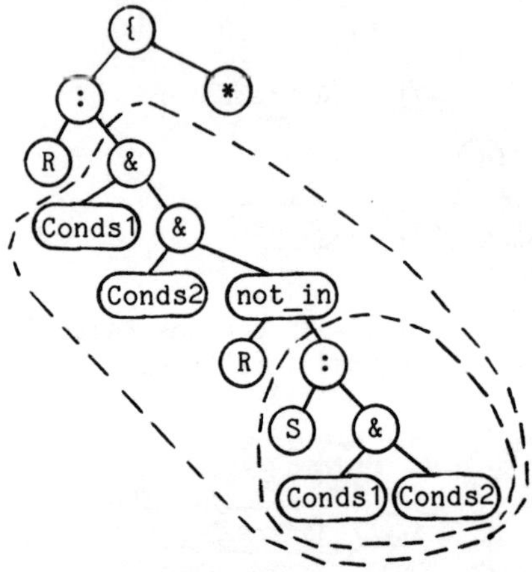

(R ++ S) : Conds [Attrs]

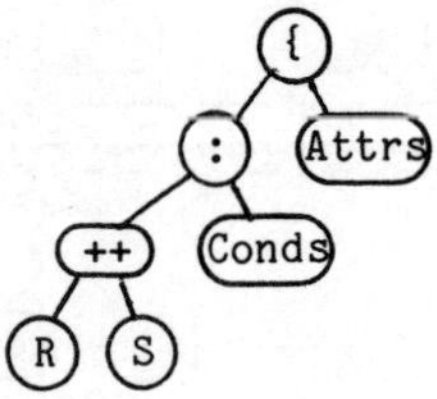

(R : Conds [Attrs])++(S : Conds [Attrs]

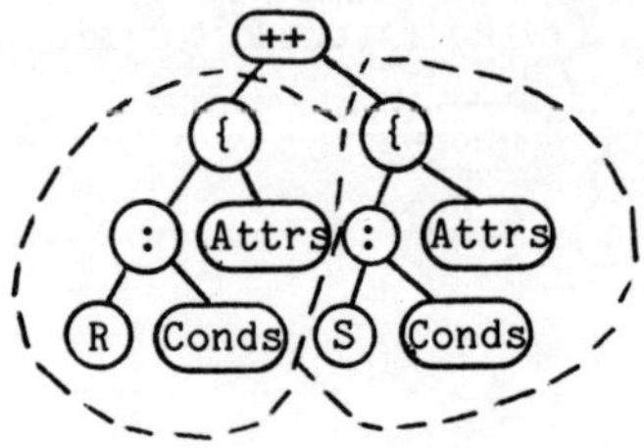

((R++S) : Conds [Attrs]) -- P
[Attrs1]

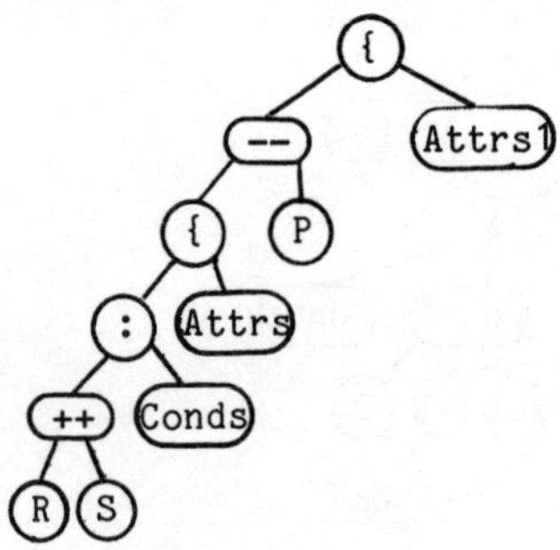

(R : Attrs not_in P { Attrs1) ++
(S : Attrs not_in P { Attrs1)

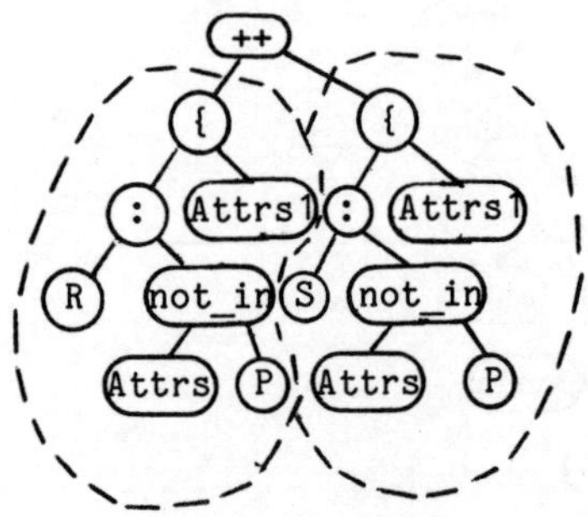

(R <=> S : Conds [Attrs1]) <=> P [Attrs2]

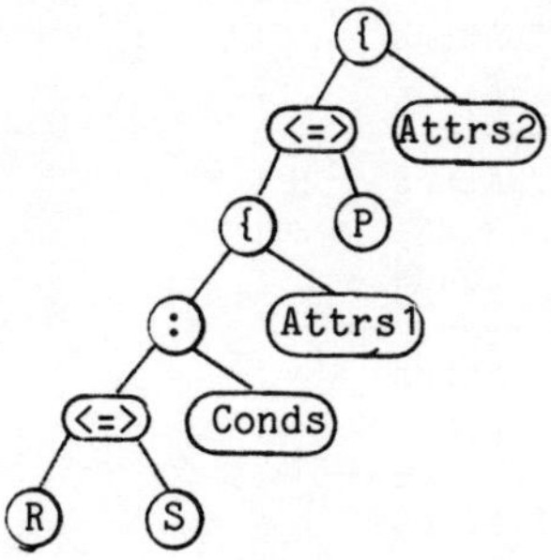

R ** S&P : equal(R,S) & Conds & equal (Attrs1,P) { Attrs2

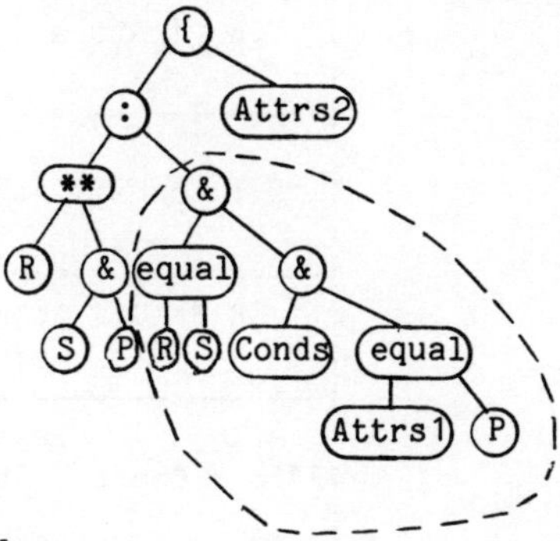

6.4 THE COMPATIBILITY BETWEEN ML AND EL

6.4.1 Five Standardised Models

After carefully studying the rule system with all the abstracted examples given above, we have come to the very important conclusion that, whatever an original algebra looks like, the standardised expression involves only at most four operations: selection, projection, Cartesian product, and union. Moreover, we observe that the standardised expressions have fixed orders of algebraic operations; there are five kinds of models, which are shown in Fig. 6.4.

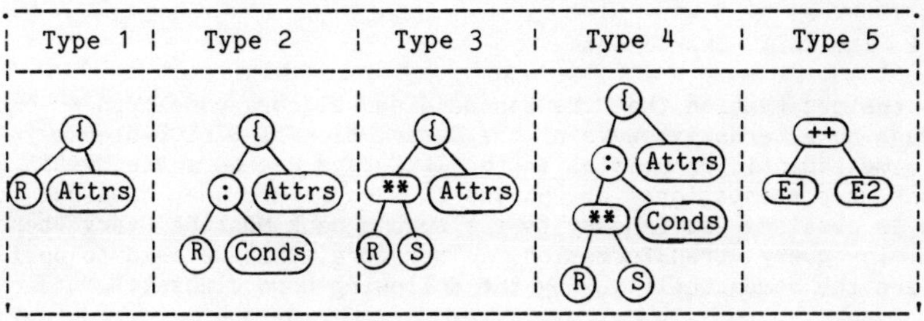

Fig. 6.4 The Standardised Models

We further observe that within the description of a selection condition Conds, there may be subexpressions whose representations again belong to these models; whereas the expressions E1 and E2 in type 5 may be any type of types 1-4.

Keeping in mind the EL fundamental SELECT-block, we surprisingly notice the correspondences between the ML models and the EL SELECT-blocks which is shown in Fig. 6.5.

M L M O D E L	E L SELECT-block
R { Attrs	SELECT Attrs FROM R
R : Conds { Attrs	SELECT Attrs FROM R WHERE Conds
R ** S { Attrs	SELECT Attrs FROM R,S
R**S : Conds { Attrs	SELECT Attrs FROM R,S WHERE Conds
E1 ++ E2	SELECT-block UNION SELECT-block

Fig. 6.5 Correspondences Between ML and EL

Of particular interest are the predicates "in" and "not_in" created by the ML unification and located in a selection condition. They happen to correspond to the EL chaining requirements which cause a SELECT-block to be nested by another SELECT-block.

6.4.2 The ILEX Shared Bank

With the observation that the standardised algebra models in ML can be viewed as alternative ways of the description of SELECT-blocks in EL, the same semantic properties in the ILEX bank can be shared with different representations by ML and EL even before the canonical logic form is obtained. It is easy to see such a bank must be very beneficial in query transformation. Therefore, what we need to do is to declare the compatibilities by the following Horn clauses:

```
compatibility({(:(**(A,B),Z),S),from(S,where(&(A,B),Z))).
compatibility({(**(A,B),S),from(S,&(A,B))).
compatibility({(:(N,Z),S),from(S,where(N,Z))).
compatibility({(N,S),from(S,N)).
```

The remaining work for the ML analyser becomes very simple. Only two things should be stressed here. Firstly, the predicate "equal" could be easily dealt with by seeking or creating equal join variables. But it does not produce any new relevant formulas at all. Secondly, in order to analyse a ML query and convert it to the canonical logic form, the subexpressions stated in union operations are standardised one by one; while the nested subexpressions described by predicates "in" and "not_in" are standardised level by level. This strategy not only makes the transformation much easier than the standardisation of a whole complicated algebra at once, but also takes the advantage of using the shared bank.

With the shared bank, the following PROLOG clauses cover all the situations.

```
m :- accept_e_m, !, analyser.

analyser :- see(q), read(X), seen, tell(que), !,
            simplify(X,Y), analyse(Y), told.
analyse(++(A,B)) :- simplify(A,T), compatibility(T,A1),
                    user_head_xs(A1,Xs),
                    get_sub_qs(A1,Xs,!), put(44),
                    write('!;'), write(Xs), put(44), !,
                    sub_analyse(B,Xs,!), put(44), write('!.'), nl.
analyse(A) :- simplify(A,T), compatibility(T,A1),
              user_head_xs(A1,Xs), get_sub_qs(A1,Xs,!),
              put(44), write('!.'), nl.

sub_analyse(++(A,B),V,K) :- simplify(A,T), compatibility(T,A1),
                            get_sub_qs(A1,V,K), put(44),
                            write('!;'), write(Xs), put(44), !,
                            sub_analyse(B,V,K).
sub_analyse(A,V,K) :- simplify(A,T), compatibility(T,A1),
                      get_sub_qs(A1,V,K).
```

The ILEX canonical logic form of an arbitrary algebra is therefore automatically obtained.

CHAPTER 7
Negation and Aggregation within System ILEX

As a formal basis, the canonical logic form for all relational query languages presented in Chapter 3 is not only free of the existential and universal quantifiers, but also extended to include aggregate functions. More structural compatibility between the proposed logic form and existing high level relational languages is therefore achieved. The Picture-like, English-like, and Mathematics-like languages, given in Chapters 4-6, have been developed and installed in the ILEX system. While a query written in any of the three query languages is mapped into the canonical logic form, the use of aggregate functions and set facilities has not been well described. Therefore, there is a need to turn back to look at the proposed logic form and discuss the precise and general definitions and implementation such as negation, aggregate functions, and set facilities.

7.1 TREATMENT OF NEGATION AS NONPROVABILITY

Many queries involve (explicitly or implicitly) the concept of negation. An example is: Find supplier names for suppliers who do not supply part P2. The request can be expressed in PL, EL, or ML as following:

In PL:

```
.--------------.                     .-------------.
| suppliers    |                     | shipment    |
----------------------------         -------------------
sno   sname   status   city          sno   pno    qty
----------------------------         -------------------
N     p.A                            ~N    p2
```

In EL:

```
SELECT sname FROM suppliers WHERE sno NOT_IN
              (SELECT sno FROM shipment WHERE pno=p2)
```

In ML:

```
(SUPPLIERS [sno] -- SHIPMENT : pno=p2 [sno]) <=> SUPPLIERS [sname]
```

The given query, regardless of whatever language written, is mapped into canonical logic form as

```
[A] &
sub_q(suppliers,[N,A,#,#],[],[],[N,A],!) &
sub_q(shipment,[N,p2,#],[],[],[N],not) &
!.
```

The logic form could further be translated into PROLOG:

```
ans((A)) :- suppliers(N,A,_,_),
            not shipment(N,p2,_).
```

7.1.1 The Open and Closed World Assumptions

Care must be taken when representing negative information, as under certain circumstances, its operational and declarative interpretations might not coincide [42]. Basically, two assumptions are possible: the open and closed world assumptions.

1) The open world assumption corresponds to the usual first order approach to query evaluation: Given a data base DB and a query Q, the only answers to Q are those which obtain from proofs of Q given DB as hypotheses. With this definition we could represent negative information explicitly, for example, by adding assertions of form "not(p)".

2) Under the closed world assumption, certain answers are admitted as a result of failure to find a proof. More specifically, if no proof of a positive ground literal exists, then the negation of that literal is assumed true. This can be viewed as equivalent to implicitly augmenting the given data base with all such negated literals.

The second approach presupposes a complete knowledge of the domain being represented. For many domains of application, this assumption is appropriate. For example, it is natural to assume that those employees who are not stated to work at Department "d1" do not work there. In other words, the individuals named in the database are the only individuals there are. For such domains, an implicit representation is usually preferable, as negative information generally outnumbers by far positive information, and it would be redundant to represent it explicitly when it can simply be established by default.

7.1.2 Negation as Failure

In dealing with how meaning can be assigned to answers to negative questions, the standard negation of first logic is problematic to implement and seems inappropriate for many purposes. By contrast, the great advantage of the closed world assumption is the ease with which it can be implemented. For pragmatic reasons PROLOG systems provide a partial implementation of non-provability. To show that P is false we do an exhaustive search for a proof of P. If every possible proof fails, not P is 'inferred'. Here is the PROLOG definition in which the combination of the built-in predicates "cut" and "fail" is used:

```
not(P) :- call(P), !, fail.
not(P).
```

Thus the query given above would be interpreted as meaning: Find supplier names for suppliers who are not known to supply part P2.

Unfortunately, dealing with closed words does not in itself guarantee negation by default to behave as expected within logic programs. Let us consider a database which contains the following definitions:

```
male(david).
male(albert).
female(susan).
female(margaret).
```

Under the closed-world assumption, "male(susan)" and "male(margaret)" must be considered to be false. But whereas the queries "not male(susan)" and "not male(margaret)" will be successfully evaluated since both "male(susan)" and "male(margaret)" will fail, the query "not male(X)" will just fail instead of retrieving susan and margaret as values for X since male(X) can be proved by matching X with either david or albert.

As this example shows, within closed-world databases, negated predicates are only safe to evaluate when they contain no free variables, i.e., when all the variables they contain have been replaced by ground terms.

One possible solution to this problem is to dynamically postpone the evaluation of some atoms in a query, according to predefined criteria. The execution of a formula "not P" can be blocked until "P" contains no free variables. We have successfully implemented this solution for the ILEX system in which query reordering served other purposes as well (see Chapter 8).

7.2 THE SECOND ORDER PREDICATES: "ALL", "GROUP" AND "UPDATE"

7.2.1 The Predicate "all"

To provide set theoretic facilities in ILEX, a fundamental concept is the second-order predicate "all" which is used to replace the universal quantifier in relational calculus at the conceptual level. The goal "all(Answer,Query,Set_of_answers)" executes "Query" and, for each solution, saves the value of "Answer". It finally builds a set of all answers and matches this set with "Set_of_answers". The PROLOG clauses for "all" are as follows:

```
all(Ans,Q,_) :- asserta(found(mark)), call(Q),
                one_of_them(Ans), fail.
all(Ans,Q,Set) :- collect_found([],Set), !.
```

```
one_of_them(Ans) :- found(Ans), !.
one_of_them(Ans) :- asserta(found(Ans)).

collect_found(S,Set) :- getnext(X), collect_found([X|S],Set).
collect_found(S,S).

getnext(X) :- retract(found(X)), !, X\==mark.
```

The "all" predicate first adds a special marker to the facts for **found**, in the form of a structure with functor found and component **mark**. This special marker serves to mark the place in the database before which all of the unique Ans's satisfying Q in the use of all will be asserted. Next, an attempt is made to satisfy Q, and each time it succeeds, then X, if it is not found in the current results, is inserted in the database by supplying it as a component to the found functor. The **fail** forces backtracking to occur, attempting to re-satisfy Q. When Q finally fails, backtracking will force the first all clause to fail, and an attempt will be made to satisfy the second one. The second clause calls collect_found to retract each found structure back out of the database, inserting its component in a list. The collect_found predicate puts each element into a variable that holds the "list so far". As soon as the component **mark** is encountered, **getnext** fails, so the second clause of collect_found is satisfied, which shares its second argument (the result) with its first (the collected list).

Here is how we could find out all the colours of parts in the relation "PARTS":

```
?- all(C,parts(_,_,C,_),Set).
```

then, the solution will be: Set = [red,blue,green]

Notice that the presence of the **found(mark)** in the database indicates a particular use of all. This means that all can be used recursively - any occurrence of all used within the second argument of another all will be treated correctly.

It is also significant that the application of the predicate "all" could be extended to cover any combination of attributes in a relation if wanted. For instance, we could find out all the part names together with weights from the relation "PARTS" by asking:

```
?- all((Name,Weight),parts(_,Name,_,Weight,_),Set).
```

then the answer would be:

```
Set = [(nut,12),(bolt,17),(screw,17),(screw,14),(cam,12),(cog,19)]
```

7.2.2 The Predicate "group"

High level query languages very often involve the partition facility which conceptually rearranges a relation into groups such that in any one group all tuples have the same value for the grouped attribute.

As we have seen, the trigger g. used in PL and the clause GROUPED_BY used in EL establish clear semantics for the "group" operation; then, quite frequently, an aggregate function over each group may be computed. It is an important operation in practice although it was not included in Codd's original relational algebra.

The predicate "group" could be implemented in much the same way as that of "all". However, we take the alternative as follows (For reasons see Chapter 8):

```
group(N,G,N) :- call(G), only(N).
only(N) :- not ffound(N), asserta(ffound), !.
```

where ffound is a functor to remember what has been grouped so far during a query execution. Note that there is a difference between the two N's which are the arguments of the second order predicate "group". If and only if the subgoal "only(N)" in which the N has instantiated by calling G succeeds, then the predicate "group" succeeds, and only at that time the second N can be matched.

Incidentally, the predicate can also be used to partition a relation over any combination of its attributes. For instance:

```
group((Dept,Mgr),employee(_,_,_,Dept,Mgr),(Dept,Mgr))
```

7.2.3 The Predicate "update"

As far as the storage operations are concerned, we introduce a predicate update with three arguments. We can consider update(Old,G,New) as saying that replace an instantiated tuple G in the database by a new tuple which is the same as G except that the occurrence of Old becomes New. Here is the definition of update.

```
update(X,G,Y) :- call(G), updated(X,G,Y), fail.
update(_,_,_) :- !.
updated(X,G,Y) :- find(Y,Y1), replace(Y1,X,G,New),
                  retract(G), asserta(New), !.
find(X,X) :- atomic(X).
find(E,R) :- R is E.
replace(New,Old,Old,New).      /* totally replaced */
replace(New,Old,Val,Val) :- atomic(Val). /* nothing to do with New */
replace(New,Old,Val,NewVal) :- functor(Val,Fn,N),
                               functor(NewVal,Fn,N),
                               subst_args(N,New,Old,Val,NewVal).
subst_args(0,_,_,_,_) :- !.
subst_args(N,New,Old,Val,NewVal) :- arg(N,Val,OldArg),
                                    arg(N,NewVal,NewArg),
                                    replace(New,Old,OldArg,NewArg),
                                    N1 is N-1,
                                    subst_args(N1,New,Old,Val,NewVal).
```

7.3 AGGREGATE FUNCTIONS IN ILEX

One of important functions of real-life DBMSs is the application of aggregate or statistical functions. The functions currently supported in ILEX are SUM, CNT, AVG, MAX, and MIN. For example, to calculate the average of the salaries in the relation EMPLOYEE in the Department "d1", we could write:

In PL:

```
.--------------.
| employee     |
---------------------------------
ename   age   salary   dept
---------------------------------
#       #     p.avg.S  d1
```

In EL:

```
SELECT AVG(salary) FROM employee WHERE dept=d1
```

In ML:

```
EMPLOYEE : dept=d1 [AVG(salary)]
```

The corresponding canonical form is:

```
[X] &
sub_q(employee,[#,#,S,d1,#],[],[],[S],avg) &
!.
```

The execution could be in the way that, first, the relation EMPLOYEE would be selected under the "d1" department; then projected on the attribute "salary"; finally, the projection would be sent to the AVG function.

7.3.1 Formal Definitions

While relational database theory has provided a sound mathematical basis for studying many database problems, the use of aggregate functions in existing relational query languages is not well understood. In particular, precise and general definitions are lacking, and their embedding into query languages is not well defined [43]. Two examples are SQL and QBE in which the definitions of aggregate functions rely unnecessarily on "sets" of tuples having duplicate members (a contradiction). This goes completely outside the set-theoretic definition of the relational model. A precise definition is therefore needed. Here we give the definition for aggregate functions, which is believed to be natural, general, and precise.

> **An aggregate function takes a set of tuples (a relation) as an argument and produce a single simple value (usually a number) as a result.**

The definition given does not require that aggregation functions be able to accept arguments with duplicates. Formally, we hypothesise:

Aggregate Function = AGGi (Relation)

where i is an attribute within R. For instance, we could have:

```
AVG salary (EMPLOYEE) -> R
SUM status (SUPPLIERS) -> R
MAX weight (PARTS) -> R
CNT sno (SUPPLIERS) -> R
```

where, R, as a result, is a single value.

7.3.2 The Implementation of Aggregate Functions

Our implementation strategy to the definitions is based on two principles:

i) Any aggregate function is based on a base relation.

ii) The query tuple involving an aggregate function in a canonical logic form will introduce an **aggregate-predicate** which incorporates the expressive power of high-order predicate calculus into the proposed canonical logic form.

Thus, the query tuple in the logic form of the above query will be implemented as an extension to PROLOG:

```
avg(S,employee(_,_,S,d1,_),X)
```

to be read as "the average of S's such that employee(_,_,S,d1,_) is provable is X". In general, The extension allows goals of the form:

```
aggregate_predicate(V,P,X)
```

to be read **the aggregate function specified by "aggregate_predicate" on V's such that P is provable is X, where P is a goal or conjunction of goals.**

With this implementation strategy, let us consider a more sophisticated query: **Find the employee names and ages for employees at the "d1" department who earn more than the average salary of those who are at the same department with age over 30.**

In PL:

```
.--------------.
| employee     |
----------------------------------
ename   age    salary     dept
----------------------------------
#       A>30   avg.S      d1
p.Name  p.A1   S1>avg.S   d1
```

In EL:

```
SELECT ename, age FROM employee WHERE dept=d1, salary >
  (SELECT AVG(salary FROM employee WHERE age>30, dept=d1)
```

The corresponding canonical form is:

```
[Name,A1] &
sub_q(employee,[#,A,S,d1],[A>30],[],[A,S],[avg,S,X]) &
sub_q(employee,[Name,A1,S1,d1],[],[S1>X],[Name,A1,S1],!)
!.
```

The final PROLOG program could be:

```
ans((Name,A1)) :- avg(S,(employee(_,A,S,d1),A>30),X),
                  employee(Name,A1,S1,d1), S1>X.
```

Generally speaking, the second-order predicate, agg(X,G,R), produces the result R based on the aggregate-predicate, agg, such that the first order predicate G is satisfied. G is an ordinary structure (say, a base relation), except that the aggregate-predicate, agg, treats it as a PROLOG goal. Also X (corresponding to an attribute in the base relation) will appear somewhere inside G. So, G can be instantiated to a PROLOG goal of arbitrary complexity.

Here is the PROLOG program showing how the current aggregate functions AVG, MAX, CNT, MIN, and SUM are implemented in a uniform manner.

```
cnt(X,G,_) :- asserta(found(mark)), call(G),
              asserta(found(X)), fail.
cnt(X,G,C) :- cnt_found(0,C), !.

sum(X,G,_) :- write_down(X,G), fail.
sum(X,G,S) :- sum_found(0,S), !.
avg(X,G,_) :- write_down(X,G), fail.
avg(X,G,A) :- avg_found(0,0,A), !.
max(X,G,_) :- write_down(X,G), fail.
max(X,G,M) :- max_found(0,M), !.
min(X,G,_) :- write_down(X,G), fail.
min(X,G,M) :- min_found(0,M), !.

cnt_found(I,J) :- getnext(X), K is I+1, cnt_found(K,J).
cnt_found(K,K).
sum_found(I,J) :- getnext(X), K is I+X, sum_found(K,J).
sum_found(K,K).
avg_found(I,J,K) :- getnext(X), M is I+1,
                    N is J+X, avg_found(M,N,K).
avg_found(M,N,A) :- A is N/M, !.
max_found(I,J) :- getnext(X),
          (X>I, max_found(X,J); max_found(I,J)).
max_found(K,K).
min_found(I,J) :- getnext(X),
          (X<I, min_found(X,J); min_found(I,J)).
```

```
min_found(K,K).

write_down(X,G) :- asserta(found(mark)),
                   call(G), asserta(found(X)).

getnext(X) :- retract(found(X)), !, X \== mark.
```

An important aspect of the implementation of the aggregate-predicate construct is that, unlike "the negation as failure inference rule", it behaves correctly in all situations. Free variables in an expression, say, (employee(_,A,S,d1,_),A>30), need not be completely instantiated at the time of execution. If they are not fully instantiated, execution of the expression will generate suitable instantiations, backtracking where necessary.

7.3.3 The Combination of Second Order Predicates

With proper order, the combination of second order predicates can be used to implement rather complicated queries. For example, the correct response to the query: **For each department, sum the salaries of all employees** is:

In PL:

```
.--------------.
| shipment     |
--------------------------------
ename   age   salary    dept
--------------------------------
#       #     #         g.Dept
#       #     p.sum.S   p.Dept
```

In EL:

```
SELECT      Dept, SUM(Salary)
FROM        employee
GROUPED_BY  Dept
```

The corresponding canonical logic form obtained from either the PL editor or the EL parser will be:

```
[X,Dept] &
sub_q(employee,[#,#,#,Dept],[],[],[Dept],[group,Dept,Dept]) &
sub_q(employee,[#,#,S,Dept],[],[],[S,Dept],[sum,S,X]) &
!.
```

then in PROLOG:

```
ans((X,Dept)) :- group(Dept,employee(_,_,_,Dept),Dept),
                 sum(S,employee(_,_,S,Dept),X).
```

Another example is: **Get part number for all parts supplied by more than two suppliers.**

In PL:

```
.--------------.
| shipment     |
------------------------
sno       pno      qty
------------------------
#         g.N
cnt.M>2   p.N
```

In EL:

```
SELECT pno FROM shipment GROUPED_BY pno HAVING CNT(sno) > 2
```

In canonical logic form:

```
[N] &
sub_q(shipment,[#,N,#],[],[],[N],[group,N,N]) &
sub_q(shipment,[M,N,#],[],[X>2],[M,N],[sum,M,X]) &
!.
```

In PROLOG:

```
ans((N)) :- group(N,shipment(_,N,_),N),
            cnt(M,shipment(M,N,_),X),
            X>2.
```

Finally, let us consider the query: **How many people earn less than $8000 in each department?**

In PL:

```
.--------------.
| employee     |
-------------------------------------
ename     age    salary   dept
-------------------------------------
#         #      #        g.D
p.cnt.N   #      S<8000   p.D
```

In EL:

```
SELECT      Dept, CNT(Ename)
FROM        Employee
GROUPED_BY  Dept
WHERE       Salary < 8000
```

In LOGIC:

```
[D,X] &
sub_q(employee,[#,#,#,D],[],[],[D],[group,D,D]) &
sub_q(employee,[N,#,S,D],[S<8000],[],[cnt,S,X]) &
!.
```

In PROLOG:

```
ans((D,X)) :- group(D,employee(_,_,_,D),D),
              cnt(N,(employee(N,_,S,D),S<8000),X).
```

7.4 EXTENSIBILITY OF THE CANONICAL LOGIC FORM

We conclude this chapter by stressing the potential expressive power of the ILEX approach. The extension is easy to make. Two examples are shown below:

1) **Set Comparison Operators.** Let A and B be any two sets, we have:

$A \in B$ If every element of A is an element of B, then A is called a subset of B.

$B \ni A$ If $A \in B$.

$A \equiv B$ If $A \in B$ and $B \in A$.

$A \subsetneq B$ If $A \in B$ and A\=B. A is called a proper subset of B.

$B \supsetneq A$ If $A \subsetneq B$.

These set comparison operators, just like the value comparison operators (=, <, >, <=, and >=) in PROLOG, could be considered as predicates with two arguments corresponding to sets. By means of the built-in predicate "op" with proper notations, they can easily be defined in PROLOG. For example, supposing 'A <<= B', or 'B >>= A', denotes A is a subset of B; {} denotes set, we might express the query **"to get supplier numbers for suppliers who supply at least all those parts supplied by supplier s2."** in EL:

```
SELECT  sno
FROM    shipment
WHERE   sno \= s2,
        {pno} >>=
              (SELECT  {pno}
               FROM    shipment
               WHERE   sno = s2)
```

or in PL:

```
.--------------.
| shipment     |
------------------------------
sno        pno          qty
------------------------------
s2          {N}
p.M=s2   {N1}>>={N}
```

2) **Quotient.** The most difficult operation in relational algebra is quotient. To operate R2 %% S2 in the mathematical database given in Chapter 3, we could have the canonical form:

```
[A,B] &
sub_q(r2,[A,B,#,#],[],[],[A,B],[group,(A,B),(A,B)] &
sub_q(s2,[C,D],[],[],[C,D],[all,(C,D),S1] &
sub_q(r2,[A,B,C,D],[],[],[A,B,C,D],[all,(C,D),S2)] &
sub_q('>>=',[S1,S2],[],[],[S1,S2],!) &
!.
```

then in PROLOG:

```
ans((A,B)) :- group((A,B),r2(A,B,_,_),(A,B)),
              all((C,D),s2(C,D),S1),
              all((C,D),r2(A,B,C,D),S2),
              '>>='(S1,S2).
```

Since the complexities of using the existential and universal quantifiers make the calculus-based query expressions hard to formulate and comprehend, most existing relational query languages use the set-theoretic facilities and aggregate functions instead of the quantifiers of relational calculus. As we have seen in ILEX, the universal quantifiers are replaced by second-order predicates such as "all" and "group". The existential quantifiers are made implicit. The aggregate functions supported greatly enhance the descriptive power. Thereby, the query expression based on the canonical logic form is straight compatible with those of existing high level relational query languages.

CHAPTER 8
Query Optimisation based on the Canonical Logic Form

It is universally accepted that trying to make user-friendly interface conflicts with trying to make it efficient. If one completely ignored any question of efficiency, one could write very comprehensible initial queries the execution of which might be highly inefficient or even unrunnable. It is therefore often desirable to preprocess a query in order to convert it into an equivalent query that takes less time to answer. Optimisation entails determining the optimal order in which the components of the query ought to be processed. The fact that no relational DBMS which incorporates no optimisation is reported means that both user-friendness and efficient implementation are crucial to the success of a DBMS. In this chapter we shall explore methods of optimising queries written in high level query languages such as PL, EL, and ML. Of particular interest is the dynamic optimisation based on the proposed canonical logic form.

8.1 THE STRATEGY FOR QUERY OPTIMISATION IN ILEX

To answer the problem how one can efficiently handle queries expressed in a high-level language that is intended to insulate the user from the details of how information is stored in the database, our strategy is to separate the concerns about user-friendness and efficiency in two stages:

1) **Semantic Query Optimisation.** Firstly, we concentrate on making the interface as user friendly as possible. Keeping in mind user orientation and application we have set up a universal interface which is able to accept a query written in any relational language supported. At the understanding level, the PL editor, EL parser, and ML analyser use knowledge information processing to insure that semantic transformations are applied selectively; therefore, the query is mapped into our canonical logic form that has the same answer but can be processed more efficiently. For instance, as to a query written in whatever language, the size of a relation being accessed is reduced as early as possible by restriction and projection; the PL editor automatically generates its own navigational advice to a non-procedural PL query; an EL

query nested to an arbitrary depth is shown to be decomposed into a collection of query tuples in its canonical form; general approaches for optimising an arbitrary algebraic expression are used in the unification of an ML query. Indeed, the canonical logic form could be considered as the result of semantic query optimisation.

2) **Dynamic Optimisation Based on the Canonical Logic Form.** Now we are in the second stage: global optimisation. Based on statistical information about the relations and their columns in the query, the ILEX system successively transforms this logic form into an efficient PROLOG version using methods guaranteed to preserve the intent of the logic form while improving its efficiency. In particular, we shall develop an "optimiser" that bridges the gap between the understanding level and the internal level while taking the canonical form into account and obtaining the best estimated orders for performing the query.

These two phases together comprise our optimising algorithm, then the third phase is the actual implementation of the result obtained by the optimiser to the executor by which the final answer(s) to a query is obtained.

8.2 A SPECIFIC COST MEASURE

8.2.1 The Significance of the Cost Measurement

It should be clear that the efficiency with which PROLOG executes a query is critically dependent on the order in which goals are expressed in a conjunction. To see how bad a query expression ignoring the cost measure can be, consider the following query: **Find the part numbers for red parts located in London and supplied by people with the same status as Smith's.**

In PL:

shipment

sno	pno	qty
M	p.N	

suppliers

sno	sname	status	city
M	#	S	
#	smith	S	

```
.--------------.
| parts        |
------------------------------------------
pno    pname    colour   weight   city
------------------------------------------
N      #        red      #        london
```

In the canonical form:

```
[N] &
sub_q(shipment,[M,N,#],[],[],[M,N],!) &
sub_q(suppliers,[M,#,S,#],[],[],[M,S],!) &
sub_q(suppliers,[#,smith,S,#],[],[],[S],!) &
sub_q(parts,[N,#,red,#,london],[],[],[N],!) &
!.
```

We could simply transform the canonical logic form of the query into PROLOG program:

```
ans((N)) :- shipment(M,N,_), suppliers(M,_,S,_),
            suppliers(_,smith,S,_), parts(N,_,red,_,london).
```

Executed exactly as it stands. Suppose only p1 and p4 are red parts located in London; the total number of tuples in relation "shipment" is 900; and the total number of suppliers is 300; the number of tuples of "shipment" in which pno is p1 or p4 is 50. This query would take a time of the order of 900 multiplied by 300, i.e. roughly 900*300=270 000. The execution would be extremely inefficient and space-consuming. However, after optimising, the query is reordered as:

```
ans((N)) :- parts(N,_,red,_,london), suppliers(_,smith,S,_),
            shipment(M,N,_), suppliers(M,_,S,_).
```

and now only takes a time of the order of 2*50=100. For queries in which the user does not care about the order or there are more variables, the optimser will generally make all the difference between an execution time which is perfectly acceptable, and one which is out of the question.

8.2.2 A Cost Formula

In order to estimate the access cost for a query, we shall develop a cost formula. By its nature, the cost formula is something which can only be estimated. There is wide scope for experiment with different methods for computing it. In conventional von Neumann type computer systems, relations, like files, are paged into and out of the main memory from secondary storage in order to accommodate searching. Basically, we have:

$$COST = I/O\ Time + W * CPU\ Time$$

The I/O time can be measured by the number of page accesses of relations (both read and written); The CPU time is calculated by the use of standard operations whose time is assumed to be known; W given in the formula is an adjustable weighting factor. Specifically, more sophisticated cost formulas could be set up: for example, take domain length and physical allocation of relations and devices into account, and calculate the costs of standard operations such as value comparisons (<, >, <=, >=, \=, etc). Since the time taken for carrying out the disk accesses, in general, dominates the time taken for run-time computation, most reasonable cost formulas, in practice, produce very similar results. We limit our attention to disk accesses. The current optimiser therefore uses a very simple formula which has nevertheless proved adequate.

Our cost formula relies on some simple statistical information about the sizes of the relations in the database and the sizes of the domains over which their arguments range. First, we review the terminology:

$|R|$ = the cardinality of relation R, i.e. the number of tuples of relation R in the database;

Di = the ith domain of the relation under consideration;

$|D|$ = the size of the domain D over which its argument ranges.

For the relations involved in the suppliers-parts-dept database, relevant statistics might be:

|shipment| = 900	|suppliers| = 300	|parts| = 400
|sno| = 300	|city| = 40	|pname|=300
|pno| = 400	|status| = 30	|colour| = 35
|qty| = 150	|sname| = 250	|weight| = 85

It assumes that the cost is given by dividing the cardinality of the relation corresponding to a goal predicate, by the product of the size of the domains of each **instantiated** argument position.

$$COST = \frac{|R|}{|D1|*|D2|*...*|Dn|}$$

For each predicate and each state of instantiation of its arguments, there is a cost factor, a numerical value. For example, "shipment(M,N,Q)" has cost:

900	if none of M, N and Q is instantiated,
900/300	if only M is instantiated,
900/400	if only N is instantiated,
900/(300*400)	if only Q is uninstantiated,
900/(300*400*150)	if M, N and Q are all instantiated.

The last case is only a test which will generally eliminate all possibilities.

8.3 DYNAMIC OPTIMISATION

8.3.1 Assumptions

There are several assumptions that we make relative to the dynamic optimisation to be described in this section.

Disjunctive Logic Form. We assume that a canonical form is in disjunctive form, that is a query consists of a disjunction of subqueries which are conjunctions of predicates. That is:

```
Q == SUB1 # SUB2 # ... # SUBi
SUBj == Hj & sub_q(...) & sub_q(...) & ... & !
```

This is a minor assumption since at the understanding level the corresponding interpreter can take an arbitrary query and transform it to this form. These subqueries will be optimised one by one.

Uniform Distribution. We assume that all tuple accesses or, more precisely, all successful matches, are equally easy to make. For this to be at all realistic, it is necessary that the database be suitably indexed. (For the ILEX application to MEMEX, the database is totally inverted [25,44]). We assume that for each argument in each relation the elements are uniformly distributed, and hence are equally likely to occur. So we assume in particular that the number of tuples in "suppliers(N,A,K,london)" is the same number of tuples in "suppliers(N,A,K,paris)" (where london and paris are in the domain of "CITY", the fourth argument of "suppliers". We also assume that when we join relations the underlying domains for the join variables are identical. So, for example, if "suppliers(N,A,K,london) & shipment(N,p2,_)" appears in a query, then the domain of the first argument of suppliers is identical with the domain of the first argument of shipment.

The Treatment of Comparisons. A goal in a canonical form "sub_q(P,Ms,Fs1,Fs2,Vs,Fu)" may not only specify a base relation but also involve comparisons stated by Fs1 and Fs2. In its corresponding PROLOG version, therefore, a base predicate is immediately followed by a set of independent formulas Fs1, if any. A relevant comparison in Fs2 which contains variables involving two base relations will be delayed until the two base relations are implemented. In other words, a relevant comparison will be postponed till it contains no uninstantiated variables at the time it is executed.

The Priority of Second-order Predicates. The cost of a second-order predicate "sub_q(P,Ms,Fs1,Fs2,Vs,Fu)" which can be distinguished by Fu is defined individually. For instance, the predicate "sub_q(P,Ms,Fs1,Fs2,Vs,not)" represents a negation, and, as stated in the previous chapter, it has to be delayed until other goals have been satisfied.

The Anonymous Variables. We assume that any anonymous variable which is not concerned and denoted by "_" will be out of consideration during optimisation.

8.3.2 Ordering Goals in a Conjunction

Under these assumptions, the intended objective of the optimiser is to minimise the number of alternatives which have to be considered during the PROLOG execution. In conventional database terms, this is equivalent to minimising the number of tuple accesses. The optimiser attempts to meet this objective by so ordering the goals that the goal to be executed next is the one which can be expected to least increase the number of alternatives being considered, or (better still) to most decrease the number, i.e. the goal to be executed next is the one with the minimal cost factor at that time. This is a dynamic process where the selection of the first and subsequent goals affects the selection from the remaining goals.

To illustrate this, the goals of our previous example have initial costs as shown below:

```
shipment(M,N,_),suppliers(M,_,S,_),suppliers(_,smith,S,_),
      900              300                  300/250
parts(N,_,red,_,london)
     900/(35*40)
```

The goal chosen is therefore "parts(N,_,red,_,london)" which will result in instantiating N, to say 'n', leaving the remaining goals with costs:

```
shipment(M,n,_),suppliers(M,_,S,_),suppliers(_,smith,S,_)
    900/400            300                  300/250
```

The test "suppliers(_,smith,S,_)" is selected for execution next, which will result in instantiating S, to say 's', leaving remaining goals with costs:

```
shipment(M,n,_),suppliers(M,_,s,_)
    900/400            300/30
```

The figures indicate that "shipment(M,n,_)" is the more restrictive of these two tests, and so this goal is chosen to be executed first. Thus the optimiser chooses what is probably the best order for executing the goals:

```
parts(N,_,red,_,london) -> suppliers(_,smith,S,_) ->
shipment(M,N,_) -> suppliers(M,_,S,_)
```

8.3.3 The Implementation of the Optimisation Method

The implementation in PROLOG of the optimiser algorithm is exactly the same; at every step of the ordering process, it will recompute and re-compare all the costs of the remaining goals. In addition to working out the goal ordering, the optimiser takes care to translate the canonical form into its corresponding PROLOG version.

The top level PROLOG clauses for the optimiser are as follows:

```
optimisation :- see(que), read(Q), seen,
             tell(query), set_up_a_law(Q), told.

set_up_a_law((H,B)) :- functor(H,'.',2),        /* A retrieval query */
                       write_head(H), order(B), write('.'), nl.
set_up_a_law((A,B)) :- write_head(storage), /* A storage operation */
                       order((A,B)), write('.'), nl.
set_up_a_law((HB;HBs)) :- set_up_a_law(HB),          /* OR/UNION/++ */
                          set_up_a_law(HBs).

write_head(storage) :- write('ans(storage) :- '), nl.
write_head(Head) :- write('ans(('), write_l(Head),
                    write(')) :- '), nl.

order((sub_q(N,Ms,Fs1,Fs2,_,Fu),!)) :-
        form_predicate(N,Ms,Fs1,Fu), write_l(Fs2).
order((sub_q(N1,M1,F1,F2,V1,S1),sub_q(N2,M2,F3,F4,V2,S2),!)) :-
             cost(S1,V1,N1,Cost1), cost(S2,V2,N2,Cost2),
             (Cost1<Cost2, form_predicate(N1,M1,F1,S1),
             put(44), form_predicate(N2,M2,F3,S2);
             form_predicate(N2,M2,F3,S2), put(44),
             form_predicate(N1,M1,F1,S1)), append(F2,F4,F),
             (F== []; put(44), write_l(F)), !.
order(Q) :- min_cost(Q,A), arg(5,A,V), remove(Q,A,V,Q1,F2),
        order(Q1), (F2== []; put(44), write_l(F2)).

min_cost((A,B,!),Z) :- arg(1,A,N1), arg(5,A,V1), arg(6,A,S1),
                       arg(1,B,N2), arg(5,B,V2), arg(6,B,S2),
                       cost(S1,V1,N1,Cost1), cost(S2,V2,N2,Cost2),
                       (Cost1<Cost2, Z=A; Z=B), !.
min_cost((A,B,C),Z) :- arg(1,A,N1), arg(5,A,V1), arg(6,A,S1),
                       arg(1,B,N2), arg(5,B,V2), arg(6,B,S2),
                       cost(S1,V1,N1,Cost1), cost(S2,V2,N2,Cost2),
                       (Cost1<Cost2, min_cost((A,C),Z);
                       min_cost((B,C),Z)), !.

remove(!,_,_,!,_).
remove((T,Q),A,V,R,Fs2) :- T==A, !,       /* "T" is exactly "A" */
                       T= sub_q(N,Ms,Fs1,Fs2,_,Fu),
                       form_predicate(N,Ms,Fs1,Fu), put(44),
                       remove(Q,A,V,R,_).
remove((T,Q),A,V,(T1,R),F2) :- T=sub_q(N,Ms,Fs1,Fs2,Vs,Fu),
                       subtract(Vs,V,V1),
                       T1=sub_q(N,Ms,Fs1,Fs2,V1,Fu),
                       remove(Q,A,V,R,F2).

form_predicate(N,M,[],!) :- write(N), put(40), write_l(M), put(41).
form_predicate(N,M,F,!) :- form_predicate(N,M,[],!),
                       put(44), write_l(F).
form_predicate(N,M,F,not) :- write('not ('),
                       form_predicate(N,M,F,!), put(41).
form_predicate(N,M,[],S) :- atom(S),    /* S= asserta; retract */
                       write(S), put(40),
                       form_predicate(N,M,[],!), put(41).
```

```
form_predicate(N,M,F,retract) :- form_predicate(N,M,F,!), put(44),
                        form_predicate(N,M,[],retract).
form_predicate(N,M,[],[K,X,G]) :- write(K), put(40), write(X),
                        put(44), form_predicate(N,M,[],!),
                        put(44), write(G), put(41).
form_predicate(N,M,F,[K,X,G]) :- write(K), put(40), write(X),
                        write(',('), form_predicate(N,M,F,!),
                        write('),'), write(G), put(41).
```

As seen in the program, the recursive process of ordering is most significant. Given a set of sub-goals which corresponds to the first argument Q of the predicate 'min_cost', the predicate will pick out the sub-goal A which has the minimal cost at that time. The predicate 'remove' with five arguments Q, A, V, R and F removes A from Q and puts the rest of Q in R. The predicate 'order' then is called recursively. In addition, the PROLOG version of the query is written by the predicate 'form_predicate' in the course of ordering.

8.4 POTENTIAL POWER FOR IMPROVING EFFICIENCY

The PROLOG version of the query we have obtained so far incorporates a simple proof procedure. However, the extralogical primitives provided by the PROLOG system, such as cut, fail, fork, etc, can play an important role in improving efficiency, since they can decide how the proof is to be carried out.

Let us consider the execution of queries. To find several solutions that will match a query, we may have:

```
react :- ..., ans(X), ..., fail.
react.
```

where the goal "ans(X)" is in the form:

```
ans(X) :- aa(...), bb(...), cc(...), dd(...), ee(...).
```

By using the built-in predicate **fail** the multiple solutions are generated. The problem is essentially that resolution treats all goals (aa, bb, cc, dd and ee) in a conjunction as being dependent. This is fine so long as the goals share uninstantiated variables. However when the rest of a conjunction no longer shares variables, they should be solved independently, or even simultaneously! In the course of trying alternative ways to solve one of independent tasks, others are needlessly repeated.

To illustrate the problem, let us look at the following example in which goals have appropriately been ordered by the optimiser:

```
ans(X1) :- aa(X1), bb(X1,Y1), cc(Y1), dd(X1,Y2), ee(Y2).
```

If PROLOG executes this as it stands, some unnecessary backtracking will happen, revealing inefficiency. For instance, if "dd" fails, "cc" and "bb" will be asked to do backtracking. It would just waste energy in doing so, since no contribution to the answer to the query could be made by such backtracking.

Once the first goal "aa(X1)" has been solved, producing an instantiation to X1, the rest of the body breaks into two independent parts, neither of which shares uninstantiated variables with each other nor with the head of the clause. Thus, we could indicate the situation in the way:

```
ans(X1) :- aa(X1), do1(X1), do2(X1).
do1(X1) :- bb(X1,Y1), cc(Y1), !.
do2(X1) :- dd(X1,Y2), ee(Y2), !.
```

The independent subproblems indicated by do1 and do2 are processed separately (even simultaneously if possible), and no more than one solution will be produced for each subproblem because of the use of cuts.

With the aid of built-in predicates "op" and "call", we could embed extralogical primitives of PROLOG into our query expression. Suppose we have had the following declaration:

```
declaration :- op(200,xf,}), op(215,fx,{).
```

and the rule:

```
{X} :- call(X), !.
```

Then, the clause:

```
ans(X1) :- aa(X1),{bb(X1,Y1),cc(Y1)},{dd(X1,Y2),ee(Y2)}.
```

achieves exactly the same effect as that of "do1" and "do2" with cut. The braces show where the normally exhaustive enumeration of possibilities can and should be overridden, and the potential concurrence is available as well.

Here, a number of abstracted examples are given in which the order of "aa(...),bb(...)...." shows the best estimated solution for execution of the query:

```
ans(X) :- aa(X),{bb(X,Y1),cc(Y1)},{dd(X,Y2),ee(Y2)}.
ans(X1,X2) :- aa(X1),bb(X1,X2,Y1),{cc(Y1)},{dd(X1,Y2),{ee(Y2)}}.
ans(X1,X2) :- aa(X1,Y1),{bb(Y1)},cc(X2,Y2),{dd(Y2,Y3)}.
ans(X) :- aa(I,J),bb(J,K),cc(K,X).
ans(X) :- aa(X),{bb(X)}.
ans(X) :- aa(X),{bb(X)},{cc(X,Y1),{dd(Y1)},{ee(Y1)}}.
ans(X) :- aa(X),{bb(X,Y),{cc(Y)},{dd(Y)}},{ee(X,Z),{ff(Z)}}.
ans(X) :- aa(Y),bb(X),{cc(X)},{dd(Y,Z),{ee(Z,Y)}}.
ans(X) :- aa(X),{bb(X)},{cc(X,Y),{dd(Y)},{ee(Y,Z),{ff(Z)},
          {gg(Z,K),{hh(K)}}}}.
```

Looking more closely at these expressions, we can find that the braces embedding extralogical control provide some concurrency information and result in increased efficiency. There could be an interesting parallel between them. For instance, the last example shown above can be carried out in the way showing the potential power for parallelism (see Fig. 8.1).

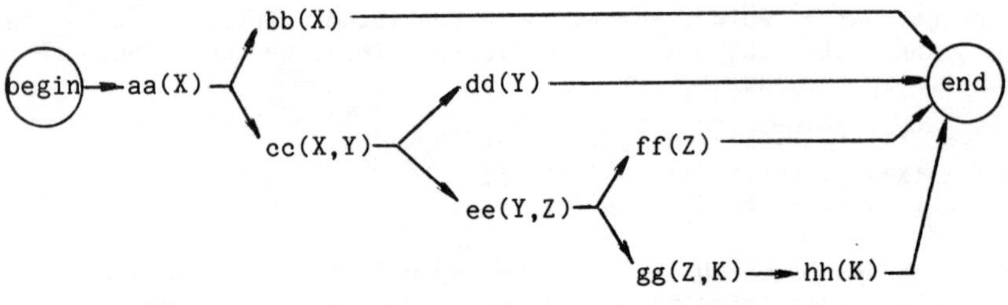

Fig. 8.1 Evaluation Process Showing Parallelism

The problem we may face is the limitation on how many sub PROLOG processes can be created by using "fork"s. The approach to query optimisation described above rests on the use of PROLOG. However expressing queries in logic does not force us to execute them with PROLOG. We are open to use any another valid method. PROLOG was not in fact designed with relational database application in mind; it was conceived purely as a programming language. The next chapter will show a way to bridge the gap between a PROLOG system and a relational database machine.

CHAPTER 9

The ILEX System Architecture based on MEMEX

Performance is an important concern in the design and implementation of relational data bases. The optimisation described in Chapter 8 is a software technique for finding proper order in accessing relations related to a query. However, moving data between main memory and secondary storage is a very time-consuming task, especially when large quantities of data are involved. There is obviously a place for associative hardware (a database machine) to optimise retrieval speed. In this chapter, we shall first consider a general proposal for bridging in first order logic the gap between a PROLOG system and a Relational Data Base Machine (RDBM), then introduce a high performance machine called MEMEX, which may significantly increase the performance of ILEX. The associative system MEMEX, originally used for serial text retrieval [44], will be examined from the viewpoint of relational associative processor implementation. Architectural and design decisions of the ILEX system based on MEMEX will be discussed. In particular, it is hoped that the selection operations can first be performed at the storage device as enhancements to the basic MEMEX machine, then more software functions will gradually be replaced by hardware.

9.1 INTERFACE BETWEEN PROLOG AND RDBM

In the ILEX system discussed so far, we have not distinguished the Internal Data Base (IDB) concerning query semantic transformation, optimisation, and certain constraints from the External Data Base (EDB) concerning the user's database. All the program including base relations is considered to be stored in main memory. Current implementation of the PROLOG assumes that all information resides in PROLOG database. So long as applications remain this small, there would be no need to positively introduce a RDBM to the ILEX system. However, when the user's relational database resides in an External Data Base (direct accessible secondary memory), several difficult interface problems appear and the utility of PROLOG diminishes. Therefore, it is necessary to combine the PROLOG system with the RDBM which is expected to be capable of storing and quickly retrieving very large relational databases. Our aim will be to introduce how, using PROLOG as a problem solver, one can interface with a large database system.

Bowen and Kowalski in their paper [45] gave a theoretical basis of amalgamating object-language and meta-language in logic programming. Based on their idea, our effort is to implement a PROLOG program named "bridge" which amalgamates object language and meta-language to avoid modifications to the PROLOG compiler or interpreter, and can handle general recursive Horn clauses, negative literals, etc. The "bridge" program expands a condition in a query so as to generate a sequence of base relation predicates all of which must be retrieved from the RDBM. The program to amalgamate meta-language and object-language is given by using meta-level statements directly written in PROLOG itself.

We illustrate, by an example shown in Fig. 9.1, how the "bridge" program and other meta-language predicates are redefined so as to simulate the effect of delaying goal statement consisting only of EDB predicate "memex". Since all base relations, say 'human(turing), human(socrates), ...', are stored in RDBM, we replace them by the new Horn clause 'ilex([human(x),memex(human,x)])' in IDB, and the deductive rule 'fallible(X):-human(X)' is translated to 'ilex([human(x),memex(human,x)])'. The meta-language program executes the question '?-bridge([fallible(x),greek(x)],Object)' and returns the objective goal 'memex(human,x),memex(greek,x)', which will be passed to a RDBM for answering the query. With this simulation, no changes are required of a PROLOG interpreter (or compiler).

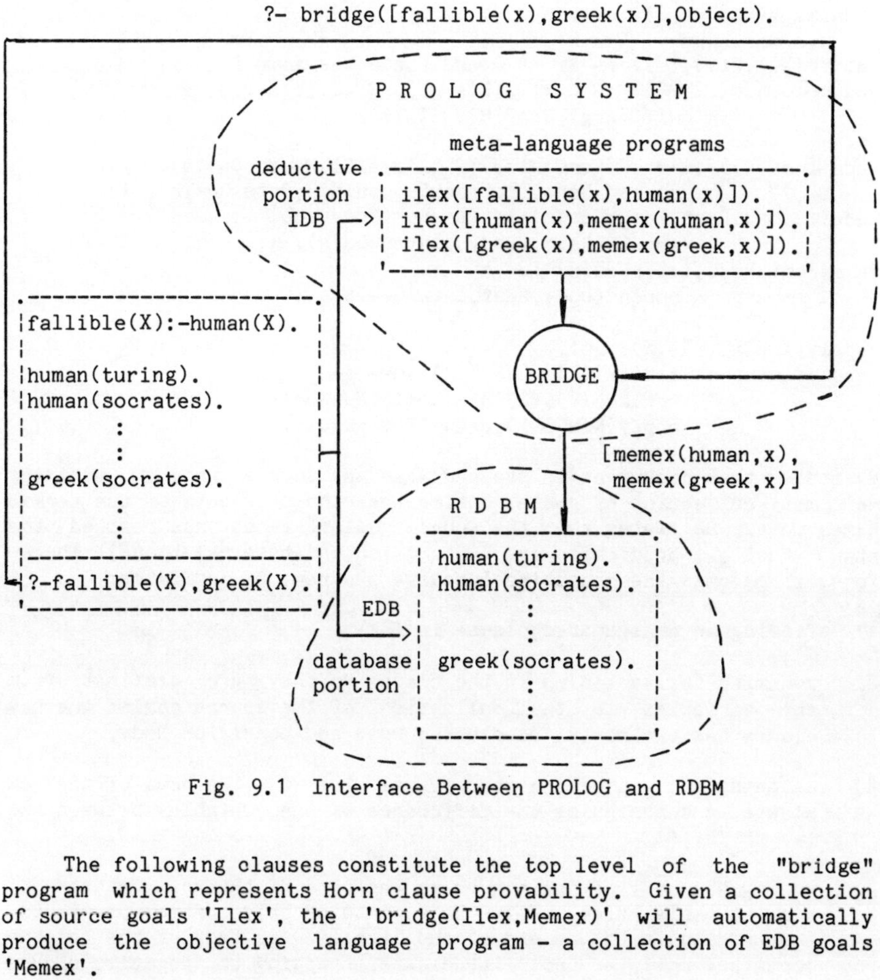

Fig. 9.1 Interface Between PROLOG and RDBM

The following clauses constitute the top level of the "bridge" program which represents Horn clause provability. Given a collection of source goals 'Ilex', the 'bridge(Ilex,Memex)' will automatically produce the objective language program - a collection of EDB goals 'Memex'.

```
bridge([],[]) :- !.                                  /* B1 */
bridge([H|B],[H|B]) :- functor(H,memex,_).           /* B2 */
bridge([Goal|Rest],Memex) :-                         /* B3 */
              ilex(Clause),
              rename_vars(Clause,[Goal|Rest],[Head|Body]),
              match(Goal,Head,Diff),
              add(Body,Rest,InterGoals),
              apply(InterGoals,Diff,NewGoals),
              bridge(NewGoals,Memex).

rename_vars([not(X)|L],_,[not(X)|L]) :- !.
rename_vars(Cl,Goals,Cl2) :-
              search_var(Cl,Var), search_var(Goals,Var),
              gen_sym(Var,V), replace(V,Var,Cl,Cl1),
```

```
               rename_vars(Cl1,Goals,Cl2), !.
rename_vars(C,_,C) :- !.

match(X,X,d([],[])) :- !. /* G and H are the same */
match(G,H,d(D1,D2)) :- G =.. [P|Arg1], H =..[P|Arg2],
               diff(Arg1,Arg2,D1,D2), !.

add([not(Cl)],Rest,InterGoals) :- bridge(Cl,NewSubGoals),
               append(Rest,[not(NewSubGoals)],InterGoals), !.
add([Body],Rest,InterGoals) :- functor(Body,edb,_),
               append(Rest,[Body],InterGoals), !.
add(Body,Rest,InterGoals) :-
               append(Body,Rest,InterGoals), !.

apply(X,d([],[]),X) :- !.
apply(InterGoals,d([V1|R1],[V2|R2]),New) :-
               replace(V1,V2,InterGoals,NewGoals),
               apply(NewGoals,d(R1,R2),New), !.
```

B1 states that recursion is stopped when the source program achieves an empty collection of goals; Noting that the predicate of the term H names memex, B2 states that the source goal statement has reached the stage that all predicates are EDB predicates (base relations). Therefore, it becomes the objective language program; B3 indicates:

1) finding an amalgamated clause in ILEX,

2) renaming the variables in the clause so they are distinct from the variables in the collection of the source goals; the new clause has two parts: conclusion Head and condition Body,

3) matching the top of the source goal list with the head of the new clause, and assigning the difference of the variables between the two to 'Diff',

4) adding the body of the clause to the rest of the goal statement; and at this time, if the body contains only a memex predicate, then adding it to the end of the list; if the body of the clause contains only a 'not' predicate, bridging the negative clause then adding it to the end of the list; otherwise, adding it to the top of the list,

5) applying the matching substitution to obtain a new collection of goals NewGoals, and

6) replacing the new goal statement, NewGoals, in the same way (recursively).

Successful application of B3 requires finding the right object level goals to apply to the selected goals. However, it is independent of the goal which is selected.

The flexibility of the meta-language representation arises from the fact that the computation and search rules of the object-language program can be modified by suitably defining the meta-language predicates, such as 'rename_vars', 'match', 'add', etc. This provides the added advantage of altering the control structure without effecting any changes to PROLOG itself, but only by the redefinition of the meta-language predicates.

9.2 Content Addressing Mechanism

It has been recognised for many years that no matter how well designed a data base management system was, there would always be limitations on the ability to manipulate the "data" supposedly "managed" by these systems. The reason for that is the von Neumann computer, though very well suited for calculations, is ill-suited for non-numerical manipulations since relevant data have to be paged into and out of the main memory from secondary storage in order to accommodate searching, while only a small fraction of it may be useful. On the other hand, the rapid advances in the development of low-cost hardware have led to many proposals for the use of the hardware to improve the performance of DBMSs. Since the user is interested in the contents of the information and not its whereabouts, what is required is a storage device that addresses by content directly. The Relational Associative Processor (RAP) is an autonomous unit to which a main frame computer can devolve information retrieval tasks. Data are searched on the secondary storage directly and only the data satisfied with given conditions are transferred into a buffer for further processing. Very complex selection criteria can be handled and very high rates of search can be achieved, typically one or two orders of magnitude greater than with conventional methods. For instance, a pattern matching program of suitable complexity may take 200 microsecs to do what associative hardware can do easily in 1 microsec. Furthermore, the CPU can be parallel and so can the normal address-by-location core memory.

9.3 A Compression Technique Based on Zipf's Law

The question arises as to what are the best methods of storing and retrieving information for a relational description. In order to minimize the space to store a relation and retrieve efficiently any required tuples or columns, the relation should be coded. An important factor is to choose a coding technique that is particularly suitable for representation, manipulation, and storage of data bases. A significant work related to our compression technique is that of Zipf, who in 1949 described the "Principle of Least Effort" [46]. His studies showed that a wide range of human affairs can be approximated by a statistical distribution known as Zipf's law:

> In a set of events, arrange the events according to their frequency of events and the most frequent event is allocated rank 1, the second most frequent rank 2, and so on; then the product of the rank R and the frequency of each event F is approximately a constant. That is:
>
> $$R * F = C$$
>
> where C is a constant depending on the size of distinct

events in the set.

Zipf first studied and described the structure of human languages, such as English, German, French, and Spanish; then Zipf's law is claimed to cover much of human activity including the distribution of city sizes, etc.

It is convenient to illustrate the experimental evidence for Zipf's law in the form of points representing frequency and rank on a logarithmic graph paper. If Zipf's law is obeyed then the points should lie on a straight line with a slop of -1. Consequently, Fig. 9.2 shows the distribution of the number of employees in U.S. insurance companies and U.S. banks.

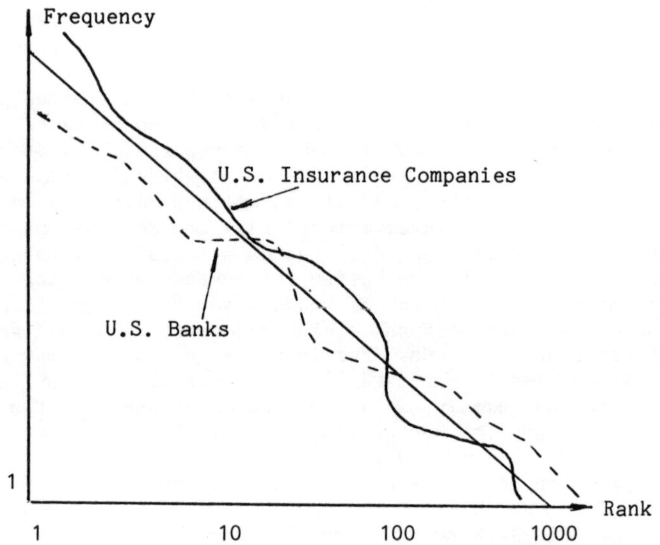

Fig. 9.2 Zipf's Plot for the U.S. Insurance Companies and Banks

It seems very reasonable to expect therefore that the components of a sizable relation, being derived from human activities, will exhibit enough of the characteristics of Zipf's law for useful compression to be achieved.

To form a compressed relational database, relation components are replaced by codes. The relation between relation components and codes is established through a dictionary (vocabulary), which must be accessed during coding and decoding of the relation. Variable binary codes are located to each relation component. The code-length assignment is inversely proportional to the probability of occurrence of basic components. That is to say that coding the most common component could be achieved by using a short code, while the infrequent one could be represented by a longer code. The statistical result shows that nearly fifty percent of written English is made up of the first 128 words. These could be represented by single bytes. Incidentally, if the reference to a standard dictionary fails, the new relation component may be inserted and the frequency of use of it can lead to the updating of the dictionary. As the cardinality of a relation increases, the number of different relation components M is related to the total number of components N by

$$M = k * N^a$$

i.e. $$\log M = a * \log N + \log k = a * \log N + b$$

where k and a are constants depending on the particular relation. The pioneer Heaps used word counts performed on title words of the Chemical Titles Tapes and came to the conclusion:

$$M = 35 * N^{\frac{1}{2}}$$

The finding reveals the growth of vocabulary is not linearly related to the growth in the database but rather expands proportional to the square root of the database size and gradually levels off (see Fig. 9.3).

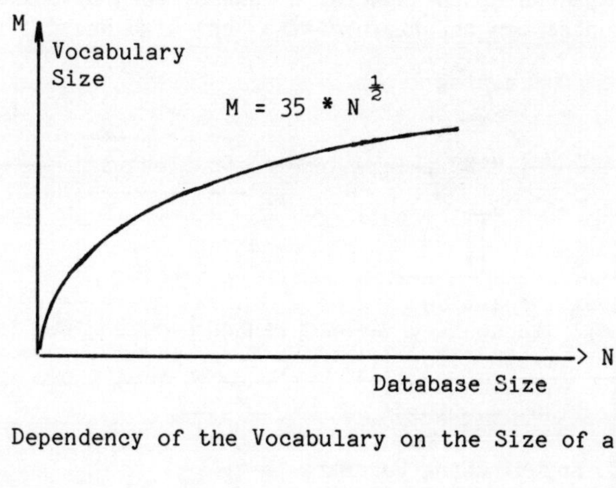

Fig. 9.3 Dependency of the Vocabulary on the Size of a Database

The main feature of the proposed technique is its ability to compress a sizable relational database to about one third of its original size. The information compression is a compromise between the complexity of the compression circuit and the compression ratio obtained. A practical design is given below:

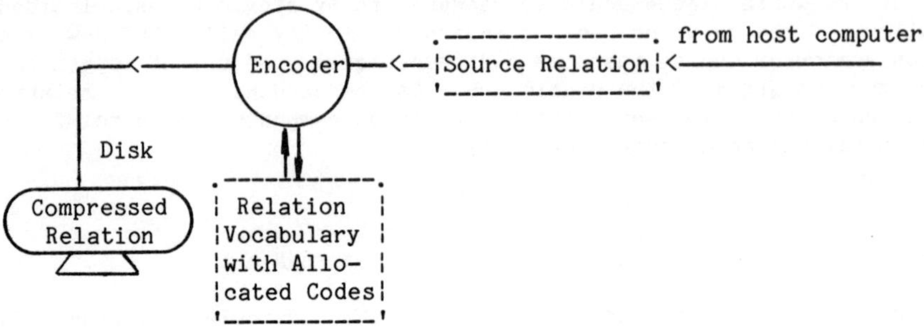

Fig. 9.4(a) The Coding Method of Relations (Storage)

The incoming relation passes first through a lexical analyser based on Zipf's principle, and resulting coded relation is treated as a UNIX file (Fig. 9.4(a)). Any queries go through the same process and therefore generate identical codes to those of the same components in the coded relational database (Fig. 9.4(b)). The addresses of any hits are stored on the special hardware, then by means of dehash the required tuples can be obtained at a very high speed.

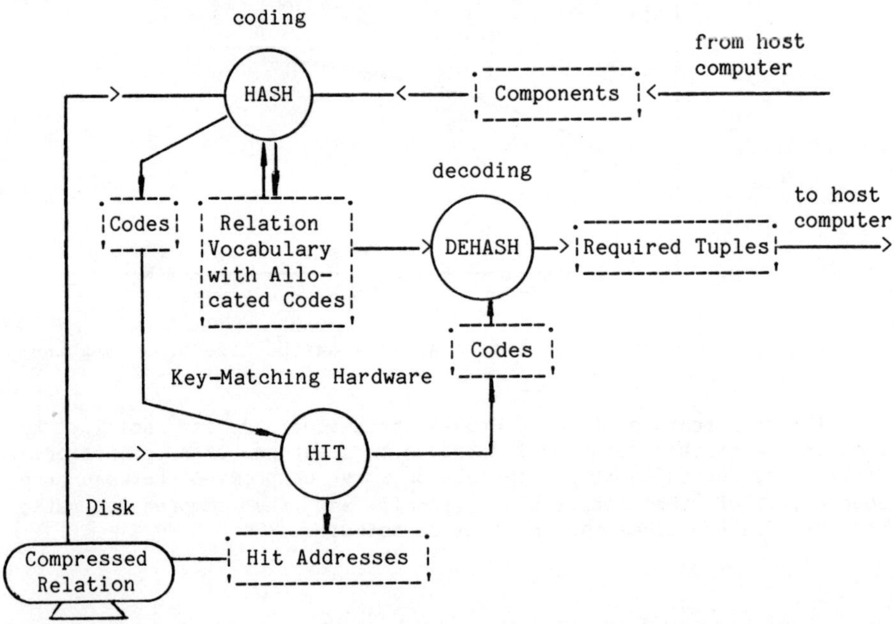

Fig. 9.4(b) The Decoding Method of Relations (Retrieval)

9.4 The Serial Associative System MEMEX

The idea of producing a large scale, associative storage system by adding content-addressing hardware to system ILEX stems from the MEMEX machine. The database machine MEMEX, which has been commercially available for two years from MEMEX Information Engines Ltd, Edinburgh UK, is designed for those who select newspapers, tabloids or periodicals which contain material stored serially on one or more files in the machine, each usually containing a few million words. Managers, without reading the bulk of the printed text, can always find any information as long as they can remember some words or numbers within it. Furthermore, they need no help from computer room staff.

A brief specification of MEMEX is given below. More details can be found in [44].

1.	Search Level:	phrase/sentence/paragraph/story/database/ section/page/entry/record/tuple
2.	Return Level:	paragraph/story/tuple/database
3.	Reading Rate:	1,000,000 English Words/ 3 Seconds
4.	Maximum Store:	80,000,000 English Words/ Disk
5.	Compress Technique:	Zipf's Law + Modified Huffman coding
6.	Compression Rate:	between 3:1 and 4:1
7.	Basic Function:	AND
8.	Extended Function:	+, -, /, ?, ??, !.
9.	Range of Search:	from 1 phrase to 8 documents
10.	Operating System:	UNIX
11.	Structure:	Disk + Special Hardware + PDP11/34A + UNIX
12.	Cost:	10p/Minute Search

9.5 A Specialized Hardware Based on MEMEX

ILEX is intended to be an integrated hardware/software database computing system based on MEMEX. Fig. 9.5 gives the outline architecture in which a Processing Ring may be used to perform some relational operations. It is hoped that more software functions will gradually be replaced by hardware.

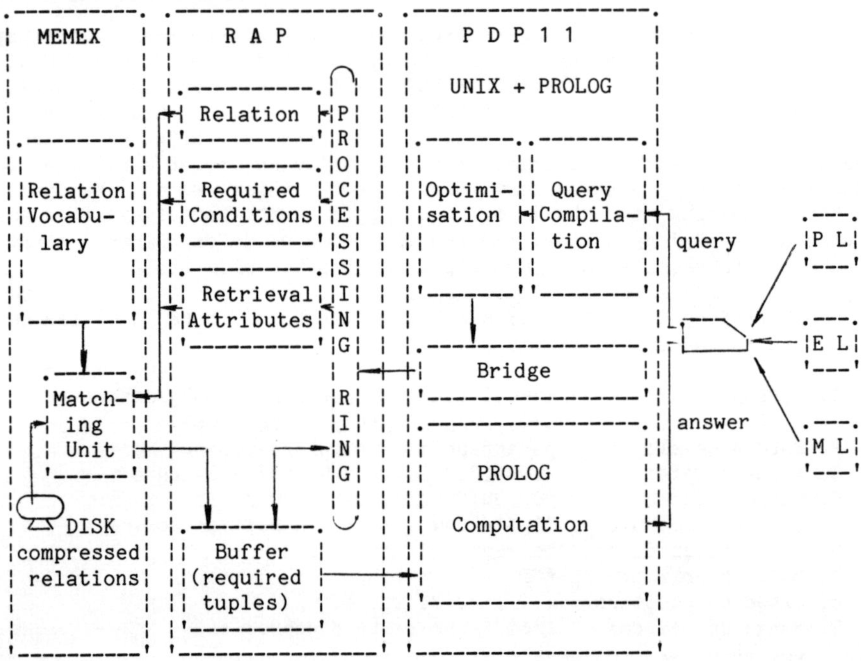

Fig. 9.5 The Architecture of ILEX Based on MEMEX

The response to a RDBM query received from 'bridge' program usually involves only a collection of tuple selections from the stored relations. For a particular stored relation, this selection is determined by some criterion based on the content of each tuple. MEMEX can use its content-addressability to perform this selection at the storage device. This ensures that only "selected" tuples are sent to the buffer for further hardware processing. As a result, the average utilisation of CPU, main storage, and buses by a query will decrease. This early tuple selection does not by itself affect the degree of PROLOG database utilisation by a query. In fact, ILEX transforms user queries so that selection operations are performed as early as possible. MEMEX can thus fully take advantage of ILEX.

There are two extended versions of the matching hardware. The design philosophy is given in Fig. 9.6(a) and Fig. 9.6(b) respectively.

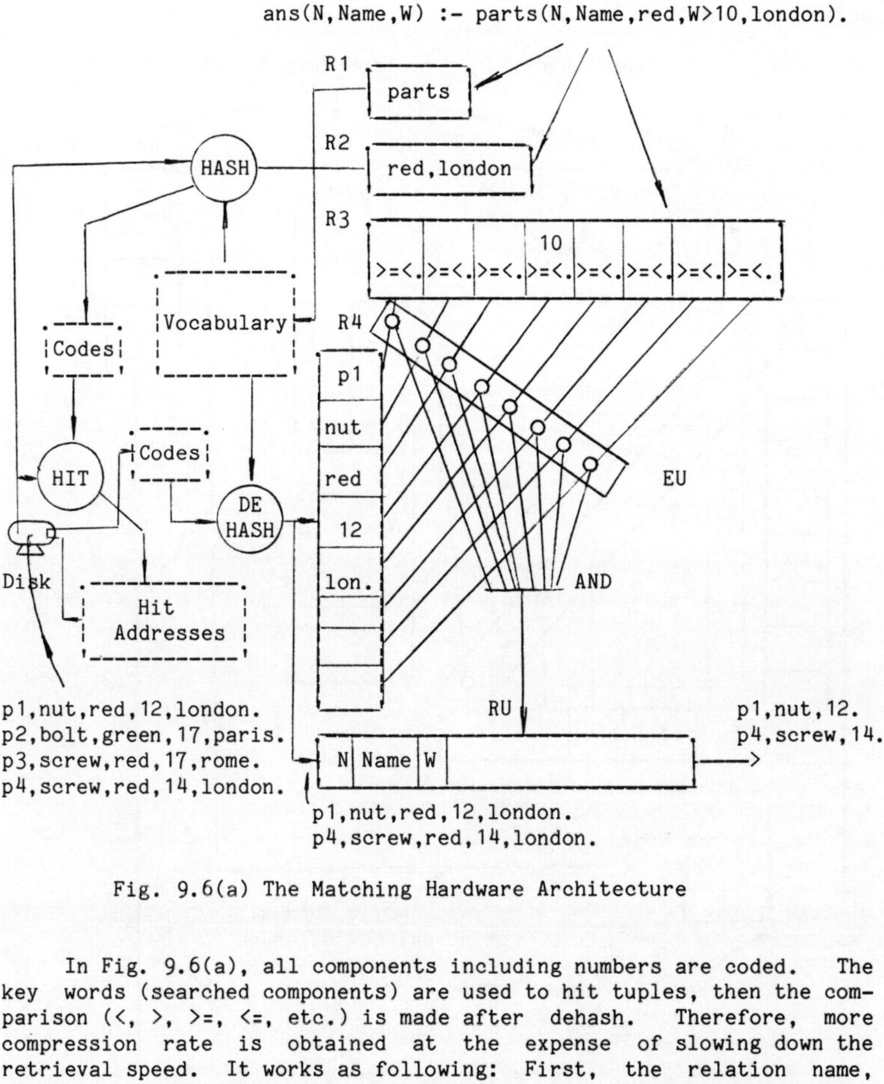

Fig. 9.6(a) The Matching Hardware Architecture

In Fig. 9.6(a), all components including numbers are coded. The key words (searched components) are used to hit tuples, then the comparison (<, >, >=, <=, etc.) is made after dehash. Therefore, more compression rate is obtained at the expense of slowing down the retrieval speed. It works as following: First, the relation name, searched components, and required comparison conditions are sent to R1, R2, and R3 respectively. In the key registers R3, corresponding latches will be set. For example, the fourth register of R3 has the integer "10" and its">" latch set while others of R3 just have "." latch set indicating an unconditional pass. During a scan, the relation name "parts" in R1 opens a corresponding vocabulary, and the tuple, "p1,nut,red,12,london", from a compressed relation "parts" on disk hits the coded search components "red" and "london" (obtained from R2) and enters the hit register R4 by dehash. Then, the output of the evaluation unit EU where logical testing is performed is set to 1 if and only if all conditions are satisfied in EU. The retrieval unit

RU then allows the components of a hit tuple under the required attributes, "p1,nut,12", to pass on to the buffer.

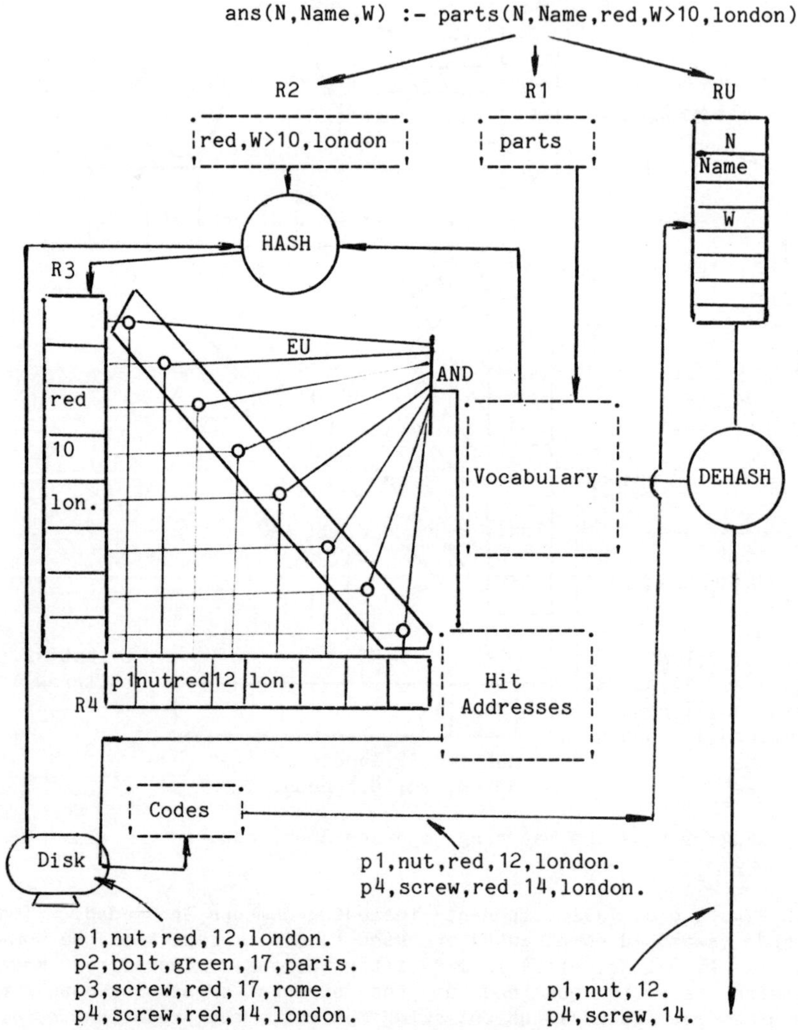

Fig. 9.6(b) The Matching Hardware Architecture

As an alternative shown in Fig. 9.6(b), numbers in a relation are not coded so that the comparison (<, >, <=, >=, =, \=, etc) can be made while the key coded words are hit. Furthermore, removing one or more columns from a relation can also be accomplished before dehash. As we can see, the relation name and required conditions (including searched components and comparison conditions) are sent to R1 and R2 respectively. In the key register R3, corresponding latches will be set in the same way as in the previous method. Since numbers are not coded, the evaluation unit U1 takes the responsibility of both hitting and testing (perhaps involving 8 comparators: >, <, >=, <=, =, \=, =, and .), and produces the hit addresses which retrieve the original information from the disk. The retrieval unit RU passes the required columns. Only after that, the dehashed tuples can be obtained by means of the dictionary. The advantages of this approach when compared with the former method are high retrieval speed and less information decoded. Compression will be somewhat affected.

In this chapter, we proposed a way in which ILEX system can be linked with large relational databases stored on peripheral devices, such as the MEMEX machine. The desired data could be created on-the-fly as the relation is scanned on the disk. Here we just touch on topics that bear much fuller investigation. Consequently a complete analysis of how the full range of relational operations could fit into the system architecture (as the processing ring in Fig. 9.5) has not been attempted. Enough has been done however to show that functions can be built into the relational engine, and the system ILEX is able to use associative hardware to very good advantage.

CHAPTER 10
Conclusions and Future Work

10.1 GENERAL CONCLUSIONS

We hope that the book has given some of the flavour of the kinds of problems in knowledge information processing, logic programming, relational database model, and associative database machine.

Investigation shows that the complex and competing requirements of making query languages user-friendly have challenged the ingenuity of language designers and stimulated a remarkably diverse set of products. Empirical studies have been undertaken to measure the ease-of-use of a query language. After comparison of a number of query languages, we have come to the conclusion that even the best formal query language would never be universally accepted. Different types of users have very different needs and skills. The choice of a language will depend upon the human circumstance of its intended use. Thus, the question to be answered may not be which language is best but under what circumstance is one language superior to another. It seems virtually certain that several different query languages such as ISBL, QBE and SQL, are going to co-exist for many years to come. So, as well as there being a growing need for different easy-to-use query languages, there is a need for query language software which solves a variety of problems in a consistent way. This application area has received less attention in the past, and no complete solution was previously known for this problem. Therefore, our most important motivation for the research work was to make an intelligent relational database very user-friendly and flexible so that all kinds of users could have a common understanding of the data, and communicate with one or another high-level query languages about the database.

In so doing, the use of knowledge information processing as a tool for formalising and implementing different aspects of query languages in a uniform manner has been discussed. Methods of artificial intelligence for deduction and understanding were combined with relational database management systems. Logic was used in this system not only as the programming tool, but also as a database formalism. The difference between "program" and "database" would then be invisible.

As a formal basis for the design, we have presented in this book the canonical logic form, in which the existential quantifiers in relational calculus are used implicitly; while the universal quantifiers are replaced by aggregate predicates. More structural compatibility between the proposed logic form and existing high level query languages is therefore achieved. It has been shown that the canonical logic representation is not only sufficient for relational completeness, but many other functions, including updating and deleting of tuples, the ability to group together certain tuples and aggregate functions such as CNT,SUM, MAX, MIN, AVG, etc, can also be converted to the uniform. Unlike QBE and SQL, the definition of aggregate functions does not violate set-theory. Besides, the canonical logic form provides "function extensibility" - i.e. the ability to extend its power, for instance, to include an arbitrary set of new built-in functions. Collection variables and collection constants are allowed to be the arguments of functions and predicates in the canonical form. This enhances the power of the logic form to be more than a first-order predicate logic. Thus the canonical logic representation appears to be sufficient for the implementation of many realistic and useful relational query languages.

In the ILEX system applications are language independent. A universal interface supporting three typical query languages: ML based on ISBL, EL based on SQL, and PL based on QBE, has been implemented entirely in PROLOG. The comparison between them is summed up in Fig. 10.1.

Language Name	Language Style	Based on	Procedurality	Interpreter
PL	Picture-Like	QBE	Non-procedural	Screen-Editor
EL	English-Like	SQL	Half-procedural	Parser
ML	Mathematics-Like	ISBL	Procedural	Analyser

Fig. 10.1 The Comparison of Three Query Languages

We observe that the various query languages are designed for communication with the real-world relational database that is relevant to the operations of an enterprise. The same semantic properties could be modelled with different representations by different query languages if these languages have adequate expressive power. A function bank has been built up to provide as much commonality of application as possible across the different query languages. The bank could be considered as the knowledge database for any query language supported, so that the software redundancy caused by the use of discrete query languages can be reduced as much as possible. However, the bank, which is consistent with the properties of data, is designed independently of any particular query language, and can be extended if necessary.

Since the independently designed query languages may drastically differ in a number of ways, such as syntactic form, procedurality, etc., contradictions between query languages may occur. Therefore, proper modification must be made. Character strings known to a query language may be changed into their internal forms, and unacceptable readings can be discarded on the grounds of a mismatch. Given a semantic description of properties which are language-independent in a DBMS, we can define a set of meaningful operations which are consistent with the properties. This set of operations can be specified individually or locally shared. For instance, in order to be able to understand a non-procedural query better, it is necessary to add a number of "criteria" by which the logic virtue of a query can be obtained so that the query can be proceduralised. Although the representations of different query languages may be very different, we can have the same semantic transformation at a considerably high level.

Representing the relational domain calculus sublanguage, the Picture-Like language, PL, could be considered as the extension of QBE. Since condition boxes used in QBE seem slightly to spoil the natural style of QBE, the effort was made to improve it by proper modification. The major task of PL is to understand a query specified by the user in the natural interactive way that the PL offers, and translate it into the canonical logic form. The screen editor of PL plays a central role for this goal. The transformation is performed in four stages. The first stage, **user-system interaction**, involves grouping the characters of the user query into a list of basic symbols called "tokens". The second stage, **conversion**, is responsible to convert the tokens into a PROLOG term. The third stage, **digestion**, produces a basic structure by analysing the PROLOG term. Finally, the effort to recognise OR-linking implied in the user query is made by the fourth stage, **recognition**, if necessary.

The SQUARE-SEQUEL-SQL route shows the development history of the query language in System R during the past ten years. Because of the attractive features of SQL it is incumbent upon us to install it into our universal interface. In terms of our implementation we call the marriage of SQL and PROLOG as an English-Like language EL. SQL uses the usual set operators - UNION, INTERSECT, and MINUS - to combine the results of independent SELECT-blocks. These operators are algebraic in nature, and are procedural components. EL dispenses with INTERSECT and MINUS by using IN and NOT_IN instead. The modification gives a better understanding to ad hoc users, while keeping up the uniformity of the language. One of the important strategies for translating an EL query into the canonical logic form is that structured English keywords in EL are considered as operators in PROLOG by declaring them in advance. These operators not only provide syntactic convenience when reading or writing, but also allow the use of simple expressions for what would otherwise have to be implemented through more complicated code containing explicit control structures such as iteration. Another important technique in writing the parser of EL is the creation of variables, which are used to determine possible instantiation states for attributes. Afterwards, all information about an attribute will be derived from where the variable appears in the canonical logic expression.

Since the relational algebra lays a foundation for relational DBMS and provides a yardstick against which other languages can be measured, we have put the algebra language, called Mathematics-Like language ML, in the ILEX system, although it is less "user-friendly". The emphasis is to show the unification of arbitrary algebraic expressions and the compatibility between algebra and calculus in the course of automatic reduction of an arbitrary ML query to its canonical form.

Note that the complexity of a query, written in PL, EL, or ML, is directly determined by the complexity of what the user wishes to do; simple request are expressed very simply. In contrast, this may not be the case with some other query languages.

In addition, any subsequent high level relational query language and its compiler are more readily incorporated into the system, since the new compiler, in addition to using the ILEX bank, could always define small independently-meaningful units (Horn clauses) which directly relate to the structure of the query language.

The advantages of logic programming and the practicability of using PROLOG for the purpose of the intelligent relational database system ILEX should be clear. It is important to take into account, not just the PL screen editor, EL parser, and ML analyser which are products, but also the work which must go into initially designing and building it and into subsequently "maintaining" it. Initially, the picture is just of a black box with queries written in a high level query language as input and the correctly translated canonical logic form as output. The specification of how the output is related to the input makes up the implementation of the translation process in PROLOG. Since context-free rules can be expressed as Horn clauses, the problem of recognising, or parsing, a string of a language is then transformed into the problem of proving that a certain theorem follows from the definite clause axioms which describe the language. What has been put to practical use in the programming language PROLOG shows how a structured query is understood by logic-program solving and demonstrates the particular advantages of PROLOG for compiler writing. The greater clarity and modularity of logic programming is a vital aid in the actual development of systems of this size and complexity. Because ILEX consists of independent rules with a declarative reading, all the resulting implementation is easy to maintain, modify, and extend.

While being very efficient at understanding queries, ILEX strives to answer queries efficiently as well. As we have seen, expressing a query in logic lays bare what its essential parts are (the logic goal), what it is that links the parts together (the logic variables), and what the crucial problem is (in what order should one to attempt to satisfy the goals). Based on a cost formula, a simple but effective dynamic strategy was described. The extralogic facilities of PROLOG could be embedded in optimised queries if desired.

Discussion is mainly at the level of the visible and conceptual concerns of the end user and the system architecture, but the actual implementation on very large data bases is not totally ignored. A general proposal for bridging the gap between a PROLOG system and a relational database machine is given, with which no changes are required of the PROLOG interpreter (or compiler). The system, therefore, is able to incorporate associative hardware, such as the MEMEX machine.

It is highly significant that we could accept a query written in a relational query language, reduce it to the canonical logic representation, optimise the logic form, and then implement the optimised query. Since this conversion is accomplished automatically, many different relational languages can be implemented using the same "underlying" software or associative database machine. This makes the unified approach very beneficial in the sense of the amount of freedom: the user's freedom, which allows the user to construct his queries from language to language, and the designer's freedom, which allows him to enhance the power of the system conveniently. Each query language supported is a cleanly-separated component and can be modified independently of the rest of the system, and the underlying software can be changed without requiring any change at the user interface. This approach should yield great benefits in reducing the cost and increasing the flexibility of implementation and application.

10.2 RECOMMENDATION FOR FURTHER STUDIES

There are several directions in which the techniques we have described could be extented. The developments of immediate practical importance for database interfaces include:

1) Enhance both practicality and expressive power to the ILEX system. For instance, allow more aggregate functions to be applied to the query output; or install a new query language, say a natural language, into the system.

2) Include in the ILEX system integrity constraints which are assertions that database instances (states) are compelled to obey. A fundamental idea concerning integrity constraints is that query languages can be used to express them. There is no doubt that first order languages can be used for that purpose.

3) Investigate ways of using the unified approach on databases defined with a non-relational DBMS, such as hierarchy and network. It is expected that the unified approach could apply to the different database structures.

4) The existing PROLOG implementations are not practical for large databases. Special hardware can help performance in certain types of applications. As back-end architectures mature, it is likely that they will incorporate more associative power. Back-end processors could execute microprograms of associative processors, thereby reducing the role of central processing unit to that of query processing. We expect the hardware to be associative in nature, and are currently pursuing this direction of research.

The success of projects like ILEX confirms the intuitive impression that predicate logic is an effective language for knowledge processing and for problem solving. Relational databases and predicate logic are closely related. The implementation of relational databases, from unification of the top level query languages to the realisation of linking a database machine, can be performed by a predicate logic language such as PROLOG. The key premise of logic programming is that computation is controlled inference. This view of computation is proving exceedingly fruitful as we believe the ILEX project demonstrates. It leads naturally to the idea that we should design computers as inference machines, an idea that the Japanese have taken as the basis for their Fifth Generation Computer Systems.

References

[1] P.Reisner "Human Factors Studies of Database Query Languages: A Survey and Assessment" Computing Survey, Vol.13, No.1, March 1981 p13-31.

[2] M.M.Zloof "Query-by-Example" in Proc. AFIPS 1975 NCC, Vol.44, p431-438.

[3] M.Zloof "Query-By-Example: A Data Base Language" IBM System J. Vol.16, No.4 p324-343, 1977.

[4] M.W.Blasgen "System R: An Architecture Overview" IBM Syst. J. vol.20, No.1, 1981 p41-62.

[5] M.M.Astrahan et al "System R, A relational Database Management System" IEEE Computer 14, No.5, p43-48, May 1979.

[6] D.Greenblatt and J.Waxman "A Study of Three Database Query Languages" in Shneiderman, p77-98, 1978.

[7] D.D.Chamberlin et al "SEQUEL: A Structured English Query Language" in Proc. 1974 ACM SIGFIDET Workshop, April 1979, p249-264.

[8] J.C.Thomas and J.D.Gould "A Psychological Study of Query-by-Example" Proc. AFIPS 1975 NCC, Vol.44, AFIPS Press, Montvale, N.J. p439-445.

[9] P.Reisner et al "Human Functors Evaluation of Two Data Base Query Languages - SQUARE and SEQUEL" in Proc. AFIPS 1975 Nat. Computer Conf. Vol.44 p447-452.

[10] R.Boyce et al "Specifying Queries as Relational Expressions: the SQUARE Data Sublanguage" Comm. ACM vol.18, no.11, p621-628 1975.

[11] F.H.Lochorsky "Data Base Management System User Performance" Tech. Rep. CSRG-90 Univ.Toronto. April 1978.

[12] D.W.Stemple et al "TABLET: The Algebra Based Language for Enquiring of Tables" Tech. Rep. 78-19, Univ. Massachusetts, Mass., Nov. 1978.

[13] C.Welty and D.W.Stemple "Human Factors Comparison of a Procedural and a Nonprocedural Query Language" ACM on Data Base Systems, Vol.6, No.4, p626-649, Dec. 1981.

[14] D.Waltraud et al "The Adaptation of Virtual Man-Computer Interface to User Requirements in Dialoges" Springer-Verlag 1981.

[15] E.F.Codd "A Relational Model for Large Shared Data Banks" communications of the ACM, Vol.13, No.6, June 1970, p377-87.

[16] E.F.Codd "A Data Base Sublanguage Based on the Relational Calculus" Proceedings 1971 ACM SIGFIDET Workshop on Data description, Access and Control, San Diego, California, Nov. 1971.

[17] S.J.P.Todd "The Peterlee Relational Test Vehicle - A System Overview" IBM Systems J. Vol.15, No.4, p285-308, 1976.

[18] S.Michael, W.Eugence, and K.Perter "The Design and Implementation of INGRES" ACM on Database Syst. Vol.1, No.3, Sept. 1976, p189-222.

[19] D.D.Chamberlin et al "A History of System R and SQL/Data System" Proc. of 7th Inter. Conf. on VLDB 1981, p456-464.

[20] M.Zloof "The System for Business Automation (SBA): Programming Language" Communication of the ACM Vol.20, No.6, June 1977 p385-396.

[21] M.M.Zloof "Office-by-Example: A Business Language that Unifies Data and Word Processing and Electronic Mail" IBM System Journal Vol.21 No.3, 1982, p272-304.

[22] Proceedings of International Conference on Fifth Generation Computer Systems Oct. 19-22 1981, Japan Information Processing Centre.

[23] J.Backus "Can Programming Be Liberated from the Von Neumann Style? A Functional Style and Its Algebra of Programs" Comm ACM 21, 8 August 1978 p613-41.

[24] W.F.Clocksin C.S.Mellish "Programming in PROLOG" Springer-Verlag Berlin Heidelberg New York, 1981.

[25] F.G.Heath "The MEMEX Information Engine" Colloquium on "Associative Methods and Data Base Engines", London England IEE, 17 May 1982, p4/1-2.

[26] J.D.Ullman "Principles of Database Systems" Pitman Publishing Limited, 1980.

[27] C.J.Date "An Introduction to Database Systems" Third Edition, Addison-Wesley Publishing Company, 1981, p92.

[28] Chin-Liang Chang and Richard Char-Tung Lee "Symbolic Logic and Mechanical Theorem Proving" 1973, Academic P.

[29] J.P.Tremblay and R.Manohar "Discrete Mathematical Structures with Applications to Computer Science" McGraw-Hill Inc. 1975.

[30] R.Kowalski "Logic for Problem Solving" Elsevier North Holland Inc. 1979.

[31] R.A.Kuwalski "PROLOG as a Logic Programming Language" AICA Congress, 23-25, Sept 1981, Vol.2, p1029-34.

[32] "The Unix PROLOG System" Version NU6 Software Report 5, Oct,1979, Dept. of Artificial Intelligence Univ. of Edinburgh.

[33] H.Gallaire "Impacts of Logic on Databases" Proceedings of the 7th International Conference on Very Large Data Bases, p248-259, 1981.

[34] R.Kowalski "Logic for Data Description" In Logic Data Bases edited by H.Gallaire and J.Minker, Plenum Press, New York, N.Y., 1978, p73-103.

[35] D.Warren "Logic Programming and Compiler Writing" Software-Practice and Experience, Vol.10 p97-125, 1980.

[36] M.H.van Emden "Computation and Deductive Information Retrieval" from "Formal Description of Programming Concepts" edited by E.J.Neuhold publishing Company, 1978.

[37] D.H.D.Warren "Efficient Processing of Interactive Relational Database queries Expressed in Logic" Proceedings of the 7th International Conference on Very Large Data Bases, July 1980, p181-203.

[38] R.Fagin "Horn Clauses and Database Dependencies" In Proc. ACM SIGACT symp. Theory of Computation, 1980, p123-134.

[39] Y.Sagiv, R.Fagin et al "An Equivalence between Relational Database Dependencies and a Fragment of Propositional Logic" J.ACM Vol.28, No.3, July 1981, p435-453.

[40] E.F.Codd "Relational Completeness of Data Base Sublanguages" in Data Base Systems, edited by R.Rustin, Prentice Hall, Englewood Cliffs, N.J. 1972, p65-98.

[41] D.D.Chamberlin "A Summary of User Experience with the SQL Data Sublanguage" Proceedings of International Conference on Data Bases, July 1980, p181-203.

[42] K.L.Clark "Negation as Failure" in the book "Logic and Data Bases" H.Gallaire and J.Minker [Eds], Plenum Press, 1978.

[43] A.Klug "Equivalence of Relational Algebra and Relational Calculus Query Languages Having Aggregate Functions" Journal of ACM, Vol.29, No.3, July 1982, p699-717.

[44] F.G.Heath "High Performance machines for Text Databases" Infotech State of The Art Review.

[45] K.A.Bowen and R.A.Kowalski "Amalgamating Language and Metalanguage in Logic Programming" in "Logic Programming" edited by K.L.Clark and S.A.Tarnlund, P153-172, 1982 Academic Press.

[46] G.K.Zipf "Human Behaviour and the Principle of Least Effort", Addison Wesley, 1949.

APPENDIX 1
Built-in Predicates and Precedences of Operators

(1) THE BUILT-IN PREDICATES IN UNIX PROLOG SYSTEM

!	Cut choices back as far as the last proper ancestor
abort	Abort all current executions
arg(N,T,A)	The Nth argument in term T is A
assert(C)	Assert clause C to the database
asserta(C)	Assert clause C in the database before others for the predicate
assertz(X)	Put clause X in the database after others for the predicate
atom(X)	X is an atom
atomic(X)	X is an atom or an integer
break	Get a new invocation of the top level interpreter
call(X)	(The goal represented by term X)
clause(H,B)	There is a clause in the database with head H and body B
consult(F)	Read clauses and goals from the file F (atom)
core	Print statistical information
debugging	Print the list of current active spy points

deny(H,B)	Remove a clause from the database which has head H and body B
display(X)	Write X on the current output in prefix format
end	Resume previous execution environment; abandon current one
fail	(A goal that always fails; backtrack immediately)
fork	Create another PROLOG process
functor(T,F,N)	T is a term whose functor is F and arity N
get(X)	The next non-blank character input is X
get0(X)	Read the next character X (integer) from the current input
integer(X)	X is an integer
length(L,M)	The length of the list L is M
listing(X)	List all clauses with atom X as predicate
listing(X,Y)	Perform "listing(X)", with output to file Y
name(X,Y)	Y is the list of the characters (integers) of X's name
next(X,Y)	Change standard input and output to X and Y
nl	A new line is taken on the current output
nodebug	Remove any spy points on predicate X (atom or list)
not(X)	(A goal that succeeds if and only if goal X fails)
notrace	Switch off tracing
op(X,Y,Z)	Declare atom Z as an operator of type Y and precedence X
pipe(X)	Create a pipe named X (atom)
portraycl(X)	Write out clause X on the current output suitably
portraygoals(X)	Write out the goals X on the current output suitably
print(X)	Write out X suitably, using "portray" if possible
put(X)	Output character X (integer expr) on the current output

read(X)	Read term X (terminated by .) from current input
reconsult(X)	Read clause from file X to change existing ones
repeat	(A goal that succeeds in infinitely many different ways)
retract(X)	Remove clause X from the database
retractall(X)	Retract all clauses that match X
see(X)	Switch current input to be from file X (atom)
seeing(X)	X is the current input file (atom)
seen	Close current input file, and switch back to standard input
shell(X)	Call shell with command X (list of characters)
skip(X)	Read character until the code X appears
spy X	Set a spy point on clause for X (atom or list)
tab(X)	Print X spaces on the current output
tell(X)	Switch current output to be to file X (atom)
telling(X)	X is the current output file (atom)
told	Close current output file, and switch back to standard output
trimcore	Release unwanted space to the operating system
true	(A goal that always succeeds)
var(X)	X is a variable (uninstantiated)
write(X)	Write term X on current output (taking account of operators)
X	(The goal given by the value of variable X)
X,Y	X and Y
X;Y	X or Y
X<Y	Integer expression X evaluates to less than integer expression Y
X=Y	X and Y are equal

X=..Y	Y is the list of the functor of X and the arguments of X
X=:=Y	Integer expressions X and Y are equal
X=<Y	Integer expression X is less than or equal to expression Y
X==Y	X and Y are identical
X=\=Y	Integer expressions X and Y are not equal
X>Y	Integer expression X is greater than integer expression Y
X>=Y	Integer expression X is greater than or equal to integer expression Y
X is Y	Integer expression Y evaluates to X
X\=Y	X and Y are not equal
X\==Y	X and Y are not identical
[$X]	Equivalent to "reconsult(X)"
[X]	Equivalent to "consult(X)"

(2) THE PROCEDENCE COMPARISON OF OPERATORS IN ILEX

```
 11 mod
 21 *, /
 31 +, -
 35 @, ~
 40 =, =, >, <, >=, <=,
    ==, =:=, ==, =..,
    is, in, not_in
 50 not, spy, nospy
 51 .
180 &
185 having
190 where, **, %%, —, ::, <=>
192 grouped_by
195 from, set, :
200 select, insert_into, delete, update, {
215 ++, union
253 ,
254 ;
255 :-, ?-
```

APPENDIX 2
Programming in PROLOG

Over the past ten years there has been a great deal of research work in logic programming. A language PROLOG (PROgramming in LOGic), based on symbolic logic, was developed and is quickly gaining popularity throughout the world. It has been used for such varied applications as symbolic calculus, database systems, computer aided design, natural language processing, abstract problem solving and many areas of artificial intelligence. The importance of PROLOG has recently been given a considerable boost by its choice by the Japanese for their fifth generation computer systems.

The suitability of logic for expressing both programs and their specifications makes it especially useful for program development. In this appendix we give a brief survey of PROLOG, both as a programming language and as a tool for some applications in automatic programming. Our aim is to help people become initiated in PROLOG and to learn it by examples.

Although PROLOG, as a programming language, can be presented only from programming concepts, its most outstanding features are drawn from its being embedded in logic. This is why we shall adopt a mixed presentation of the PROLOG language from both points of view. The main interest of PROLOG resides in its ability to let the programmer express definitions of relations with more emphasis on the definitions than on the ways to compute the relations. In other words, the PROLOG approach is rather to describe known facts and relationships about a problem, than to prescribe the sequence of steps taken by a computer to solve the problem. Of course it is not so simple to separate 'what' from 'how' and PROLOG goes only one step in that direction.

1. SYNTAX

A PROLOG program consists of a set of clauses, where each clause is either a fact about the given information or a rule about how the solution may relate to or be inferred from the given facts.

Look at the following examples of facts, together with

explanations in '/* */'.

```
likes(albert,diana).            /* Albert likes Diana  */
female(diana).                  /* Diana is female     */
play(albert,diana,badminton).   /* Albert and Diana play badminton */
```

The name of the relationship, which comes just before the round brackets in each fact, is called the predicate; The names of the objects that are included within the round brackets are called the arguments.

In PROLOG, a rule consists of a head and a body. The head and the body are connected by the symbol ':-' which is pronounced 'if'. The body describes the conjunction of goals that must be satisfied, one after the other, for the head to be true. Rules are used to express definitions or to specify that a fact depends on a group of other facts or rules. For example: **Albert likes whatever Diana likes** becomes in PROLOG:

```
likes(albert,X) :- likes(diana,X).
```

The program stating that **X is a sister of Y if X is female, and X and Y have the same parents** in PROLOG is:

```
sister(X,Y) :- female(X),
               parents(X,Z),
               parents(Y,Z).
```

Whenever we look at a PROLOG rule, we should take notice of where the variables (distinguished by an initial capital letter from constants) are. In the above rule the variable X is used three times. As soon as X becomes instantiated to some object all X's are instantiated within the scope of X. In general, a predicate will be defined by a mixture of facts and rules. Variables in different clauses are distinct even if they have the same names.

PROLOG provides a uniform data structure, called the term, out of which all data, as well as PROLOG programs, are constructed. A clause is a term. A predicate or a goal with their respective arguments, and the arguments themselves, are terms. A term is either a variable, a constant, or a structure. A structure comprises a functor and a sequence of N terms as its arguments. A term of the form [H¦T] is treated as a list (H,T), whose head is H and tail is T. The empty list is denoted []. The list [H¦T] is a very common data structure in non-numeric programming. The elements of a list may be any other terms, including other lists. A judicious use of variables can provide a way to put 'holes' in lists that can be filled with data at a later time. More examples of the list syntax are as follows:

```
[a¦[b¦[c]]] == [a,b¦[c]] == [a,b,c]
[[a,b]¦[c]] == [[a,b],c] =\= [a,b,c]
[a,[b,c],d] =\= [a,b,c,d]

[X¦Y] or [X¦[Y¦Z]] can match [a,b,c,d]
but [X,Y,Z] can not match [a,b,c,d]
```

Here is a PROLOG program. consisting of two clauses, for specifying the concatenation relation of two lists:

```
append([],L,L).                                /* clause 1 */
append([H|T],L2,[H|L3]) :- append(T,L2,L3).  /* clause 2 */
```

The second clause above is just infix notation for the term:

```
:-(append([H|T],L2,[H|L3]),append(T,L2,L3))
```

where ':-' is a binary functor. The functor takes the head 'append([H|T],L2,[H|L3])' and the body 'append(T,L2,L3)' as its two arguments. If a body has more than one goal the comma separating the goals is just another binary functor used in infix notation. For instance:

```
head :- goal1, goal2, goal3.
```

is equivalent to:

```
:-(head,,(goal1,,(goal2,goal3))).
```

The structure can be shown as a tree:

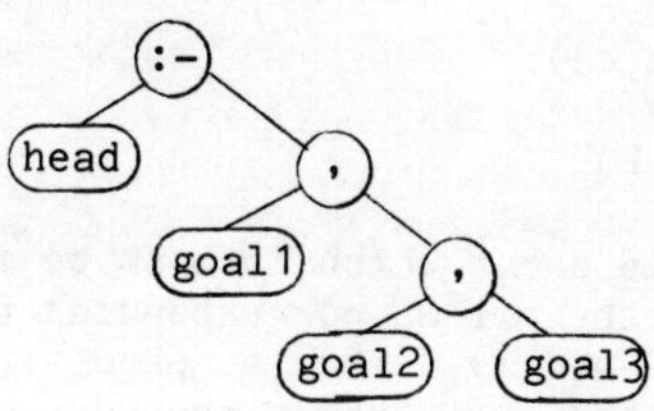

2. SEMANTICS

PROLOG differs from most programming languages in that there are two quite distinct ways to understand its semantics: a logic interpretation, and a procedural interpretation.

2.1. A Logic Interpretation

Corresponding to the definitions of concatenation above, Clause 1 can be read as: Concatenation of an empty list [] with the list L yields L. Clause 2 can be read as: List [H|T], concatenated with list L2, yields list [H|L3] if list T, concenated with L2, yields list L3.

Such a program is a <u>declarative</u> definition of concatenation rather than a procedural one, i.e. it does not really say how concatenation should be computed. It simply defines (recursively) the set of terms which are asserted to be true. A term is true if it is the head of some clause instance and each of the goals (if any) of that clause is obtained by substituting, for each of zero or more of its variables, a new term for all occurrences of the variable.

Thus the only instance of the goal

```
append([a,b],[c,d],L)
```

which is true is

```
append([a,b],[c,d],[a,b,c,d]).
```

In this way the logic interpretation gives one some understanding of a PROLOG program without looking into details of how it is executed. It is the logic aspect of PROLOG which is responsible for promoting clear, rapid, accurate programming. It allows a program to be broken down into small, independently meaningful units (clauses). Therefore, we could also consider a clause such that the head of the clause is a problem to be solved; its body is then the conjunction of subproblems to be solved for solving the given problem. This is the problem reduction formulation of problem resolution systems.

With the logic interpretation, queries about relation concatenation can be asked. Given any couple of arguments does there exist a third argument such that the triple belong to 'append'? given any triple of arguments do they belong to 'append'? and so on.

```
?- append(X,[c,d],[a,b,c,d]).
?- append([a,b],X,[a,b,c]).
?- append(X,Y,[a,b,c]).
?- append([a,b],[c,d],L).
```

Such a query is a formula about which it must be shown that it is a logic consequence of the axioms corresponding to the definitions of concatenation (clauses 1 and 2). Thus a proof procedure, which in PROLOG case happens to be a refutation procedure (resolution) when it succeeds, ought to yield values for variables which make the query a consequence of the axioms. Thus instead of computing values, using assignment, PROLOG interprets A :- B as the logical implication B -> A, and relies upon the substitution or unification to get the necessary matching.

2.2. A Procedural Interpretation

The procedural interpretation describes the way a goal is executed. The object of the execution is to produce true instance of the goal. Let us now see clauses 1 and 2 as procedure calls.

```
append([],L,L).                               /* clause 1 */
append([X|T],L2,[X|L3]) :- append(T,L2,L3).   /* clause 2 */
```

The left hand side of clause 2 is a procedure head, with the right hand side as a body of the procedure. It is important to notice that the ordering of clauses in a program, and goals in a clause, which are irrelevant as far as the logic interpretation is concerned, constitute crucial control information for the procedural semantics.

To execute a goal, the system, in top-down way, searches for the first clause whose head matches or unifies with the goal. The unification process finds the most general common instance of the three terms. If a match is found, the matching clause instance is then activated by executing in turn, from left to right, each of the goals of its body (if any). If at any time the system fails to find a match for a goal, it backtracks, i.e. it rejects the most recently activated clause, undoing any substitutions made by the match with the head of the clause. Next it reconsiders the original goal which activated the rejected clause, and tries to find a subsequent clause which also matches the goal.

Let us now briefly look at how the goal:

```
?- append([a,b],[c,d],L).
```

is actually executed. The goal only matches the second of the two clauses for 'append'. The body of the matching clause instance is

```
append([b],[c,d],L3)
```

The result of executing the goal produces a recursive procedural call matching the second clause again, with L3 bound to [b|L3] (a different L3, of course). The recursive call

```
append([],[c,d],L3)
```

is evaluated. Clause 1 applies, giving L3 = [c,d]. Unwinding the results we have

```
L = [a|[b|[c,d]]] = [a,b,c,d]
```

as desired.

To sum up, the basic computational mechanism is a pattern matching process (unification) operating on general terms. The execution is a top-down, left-to-right, depth-first process. Unification always provides the most general common instance between a goal and a matching clause, and all the general true instances of a goal can potentially be found.

3. EXAMPLES

It is difficult to give a representative set of examples of a programming language in a restricted space. The examples given below are intended to show the PROLOG's way of representing the world and its expressiveness and power. Although programming can not be learned without practising, what is important is to gain an understanding of programming techniques available to the PROLOG programmer. In some of the examples an explanation of how the program is written or how it will be used is briefly described.

1) Write a program to find an element in a given list which has property p.

```
element_property(H,[H|_]) :- p(H).
element_property(H,[_|T]) :- element_property(H,T).
```

2) Write a program to find the first element in a given list which has property p.

```
element_property(H,[H|_]) :- p(H), !.
element_property(H,[_|T]) :- element_property(H,T).
```

Note that other potential solutions are discarded on account of the cut '!' included in the first clause.

3) Find the Nth element in a given list.

```
member(1,X,[X|_]).
member(N,X,[_|Y]) :- member(M,X,Y), N is M+1.
```

The result produced by executing '?- member(3,X,[a,b,c,d])' is X=C. Similarly:

```
?- member(N,b,[a,b,c,d]). N=2
?- member(N,X,[a,b,c]).   N=1, X=a; N=2, X=b; N=3, X=c
```

4) Pick up specified elements from a given list.

```
pick_up([],_,[]).
pick_up([M|N],L,[X|Y]) :- member(M,X,L), pick_up(N,L,Y).

?- pick_up([2,4],[a,b,c,d,e],L).  L = [b,d]
?- pick_up(M,[a,b,c,d,e],[d,b]).  M = [2,4]
```

5) Find whether Y is a descendant of X.

```
descendant(X,Y) :- parent(X,Y).
descendant(X,Y) :- parent(X,Z), descendant(Z,Y).
```

6) Map a list into another one, according to a set of changing rules specified in a predicate P.

```
mapping(_,[],[]).
mapping(P,[A|B],[C|D])  :-  Q  =..  [P,A,C],  call(Q),
mapping(P,B,D).
```

Note the second clause uses the built-in operator '=..' to form a goal from the given predicate P, the input A, and the output C which is assumed to be instantiated to the modified element.

7) Compute the intersection of two lists.

```
intersect([H|T],L,[H|U]) :- member(H,L), intersect(T,L,U).
intersect([_|T],L,U) :- intersect(T,L,U).
intersect(_,_,[]).

?- intersect([a,b,c,d],[aa,b,d],L).  L = [b,d]
```

8) Search the reverse of list L.

```
   /* program 1 */
reverse([],[]).
reverse([H|T],L) :- reverse(T,R), append(R,[H],L).

   /* program 2 */
reverse(U,V) :- reverse_append(U,[],V).
reverse_append([H|T],L,V) :- reverse_append(T,[H|L],V).
reverse_append([],L,L).

?- reverse([1,2,3,4],L).  L = [4,3,2,1]
```

9) Check whether L1 is a subset of L2.

```
subset([A|X],Y) :- member(A,Y), subset(X,Y).
subset([],_).
```

10) Delete all occurrences of an element from a given list, constructing a new one.

```
delete(_,[],[]).
delete(X,[X|U],L) :- delete(X,U,L).
delete(X,[Y|U],[Y|V]) :- delete(X,U,V).

?- delete(b,[a,b,d,c,b,e],L).   L = [a,d,c,e]
```

11) Given a number M, split a list into two lists U1 and U2, where all the elements of U1 are <= M, all the elements of U2 are grater than M, and the original order is preserved.

```
split(M,[H|T],[H|U1],U2) :- H=<M, split(M,T,U1,U2).
split(M,[H|T],U1,[H|U2]) :- split(H,T,U1,U2).
split(_,[],[],[]).

?- split(4,[3,5,2,7,8,1],U1,U2).  U1 = [3,2,1] and U2 = [5,7,8]
```

12) Define a quick-sort relation using append.

```
sort([],[]).
sort([H|T],S) :- split(H,T,U1,U2),
                 sort(U1,V1), sort(U2,V2),
                 append(V1,[H|V2],S).

?- sort([3,4,2,7,8,1],S).  S = [1,2,3,4,7,8]
```

13) If-then-else

```
task :- condition, !, task1.
task :- task2.
```

If the condition succeeds, task1 is evaluated; If the condition fails, task2 is evaluated. However, even if task1 fails, it never propagates to task2 because of the cut '!'. So this is a kind of if-then-else.

14) An iterative loop in a conventional language can be expressed by the procedure 'cycle'.

```
cycle(State) :- transform(State,State1), cycle(State1).
```

"WHILE LOOPS" have a logic which can be expressed in terms of what is true before and after the loop is executed. Backtracking can be exploited to do certain kinds of loop. A file transducer might be written thus:

```
filecopy(F1,F2) :- see(F1), tell(F2),
                   repeat, read(X),
                   (X = end_of_file, !, told(F2), seen(F1));
                   (write(X), fail).
```

<u>repeat</u> always succeeds and can be backtracked to an infinite number of times. (<u>p;q</u>) tries <u>p</u> and, if <u>p</u> fails propagates out of <u>p</u>, then tries <u>q</u>. So in <u>filecopy</u>, if X doesn't equal end_of_file, it is written to F2, and the <u>fail</u> causes a backtrack to the <u>repeat</u>. Note that the <u>read</u> and <u>write</u> are not undone on failure. When X does equal end_of_file, the cut '!' throws away the backtracking history and the output file F2 and the input file F1 are closed.

15) Write a program not(P) which succeeds if and only if program P fails.

```
not(P) :- call(P), !, fail.
not(P).
```

PROLOG implements the negation by failure principle. The definition of <u>not</u>, containing the 'cut-fail' combination, involves invoking the argument P as a goal, and the 'cut-fail' combination should thereupon abandon satisfying the <u>not</u> goal if call(P) can be satisfied. Hence, the goal not(P) will succeed if and only if P is not provable.

16) Setof. The 'setof(X,P,S)' constructs a set S consisting of all the instances X's such that P is provable. The term P specifies a goal or goals. Note that variables appearing in the term X should not appear anywhere else in the clause except within the term P. Obviously, the set to be enumerated should be finite.

```
setof(X,P,_) :- asserta(found(mark)), call(P),
                one_of_them(X), fail.
setof(_,_,L) :- collect_found([],L).
one_of_them(X) :- found(X), !.
one_of_them(X) :- asserta(found(X)).
collect_found(S,L) :- getnext(X), !, collect_found([X|S],L).
collect_found(L,L).
getnext(X) :- retract(found(X)), !, X \== mark.
```

Supposing there a set of suppliers' information in the database specified in the form s(SNO,SNAME,STATUS,CITY), then the predicate 'setof' can be used in different ways:

```
?- setof(Sno,s(Sno,_,_),L).
```

will unconditionally collect all supplier numbers;

```
?- setof(Sname,s(_,Sname,_,london),L).
```

will collect all the suppliers' names who live in London;

```
?- setof((Sname,Status),s(_,Sname,Status,london),L).
```

will collect all the suppliers' names and their status for suppliers who live in London.

17) Write a program to simplify a list whose members are lists, and to transform it into a list of single members. Note that each member is a node of a tree and that simplification means to extract all redundancies, even those brought up by domination of a node over several nodes. In this case, the dominant node is redundant.

```
simplify([],[]).
simplify([X|Y],[X|B]) :- atomic(X).
simplify(F,L) :- arg(1,F,X), simplify(X,V1),
                 arg(2,F,Y), simplify(Y,V2),
                 append(V1,V2,L).

?- simplify([a,[b],[c,[[d]],e],f]],L).  L = [a,b,c,d,e,f]
?- simplify([a,[b],[[c]],d],L).  L = [a,b,c,d]
```

The program can also be used to pick up all the basic arguments from a complicated structure. For example:

```
?- simplify((a+b)*(c-d),L).  L = [a,b,c,d]
```

18) Pick up all the variables from a term and collect them in a list.

```
extract(X,[]) :- atomic(X).
extract(X,[X]) :- var(X).
extract(T,L) :- arg(1,T,X), extract(X,[],L1),
                arg(2,T,Y), extract(Y,[],L2),
                append(L1,L2,L).

?- extract(2*X+3-Y,L).  L = [X,Y]
```

19) Define factorial function.

```
    /* program 1 */
factorial(0,1).
factorial(M,R) :- M is N-1, factorial(M,R1), R is N*R1.
```

```
  /* program 2 */
factorial(M,R) :- bottom_up(0,1,M,R).
bottom_up(N,R,N,R).
bottom_up(N,R1,M,R) :- K is N+1, T is T*R1,
                       bottom_up(K,T,M,R).

?- factorial(5,R).  R = 120
```

20) Top-down design. Many problem domains can naturally be formalised as a world with a set of actions which transform that world from one state to another. Therefore, a top-down design is specified by describing an initial state and a desired goal state. The problem solver is required to generate a simple sequences of actions.

```
task(Initial_state,Goal_state) :-
                        action1(Initial_state,Middle_state),
                        action2(Middle_state,Goal_state).
action1(Initial,Goal) :- action11(Initial, Middle),
                        action12(Middle,Goal).
action2(Initial,Goal) :- action21(Initial,Middle),
                        action22(Middle,Goal).
.......
```

4. THE ATTRACTIVE FEATURES OF PROLOG

The logic programming in PROLOG is an attempt to solve the problem in the human-oriented logic way. We shall briefly highlight the bright features of PROLOG.

1). Specification is programming. The specification language is machine-intelligible, and itself is a programming language. Of course, debugging of specifications is more effective than debugging of programs. An unlimited number of different clauses may be used, and predicates with any number of arguments are possible. There is no distinction between program and data. Clauses can usefully be employed for expressing data. The suitability of logic for expressing both programs and their specifications makes it especially useful for program development. Programs derived from specifications by clauses (facts and rules) are logically implied by their specifications.

2). Deductive Capacity. Computation is viewed as inference. Program becomes proof: a logical proof of the solution of the given problem.

3). Nondeterminism. Procedures may have multiple outputs as well as multiple inputs. Procedures may generate, through backtracking, a sequence of alternative results.

4). Double Role (Input/Output) of any arguments, i.e. bidirectional computation. The input and output arguments of a procedure do not have to be distinguished in advance, but may vary from one call to another. Procedures can thus be multi-purpose. The computation can be done forwards or backwards depending on the given environments. We can check the computation in a wide variety of methods. And the existing program is extensively utilized because of the bidirectional property of the logic program.

5). Double Interpretation. As we have already seen, there is a natural declarative semantics inherited from logic in addition to the usual procedural semantics.

6). Recursion in PROLOG is the normal and natural way of viewing data structures and programs. However, there are no explicit 'for' and 'while' loops. PROLOG also dispenses with goto and assignment statements. A data structure containing free variables may be returned as a procedure's output. The free variables can later be filled in by other procedures giving the effect of implicit assignments to a data structure. Where necessary, free variables are automatically linked together by invisible references. Therefore, the logical variables incorporate much of the power of assignment and references in other languages. This is reminiscent of the way most uses of goto can be obviated in a language with well-structured control primitives, and enables us to take advantage of the possibility of parallel execution.

The key premise of logic programming is that computation is a controlled inference. This view of computation is proving exceedingly fruitful. It leads naturally to the idea that we should design computers as inference machines, an idea that the Japanese have taken as the basis for the design of their fifth generation computer systems.

APPENDIX 3
The Relational Completeness of the Canonical Form

THE MATHEMATICAL DATABASE

r1

aa	bb	cc
a	b	c
d	a	f
c	b	d

s1

dd	ee	ff
b	g	a
d	a	f

r2

aa	bb	cc	dd
a	b	c	d
a	b	e	f
b	c	e	f
e	d	c	d
e	d	e	f
a	b	d	e

s2

cc	dd
c	d
e	f

r3

aa	bb	cc
1	2	3
4	5	6
7	8	9

s3

dd	ee
3	1
6	2

```
.--------------.                          .--------------.
| r4           |                          | s4           |
------------------------                  ------------------------
aa       bb       cc                      bb       cc       dd
------------------------                  ------------------------
a        b        c                       b        c        d
b        b        f                       b        c        e
c        a        d                       a        d        b
```

(1) U N I O N

In PL:

```
.--------------.                .--------------.
| r1           |                | s1           |
------------------------        --------------------------
aa       bb       cc            aa         bb          cc
------------------------        --------------------------
A        B        C             X          Y           Z

.--------------.
| *            |
------------------------
11       22       33
------------------------
A        B        C
X        Y        Z
```

In EL:

```
    SELECT      *
    FROM        r1
 UNION
    SELECT      *
    FROM        s1
```

In ML:

```
R1 ++ S1
```

In LOGIC:

```
[X1,X2,X3] &
sub_q(r1,[X1,X2,X3],[],[],[X1,X2,X3],!) &
! #
[X1,X2,X3] &
sub_q(s1,[X1,X2,X3],[],[],[X1,X2,X3],!) &
!.
```

In PROLOG:

```
ans((_591,_593,_595)) :-
        r1(_591,_593,_595).
ans((_591,_593,_595)) :-
        s1(_591,_593,_595).
```

RESULT:

```
        ------------------------
        aa       bb       cc
        ------------------------
        a        b        c
        d        a        f
        c        b        d
        b        g        a
```

(2) SET DIFFERENCE

In PL:

```
        .--------------.                       .---------------.
        | r1           |                       | s1            |
        ------------------------               ------------------------
        aa       bb       cc                   aa       bb       cc
        ------------------------               ------------------------
        p.X      p.Y      p.Z                  ~X       Y        Z
```

In EL:

```
        SELECT   aa,bb,cc
        FROM     r1
        WHERE    (aa,bb,cc) NOT_IN
                           (SELECT   aa,bb,cc
                            FROM     s1)
```

In ML:

```
        R1 -- S1
```

In LOGIC:

```
        [X,Y,Z] &
        sub_q(r1,[X,Y,Z],[],[],[X,Y,Z],!) &
        sub_q(s1,[X,Y,Z],[],[],[X,Y,Z],not) &
        !.
```

In PROLOG:

```
        ans((_681,_683,_685)) :-
                r1(_681,_683,_685),
                not (s1(_681,_683,_685)).
```

RESULT:

```
        ------------------------
        aa       bb       cc
        ------------------------
        a        b        c
        c        b        d
```

(3) CARTESIAN PRODUCT

In PL:

```
.--------------.                                 .--------------.
| r1           |                                 | s1           |
-----------------------                          -----------------------
aa       bb       cc                             aa       bb       cc
-----------------------                          -----------------------
A        B        C                              X        Y        Z


.--------------.
| *            |
---------------------------------------------
11       22       33       44       55       66
---------------------------------------------
A        B        C        X        Y        Z
```

In EL:

```
SELECT  *
FROM    r1, s1
```

In ML:

```
  R1 ** S1
```

In LOGIC:

```
[X,Y,Z,A,B,C] &
sub_q(r1,[X,Y,Z],[],[],[X,Y,Z],!) &
sub_q(s1,[A,B,C],[],[],[A,B,C],!) &
!.
```

In PROLOG:

```
ans((_929,_931,_933,_944,_946,_948)) :-
        r1(_929,_931,_933),
        s1(_944,_946,_948).
```

RESULT:

11	22	33	44	55	66
a	b	c	b	g	a
a	b	c	d	a	f
d	a	f	b	g	a
d	a	f	d	a	f
c	b	d	b	g	a
c	b	d	d	a	f

(4) PROJECTION

In PL:

```
.--------------.
| r1           |
-------------------------
aa      bb      cc
-------------------------
p.X     #       p.Y
```

In EL:

```
SELECT  aa,cc
FROM    r1
```

In ML:

```
R1 [aa,cc]
```

In LOGIC:

```
[A,C] &
sub_q(r1,[A,#,C],[],[],[A,C],!) &
!.
```

In PROLOG:

```
ans((_342,_346)) :-
        r(_342,_,_346).
```

RESULT:

aa	cc
a	c
d	f
c	d

(5) SELECTION

In PL:

```
.--------------.
| r1           |
-------------------------
aa      bb      cc
-------------------------
p.X     p.b     p.Z
```

In EL:

```
SELECT  *
FROM    r1
WHERE   bb = b
```

In ML:

```
R1 : bb = b
```

In LOGIC:

```
[X,Y,Z] &
sub_q(r1,[X,Y,Z],[Y=b],[],[X,Y,Z],!) &
!.
```

In PROLOG:

```
ans((_500,_508,_504)) :-
        r(_500,_508,_504),_508=b.
```

RESULT:

aa	bb	cc
a	b	c
c	b	d

(6) INTERSECTION

In PL:

```
.---------------.                    .---------------.
| r1            |                    | s1            |
------------------------             ------------------------
aa      bb      cc                   aa      bb      cc
------------------------             ------------------------
X       Y       Z                    p.X     p.Y     p.Z
```

In EL:

```
SELECT    aa,bb,cc
FROM      r1
WHERE     (aa,bb,cc) IN
                     (SELECT  aa,bb,cc
                      FROM    s1)
```

In ML:

```
R1 :: S1
```

In LOGIC:

```
[X1,X2,X3] &
sub_q(r1,[X1,X2,X3],[],[],[X1,X2,X3],!) &
sub_q(s1,[X1,X2,X3],[],[],[X1,X2,X3],!) &
!.
```

In PROLOG:

```
ans((_681,_683,_685)) :-
        r1(_681,_683,_685),
        s1(_681,_683,_685).
```

RESULT:

aa	bb	cc
d	a	f

(7) JOIN

In PL:

```
.--------------.                                    .--------------.
| r3           |                                    | s3           |
-----------------------                             ------------------
aa      bb      cc                                  dd       ee
-----------------------                             ------------------
A       B       C                                   D>B      E


.--------------.
| *            |
--------------------------------------
11      22      33      44      55
--------------------------------------
A       B       C       D       E
```

In EL:

```
SELECT  r3.aa, r3.bb, r3.cc, s3.dd, s3.ee
FROM    r3, s3
WHERE   s3.dd > r3.bb
```

In ML:

```
R3 ** S3 : s3.ddd > r3.bb
[r3.aa, r3.bb, r3.cc, s3.d, s3.ee]
```

In LOGIC:

```
[X1,X2,X3,X4,X5] &
sub_q(r3,[X1,X2,X3],[],[],[X1,X2,X3],!) &
sub_q(s3,[X4,X5],[],[X4>X2],[X4,X5],!) &
!.
```

In PROLOG:

```
ans((_1871,_1896,_1875,_1894,_1898)) :-
        s3(_1894,_1898),
        r3(_1871,_1896,1875,_1894),
        _1894>_1896.
```

RESULT:

aa	bb	cc	dd	ee
1	2	3	3	1
1	2	3	6	2
4	5	6	6	2

(8) NATURAL JOIN

In PL:

```
.--------------.                          .--------------.
| r4           |                          | s4           |
-----------------------                   -----------------------
aa      bb      cc                        bb      cc      dd
-----------------------                   -----------------------
A       B       C                         B       C       D


.--------------.
| *            |
-------------------------------
11      22      33      44
-------------------------------
A       B       C       D
```

In EL:

```
SELECT  r4.aa, r4.bb, r4.cc, s4.dd
FROM    r4, s4
WHERE   r4.bb = s4.bb,
        r4.cc = s4.cc
```

In ML:

```
R4 <=> S4 [aa,bb,cc,dd]
```

In LOGIC:

```
[A,B,C,D] &
sub_q(r4,[A,B,C],[],[],[A,B,C],!) &
sub_q(s4,[B,C,D],[],[],[B,C,D],!) &
!.
```

In PROLOG:

```
ans((_858,_873,_875,_877)) :-
        s4(_873,_875,_877),
        r4(_858,_873,_875).
```

RESULT:

aa	bb	cc	dd
a	b	c	d
a	b	c	e
c	a	d	b

(9) QUOTIENT

In ML:

```
R2 %% S2
```

In LOGIC:

```
[A,B] &
sub_q(r2,[A,B,C,D],[],[],[A,B,C,D],([group,[A,B],[A,B]])&
sub_q(s2,[C,D],[],[],[C,D],([all,[C,D],L1]) &
sub_q(r2,[A,B,C,D],[],[],[A,B,C,D],([all,[A,B,C,D],L2])&
sub_q(subset,[L1,L2],[],[],[L1,L2],!) &
!.
```

In PROLOG:

```
ans((_611,_613)) :-
        group([_611,_613],r2(_611,_613,_,_),[_611,_613]),
        all([_623,_625],r2(_611,_613,_623,_625),_643),
        all([_623,_625],s2(_623,_625),_641),
        subset(_641,_643).
```

RESULT:

```
------------------
aa      bb
------------------
a       b
e       d
```

APPENDIX 4
Sample Queries

THE SUPPLIERS-PARTS-DEPT DATABASE

suppliers

sno	sname	status	city
s1	smith	20	london
s2	jones	10	paris
s3	blake	30	paris
s4	clark	20	london
s5	adams	30	athens

shipment

sno	pno	qty
s1	p1	300
s1	p2	200
s1	p3	400
s1	p4	200
s1	p5	100
s1	p6	100
s2	p1	300
s2	p2	400
s3	p2	200
s4	p2	200
s4	p4	300
s4	p5	400

parts				
pno	pname	colour	weight	city
p1	nut	red	12	london
p2	bolt	green	17	paris
p3	screw	blue	17	rome
p4	screw	red	14	london
p5	cam	blue	12	paris
p6	cog	red	19	london

stock		
dept	pno	qty
d1	p1	600
d1	p2	350
d2	p1	450
d3	p1	500
d3	p4	220

department		
dept	city	manager
d1	london	smith
d2	perth	long
d3	london	lee

employee			
ename	age	salary	dept
john	34	8600	d1
morgan	24	6300	d2
lewis	42	9000	d3
long	34	8500	d2
henry	29	12300	d1
thomas	31	7300	d3
martin	45	7500	d1

Here we attempt to offer some kinds of queries successfully run by ILEX under UNIX on PDP 11/45. The examples below show the query, its representations in PL, EL, and ML, the canonical logic form, the PROLOG form, and the actual answer. Note that it is up to the user to decide which language it is intended to use, and queries can be given from language to language as well.

Q1: Get part numbers for all parts supplied.

In PL:

```
.--------------.
| shipment     |
-----------------------
sno     pno     qty
-----------------------
#       p.No    #
```

In EL:

```
SELECT  pno
FROM    shipment
```

In ML:

```
SHIPMENT [pno]
```

In LOGIC:

```
[No] &
sub_q(shipment,[#,No,#],[],[],[No],!) &
!.
```

In PROLOG:

```
ans((_605)) :-
        shipment(_,_605,_).
```

RESULT:

```
--------
pno
--------
p1
p2
p3
p4
p5
p6
```

Q2: **Get full details of all employees.**

In PL:

```
.---------------.
| p.employee    |
```

In EL:

```
SELECT  *
FROM    employee
```

In ML:

```
EMPLOYEE
```

In LOGIC:

```
[A,B,C,D] &
sub_q(employee,[A,B,C,D],[],[],[A,B,C,D],!) &
!.
```

In PROLOG:

```
ans((_743,_745,_747,_749)) :-
        emp(_743,_745,_747,_749).
```

RESULT:

ename	age	salary	dept
john	34	8600	d1
morgan	24	6300	d2
lewis	42	9000	d3
long	34	8500	d2
henry	29	12300	d1
thomas	31	7300	d3
martin	45	7500	d1

Q3: List supplier names and status for suppliers in Paris with status>20.

In PL:

```
.-------------.
| suppliers   |
--------------------------------
sno     sname   status  city
--------------------------------
#       p.Name  p.S>20  paris
```

In EL:

```
SELECT  sname, status
FROM    suppliers
WHERE   status > 20,
        city = Paris
```

In ML:

```
SUPPLIERS : Status>20, City=Paris [Sname,Status]
```

In LOGIC:

```
[Name,S] &
sub_q(suppliers,[#,Name,S,paris],[S>20],[],!) &
!.
```

In PROLOG:

```
ans((_777,_779)) :-
```

```
        suppliers(_,_777,_779,paris), _779>20.
```

RESULT:

```
---------------
sname   status
---------------
blake   30
```

Q4: Get supplier numbers and names for suppliers who are located in Paris or have status > 20.

In PL:

```
.-------------.
| suppliers   |
--------------------------------
sno     sname   status  city
--------------------------------
p.M     p.A     #       paris
p.N     p.B     S>20
```

In EL:

```
   SELECT  sno, sname
   FROM    suppliers
   WHERE   city = paris
UNION
   SELECT  sno, sname
   FROM    suppliers
   WHERE   status > 20
```

In ML:

```
(SUUPLIERS : City=Paris [Sno,Sname]) ++
(SUPPLIERS : Status>20 [Sno,Sname])
```

In LOGIC:

```
[M,A] &
sub_q(suppliers,[M,A,#,paris],[],[],[M,A],!) &
! #
[N,B] &
sub_q(suppliers,[N,B,S,#],[S>20],[],[N,B,S],!) &
!.
```

In PROLOG:

```
ans((_1230,_1232)) :-
        suppliers(_1230,_1232,_,paris).
ans((_1261,_1263)) :-
        suppliers(_1261,_1263,_1265,_), _1265>20.
```

RESULT:

sno	sname
s2	jones
s3	blake
s5	adams

Q5: Get those part numbers whose weight is greater than 18, or located in Paris, or supplied by Jones.

In PL:

```
.--------------.
| parts        |
------------------------------------------
pno     pname    colour  weight   city
------------------------------------------
p.X     #        #       W>18
p.Y     #        #       #        paris


.--------------.
| shipment     |
----------------------
sno     pno      qty
----------------------
M       p.Z


.--------------.
| suppliers    |
-------------------------------
sno     sname    status  city
-------------------------------
M       jones
```

In EL:

```
   SELECT  pno
   FROM    parts
   WHERE   weight>18
UNION
   SELECT  pno
   FROM    parts
   WHERE   city=Paris
UNION
   SELECT  pno
   FROM    shipment
   WHERE   sno IN
                (SELECT  sno
                 FROM    suppliers
                 WHERE   sname = Jones)
```

In ML:

```
(PARTS : Weight>18 [Pno]) ++
(PARTS : City = Paris [Pno]) ++
(SHIPMENT <=> (SUPPLIERS : Sname=Jones) [Pno])
```

In LOGIC:

```
[X] &
sub_q(parts,[X,#,#,W,#],[W>18],[],[X,W],!) &
! #
[Y] &
sub_q(parts,[Y,#,#,#,paris],[],[],[Y],!) &
! #
[Z] &
sub_q(shipment,[M,Z,#],[],[],[M,Z],!) &
sub_q(shipment,[M,jones,#,#],[],[],[M],!) &
!.
```

In PROLOG:

```
ans((_2730)) :-
        parts(_2730,_,_,_2732,_), _2732>18.
ans((_2758)) :-
        parts(_2758,_,_,_,paris).
ans((_2781)) :-
        suppliers(_2799,jones,_,_),
        shipment(_2799,_2781,_).
```

RESULT:

```
--------
pno
--------
p6
p2
p5
p1
```

Q6: Find supplier numbers for suppliers who supply both p1 and p2.

In PL:

```
.--------------.
| shipment     |
--------------------------
sno      pno      qty
--------------------------
p.N      p1
  N      p2
```

In EL:

```
SELECT   sno
FROM     shipment
WHERE    pno = p1,
         sno IN
              (SELECT   sno
```

```
                    FROM     shipment
                    WHERE    pno = p2)
```

In ML:

```
(SHIPMENT : Pno=P1 [Sno]) :: (SHIPMENT : Pno=P2 [Sno])
```

In LOGIC:

```
[N] &
sub_q(shipment,[N,p1,#],[],[],[N],!) &
sub_q(shipment,[N,p2,#],[],[],[N],!) &
!.
```

In PROLOG:

```
ans((_846)) :-
        shipment(_846,p2,_),
        shipment(_846,p1,_).
```

RESULT:

```
--------
sno
--------
s1
s2
```

Q7: Get supplier names and status for suppliers who live in London and supply at least one red part.

In PL:

```
.---------------.
| suppliers     |
---------------------------------
sno     sname   status  city
---------------------------------
M       p.Name  p.S     london


.---------------.
| shipment      |
-------------------------
sno     pno     qty
-------------------------
M       N


.---------------.
| parts         |
------------------------------------------
pno     pname   colour  weight  city
------------------------------------------
N       #       red
```

In EL:

```
SELECT  sname, status
FROM    suppliers
WHERE   city = London,
        sno IN
             (SELECT  sno
              FROM    shipment
              WHERE   pno IN
                           (SELECT pno
                            FROM   parts
                            WHERE  colour = red))
```

In ML:

```
(PARTS : colour=red) <=> SHIPMENT <=>
(SUPPLIERS : city=London) [sname,status]
```

In LOGIC:

```
[Name,S] &
sub_q(suppliers,[M,Name,S,london],[],[],[M,Name,S],!) &
sub_q(shipment,[M,N,#],[],[],[M,N],!) &
sub_q(parts,[N,#,red,#,#],[],[],[N],!) &
!.
```

In PROLOG:

```
ans((_2086,_2088)) :-
        parts(_2126,_,red,_,_),
        shipment(_2104,_2126,_),
        suppliers(_2104,_2086,_2088,london).
```

RESULT:

```
----------------
sname  status
----------------
smith  20
clark  20
```

Q8: Get supplier numbers for suppliers not currently supplying any parts.

In PL:

```
.--------------.
| suppliers    |
--------------------------------
sno    sname   status  city
--------------------------------
p.No
```

```
.--------------.
| shipment     |
------------------------
sno    pno    qty
------------------------
~No
```

In EL:

```
SELECT  sno
FROM    suppliers
WHERE   sno NOT_IN
                (SELECT  sno
                 FROM    shipment)
```

In ML:

```
(SUPPLIERS [Sno]) -- (SHIPMENT [Sno])
```

In LOGIC:

```
[No] &
sub_q(suppliers,[No,#,#,#],[],[],[No],!) &
sub_q(shipment,[No,#,#,#],[],[],[No],not) &
!.
```

In PROLOG:

```
ans((_1251)) :-
        suppliers(_1251,_,_,_),
        not shipment(_1251,_,_).
```

RESULT:

```
--------
sno
--------
s5
```

Q9: Get supplier names and status for suppliers who do not supply part P2.

In PL:

```
.--------------.
| suppliers    |
---------------------------------
sno     sname   statue  city
---------------------------------
N       p.A     p.S
```

```
.--------------.
| shipment     |
------------------------
sno     pno     qty
------------------------
~N      p2
```

In EL:

```
SELECT  sname, status
FROM    suppliers
WHERE   sno NOT_IN
               (SELECT  sno
                FROM    shipment
                WHERE   pno = p2)
```

In ML:

```
((SUPPLIERS [Sno]) -- (SHIPMENT : Pno=P2 [Sno]))
<=> SUPPLIERS [Sname,Status]
```

In LOGIC:

```
[A,S] &
sub_q(suppliers,[N,A,S,#],[],[],[N,A,S],!) &
sub_q(shipment,[N,p2,#],[],[],[N],not) &
!.
```

In PROLOG:

```
ans((_1290,_1292)) :-
        suppliers(_1308,_1290,_1292,_),
        not shipment(_1308,p2,_).
```

RESULT:

```
----------------
sname  status
----------------
adams  30
```

Q10: List the suppliers' names and locations for supplier whose status is greater than Smith's.

In PL:

```
.--------------.
| suppliers    |
--------------------------------
sno     sname   status  city
--------------------------------
#       smith   S
#       p.Name  X>S     p.City
```

In EL:

```
SELECT  sname, city
FROM    suppliers
WHERE   status >
                (SELECT  status
                 FROM    suppliers
                 WHERE   sname = smith)
```

In LOGIC:

```
[Name,City] &
sub_q(suppliers,[#,Name,X,City],[],[X>S],[Name,X,City],!) &
sub_q(suppliers,[#,smith,S,#],[],[],[S],!) &
!.
```

In PROLOG:

```
ans((_1094,_1098)) :-
        suppliers(_,smith,_1091,_),
        suppliers(_,_1094,_1096,_1098), _1096>_1091.
```

RESULT:

sname	city
blake	paris
adams	athens

Q11: Collect suppliers' names, part names, and quantities supplied for suppliers in London.

In PL:

```
.--------------.
| suppliers    |
--------------------------------
sno      sname    status  city
--------------------------------
M        Name     #       london


.--------------.
| shipment     |
-------------------------
sno      pno      qty
-------------------------
M        N        Qty
```

```
.--------------.
| parts        |
-----------------------------------------
pno     pname   colour  weight  city
-----------------------------------------
N       Part
```

```
.--------------.
|   *          |
--------------------------
supplier  part   quantity
--------------------------
Name      Part   Qty
```

In EL:

```
SELECT  sname, pname, qty
FROM    suppliers, shipment, parts
WHERE   suppliers.city = London,
        suppliers.sno = shipment.sno,
        shipment.pno = parts.pno
```

In ML:

```
(SUPPLIERS : city=London) <=> SHIPMENT
 <=> PARTS [sname,pname,qty]
```

In LOGIC:

```
[Name,Part,Qty] &
sub_q(suppliers,[M,Name,#,london],[],[],[M,Name],!) &
sub_q(shipment,[M,N,Qty],[],[],[M,N,Qty],!) &
sub_q(parts,[N,Part,#,#,#],[],[],[N,Part],!) &
!.
```

In PROLOG:

```
ans((_2640,_2682,_2660)) :-
        parts(_2680,_2682,_,_,_),
        shipment(_2656,_2680,_2660),
        suppliers(_2656,_2640,_,london).
```

RESULT:

supplier	part	quantity
smith	nut	300
smith	bolt	200
clark	bolt	200
smith	screw	400
smith	screw	200

```
clark   screw   300
smith   cam     100
clark   cam     400
smith   cog     100
```

Q12: How many suppliers in London?

In PL:

```
.--------------.
| suppliers    |
------------------------------------------
sno               sname    status   city
------------------------------------------
p.cnt.N           #        #        london
```

In EL:

```
SELECT  CNT(sno)
FROM    suppliers
WHERE   city = London
```

In ML:

```
SUPPLIERS : City=London [CNT(sno)]
```

In LOGIC:

```
[X] &
sub_q(suppliers,[N,#,#,london],[],[],[N],[cnt,N,X]) &
!.
```

In PROLOG:

```
ans((_803)) :-
        cnt(_801,suppliers(_801,_,_,london),_803).
```

RESULT:

```
--------
sno
--------
2
```

Q13: How many people earn more than $8000 in the Department "d1"?

In PL:

```
.--------------.
| employee     |
----------------------------------
ename     age   salary    dept
----------------------------------
p.cnt.A   #     S>8000    d1
```

In EL:

```
SELECT  cnt(ename)
FROM    employee
WHERE   salary > 8000,
        dept = d1
```

In LOGIC:

```
[X] &
sub_q(employee,[A,#,S,d1],[S>8000],[],[A,S],[cnt,A,X]) &
!.
```

In PROLOG:

```
ans((_949)) :-
        cnt(_947,(emp(_947,_,_942,d1),_942>8000),_949).
```

RESULT:

```
--------
ename
--------
2
```

Q14: Find the names of employees who are under 35 years of age and are paid more than the average salary for all employees.

In PL:

```
.--------------.
| employee     |
-------------------------------------
ename   age     salary   dept
-------------------------------------
#       #       avg.S
p.Name  A<35    S1>avg.S
```

In EL:

```
SELECT  ename
FROM    employee
WHERE   age < 35,
        salary >
                (SELECT  AVG(salary)
                 FROM    employee)
```

In LOGIC:

```
[Name] &
sub_q(employee,[Name,A,S1,#],[A<35],[S1>X],[Name,A,S1],!) &
sub_q(employee,[#,#,S,#],[],[],[S],[avg,S,X]) &
!.
```

In PROLOG:

```
ans((_1340)) :-
        avg(_1311,emp(_,_,_1311,_,_),_1337),
        emp(_1340,_1342,_1344,_,_), _1342<35,
        _1344>_1337.
```

RESULT:

```
--------
ename
--------
john
henry
```

Q15: **Find employees' names and their managers' names for employees who are under 30 years of age, work in London, and are paid more than the average salary for all employees with age over 40.**

In PL:

```
.--------------.
¦ employee     ¦
---------------------------------------
ename    age     salary      dept
---------------------------------------
#        M>40    avg.S
Name     A<30    S1>avg.S    D


.--------------.
¦ department   ¦
-----------------------------
dept     city    manager
-----------------------------
D        london  Mgr


.--------------.
¦ *            ¦
------------------
employee  manager
------------------
Name      Mgr
```

In EL:

```
SELECT  ename, manager
FROM    employee, department
WHERE   employee.dept = department.dept,
        city = london,
        ename IN
                (SELECT  ename
                 FROM    employee
                 WHERE   age < 30,
                         salary >
                                 (SELECT  AVG(salary)
```

```
                                      FROM     employee
                                      WHERE    age > 40 ))
```

In LOGIC:

```
[Name,Mgr] &
sub_q(employee,[#,M,S,#],[M>40],[],[M,S],[avg,S,X]) &
sub_q(employee,[Name,A,S1,D],[A<30],[S1>X],[Name,A,S1,Mgr,D],!)&
sub_q(department,[D,london,Mgr],[],[],[D,Mgr],!) &
!.
```

In PROLOG:

```
ans((_2393,_2417)) :-
        avg(_2366,(employee(_,_2359,_2366,_),_2359>40),_2390),
        department(_2415,london,_2417),
        employee(_2393,_2395,_2397,_2415),
        _2395<30, _2397>_2390.
```

RESULT:

```
----------------
e_name  manager
----------------
henry   smith
```

Q16: For each part supplied, get the part number and the total quantity supplied of that part.

In PL:

```
.--------------.
| shipment     |
------------------------
sno     pno     qty
------------------------
#       g.N
#       p.N     p.sum.Q
```

In EL:

```
SELECT      pno, SUM(qty)
FROM        shipment
GROUPED_BY  pno
```

In LOGIC:

```
[N,X] &
sub_q(shipment,[#,N,#],[],[],[N],[group,N,N]) &
sub_q(shipment,[#,N,Q],[],[],[N,Q],[cnt,N,X]) &
!.
```

In PROLOG:

```
ans((_926,_935)) :-
```

```
group(_926,shipment(_,_926,_),_926),
sum(_933,shipment(_,_926,_933),_935).
```

RESULT:

pno	qty
p1	600
p2	1000
p3	400
p4	500
p5	500
p6	100

Q17: How many people earn less than $8700 in each department?

In PL:

```
.--------------.
| employee     |
----------------------------------
ename     age    salary  dept
----------------------------------
#         #      #       g.D
p.cnt.N   #      S<8700  p.D
```

In EL:

```
SELECT       dept, CNT(ename)
FROM         employee
GROUPED_BY   dept
WHERE        salary < 8700
```

In LOGIC:

```
[D,X] &
sub_q(employee,[#,#,#,D],[],[],[D],[group,D,D]) &
sub_q(employee,[N,#,S,D],[S<8700],[],[N,S,D],[cnt,N,X]) &
!.
```

In PROLOG:

```
ans((_1162,_1155)) :-
  group(_1155,employee(_,_,_,_1155),_1155),
  cnt(_1160,(employee(_1160,_,_1153,_1155),_1153<8700),_1162).
```

RESULT:

dept	ename
d1	2
d2	2
d3	1

Q18: Add part p7 (name WASHER, colour GREY, weight 2, city ATHENS) to table "parts".

In PL:

```
.-------------.
| parts       |
-----------------------------------------
pno     pname   colour  weight  city
-----------------------------------------
i.p7    washer  grey    2       athens
```

In EL:

```
INSERT_INTO parts:
            (p7, washer, grey, 2, athens)
```

In LOGIC:

```
sub_q(parts,[p7,washer,grey,2,athens],[],[],[],asserta) &
!.
```

In PROLOG:

```
ans(storage) :-
        asserta(parts(p7,washer,grey,2,athens)).
```

Q19: Double the salaries of all employees in the Department "d1".

In PL:

```
.-------------.
|employee     |
------------------------------
ename   age     salary    dept
------------------------------
#       #       u.S:2*S   d1
```

In EL:

```
UPDATE  employee
SET     salary = 2*Salary
WHERE   dept = d1
```

In LOGIC:

```
sub_q(employee,[#,#,S,#,d1],[S],[],[u,S,2*S]) &
!.
```

In PROLOG:

```
ans(storage) :-
        u(_900,employee(_,_,_900,d1,_),2*_900).
```

Q20: Delete parts supplied by Smith from table "parts" whose colour is red and weight is less than 15.

In PL:

```
.-------------.
¦ parts       ¦
------------------------------------------
pno     pname   colour  weight  city
------------------------------------------
d.K     #       red     W<15


.-------------.
¦ shipment    ¦
------------------------
sno     pno     qty
------------------------
M       K


.-------------.
¦ suppliers   ¦
--------------------------------
sno     sname   status  city
--------------------------------
M       smith
```

In EL:

```
DELETE  parts
WHERE   colour = red,
        weight < 15,
        pno IN
             (SELECT  pno
              FROM    shipment
              WHERE   sno IN
                           (SELECT  sno
                            FROM    suppliers
                            WHERE   sname = Smith))
```

In LOGIC:

```
sub_q(parts,[K,#,red,W,#],[W<15],[],[K,W],!) &
sub_q(shipment,[M,K,#],[],[],[M,K],!) &
sub_q(suppliers,[M,smith,#,#],[],[],[M],!) &
!.
```

In PROLOG:

```
ans(storage) :-
        suppliers(_2092,smith,_,_),
        shipment(_2092,_2074,_),
        parts(_2074,_,red,_2056,_), _2056<15,
        retract(p(_2074,_,red,_2056,_)).
```

Q21: Set the quantity to zero for all suppliers in London.

In PL:

```
.--------------.
| suppliers    |
--------------------------------
sno    sname   status  city
--------------------------------
K      #       #       london


.--------------.
| shipment     |
------------------------
sno    pno     qty
------------------------
K      #       u.Q:0
```

In EL:

```
UPDATE  shipment
SET     qty = 0
WHERE   sno IN
              (SELECT  sno
               FROM    suppliers
               WHERE   city = London)
```

In LOGIC:

```
sub_q(suppliers,[K,#,#,london],[],[],[K],!) &
sub_q(shipment,[K,#,Q],[],[],[K,Q],[u,Q,0]) &
!.
```

In PROLOG:

```
ans(storage) :-
        suppliers(_1312,_,_,london),
        u(_1319,shipment(_1312,_,_1319),0).
```

Q22: Calculate the average salary at the Department "d2".

In PL:

```
.--------------.
| employee     |
--------------------------------
ename   age   salary   dept
--------------------------------
#       #     p.avg.S  d2
```

In EL:

```
SELECT AVG(salary)
FROM   employee
WHERE  dpt=d2
```

In ML:

```
EMPLOYEE : dept=d2 [AVG(salary)]
```

In LOGIC:

```
[X] &
sub_q(employee,[#,#,S,d2],[],[],[S],[avg,S,X]) &
!.
```

In PROLOG:

```
ans((_780)) :-
        avg(_778,employee(_,_,_778,d2),_780).
```

RESULT:

```
--------
salary
--------
7400
```

Q23: **Find the employee names and ages for employees at the "d1" department who earn more than the average salary of those who are at the same department with age over 30.**

In PL:

```
.--------------.
| employee     |
---------------------------------
ename   age    salary     dept
---------------------------------
#       A>30   avg.S      d1
p.Name  p.A1   S1>avg.S   d1
```

In EL:

```
SELECT ename, age
FROM   employee
WHERE  dept = d1,
       salary >
             (SELECT AVG(salary)
              FROM   employee
              WHERE  age>30,
                     dept = d1)
```

In LOGIC:

```
[Name,A1] &
sub_q(employee,[#,A,S,d2],[A>30],[],[A,S],[avg,S,X]) &
sub_q(employee,[Name,A1,S1,d2],[],[S1>X],[Name,A1,S1],!)
!.
```

In PROLOG:

```
ans((_1237,_1239)) :-
        avg(_1214,(employee(_,_1239,_1214,d1),_1239>30),_1234),
        empployee(_1237,_1239,_1241,d1), _1241>_1234.
```

RESULT:

ename	age
john	34
henry	29

Q24: Get part number for all parts supplied by more than two suppliers.

In PL:

```
.--------------.
| shipment     |
-------------------------
sno       pno       qty
-------------------------
#         g.N
cnt.M>2   p.N
```

In EL:

```
SELECT      pno
FROM        shipment
GROUPED_BY  pno
HAVING      CNT(sno) > 2
```

In LOGIC:

```
[N] &
sub_q(shipment,[#,N,#],[],[],[N],[group,N,N]) &
sub_q(shipment,[M,N,#],[],[X>2],[M,N],[sum,M,X]) &
!.
```

In PROLOG:

```
ans((_947)) :-
        group(_947,shipment(_,_947,_),_947),
        cnt(_952,shipment(_952,_947,_),_954),
        _954>2.
```

RESULT:

pno
p2

Q25: Find the maximum salary for young employees aged under 35 at each department.

In PL:

```
.--------------.
| employee     |
-------------------------------------
ename    age    salary   dept
-------------------------------------
#        #      #        g.D
#        A<35   p.max.S  p.D
```

In EL:

```
SELECT      Dept, MAX(Salary)
FROM        Employee
GROUPED_BY  Dept
WHERE       Age < 35
```

In LOGIC:

```
[D,X] &
sub_q(employee,[#,#,#,D],[],[],[D],[group,D,D]) &
sub_q(employee,[#,A,S,D],[A<35],[],[max,S,X]) &
!.
```

In PROLOG:

```
ans((_1355,_1348)) :-
   group(_1348,employee(_,_,_,_1348,_),_1348),
   max(_1353,(employee(_,_1344,_1353,_1348,_),_1344<35),_1355).
```

RESULT:

salary	dept
12300	d1
8500	d2
7300	d3

Q26: Find the department, and its location, where there is at least one part the quantity of which happens to be the total number of the same part supplied by all suppliers.

In PL:

```
.---------------.
| department    |
------------------------
dept    city    manager
------------------------
p.D     p.C
```

```
.--------------.
| stock        |
------------------------
dept    pno     qty
------------------------
D       M       Q1


.--------------.
| shipment     |
------------------------
sno     pno     qty
------------------------
#       g.M
#       M       sum.Q=Q1
```

In EL:

```
SELECT  dept, city
FROM    department
WHERE   dept IN
           (SELECT  dept
            FROM    stock
            WHERE   (pno, qty) IN
                               (SELECT     pno, SUM(qty)
                                FROM       shipment
                                GROUPED_BY pno ))
```

In LOGIC:

```
[D,C] &
sub_q(department,[D,C,#],[],[],[D,C],!) &
sub_q(stock,[D,M,Q1],[],[],[D,M,Q1],!) &
sub_q(shipment,[#,M,#],[],[],[M],[group,M,M]) &
sub_q(shipment,[#,M,Q],[],[X=Q1],[sum,Q,X]) &
!.
```

In PROLOG:

```
ans((_2049,_2033)) :-
        group(_2095,shipment(_,_2095,_),_2095),
        sum(_2102,shipment(_,_2095,_2102),_2104),
        stock(_2049,_2095,_2104),
        department(_2049,_2033,_).
```

RESULT:

dept	city
d1	london

Index

Entries marked with an asterisk are built-in predicates in the ILEX system.